Air Power Confronts an Unstable World

Also available from Brassey's:

BRASSEY'S/CENTRE FOR DEFENCE STUDIES
Brassey's Defence Yearbook 1997

OXLEE
Aerospace Reconnaissance

MASON
Air Power: A Centennial Appraisal

SHEFFIELD (Ed.)
Leadership and Command: The Anglo-American Military Experience Since
1861

Air Power Confronts an Unstable World

Edited by

Richard P Hallion

BRASSEY'S

London * Washington

First English Edition 1997

UK editorial offices: Brassey's, 33 John Street, London WC1N 2AT
UK orders: Marston Book Services, PO Box 269, Abingdon, OX14 4SD

North American orders: Brassey's Inc., PO Box 960,
Herndon, VA 22070, USA

Library of Congress Cataloging in Publication Data
available

British Library Cataloguing in Publication Data
A catalogue record for this book is available from the British Library

ISBN 1 85753 238 4 Hardcover

Typeset by Harold, Martin and Redman Ltd
Printed in Great Britain by Redwood Books, Trowbridge, Wiltshire

This book is dedicated, with affection
and respect, to the memory of

Major General Robert E Linhard, USAF
1947–1996

Strategist and scholar, a gifted planner and student of air power, Bob Linhard served the United States and the Free World during the long watch of the Cold War with uncommon dedication and accomplishment as a missile operations officer, strategic force planner, senior defence programs director of the National Security Council and special assistant to President Ronald Reagan for nuclear issues and arms control.

He commanded the 57th Air Division and served as deputy chief of staff for plans and resources, and director of plans and policy for the Strategic Air Command, before returning to Headquarters USAF as plans director and deputy chief of staff for plans and operations.

In all of these ways and, finally, as special assistant to the Chief of Staff, United States Air Force, for long-range planning, he was instrumental in helping shape the nature of air power for the 21st Century. He truly was, in the words of one colleague, 'a national asset'. His work and influence will long outlive him, and his memory will brighten the recollections of those of us who knew him.

CONTENTS

BIOGRAPHICAL NOTES

Dr Richard P Hallion has been the Air Force Historian at HQ United States Air Force since 1991. He is responsible for directing the worldwide USAF historical and museum programmes. He has broad experience in museum development, historical research and management analysis, and has served as consultant to a variety of professional organisations. Dr Hallion is the author of 14 books relating to aerospace history, and teaches and lectures widely.

Air Commodore Andrew G B Vallance is an RAF pilot who has flown bomber, strategic reconnaissance and tanker aircraft in the course of some 4,000 hours of flying. In 1993-95, as officer commanding RAF Wyton, he led a wing of four reconnaissance and electronic warfare squadrons and several operational ground units. A former Director of Defence Studies for the RAF, he is presently Chief of the Special Weapons Branch at Supreme Headquarters Allied Powers Europe.

Lieutenant Colonel Barry D Watts is a former USAF pilot whose service has included combat duty in South-East Asia, teaching at the USAF Academy and three years as a Soviet threat specialist with the Air Staff's Project *Checkmate*. Now Senior Analyst at the Northrop Grumman Analysis Center, in 1991-93 he headed the Gulf War Air Power Survey's work on operations and effectiveness. His most recent publication was *Clausewitzian Friction and Future War* (McNair Paper 52).

Colonel Phillip S Meilinger is an airlift pilot who has flown in both Europe and the Pacific, and served on the Air Staff in the Pentagon. He received a PhD from the University of Michigan and served for four years as Dean of the USAF's School of Advanced Airpower Studies. He is the author of a biography of General Hoyt S Vandenberg, and is currently a professor of strategy at the US Naval War College.

Group Captain Andrew P N Lambert is an RAF fighter navigator and Qualified Weapons Instructor. He participated in the UK battle planning for Operation DESERT SHIELD/DESERT STORM at HQ Strike Command and has commanded a Tornado F-3 squadron on Operation DENY FLIGHT over Bosnia. He took an MPhil course at the University of Cambridge in 1993–94 before assuming his current post as Director of Defence Studies for the RAF.

Rear Admiral James A Winnefeld is a carrier aviator and veteran of the Korean and Vietnam wars. He has participated in and helped direct joint operations in both war and peace. He has been a program director for the RAND Corporation and has participated in many strategic, command and control and air power studies. He has written many books and articles relating to air power, and won the US Naval Institute's Arleigh Burke Award in 1989 and 1995.

Air Vice-Marshal Tony Mason was the RAF's first Director of Defence Studies and was Air Secretary, 1986–89. For 20 years he has published and lectured worldwide on air power in international security. He is a frequent defence analyst for the BBC and other media. His most recent book is *Air Power: A Centennial Appraisal*, published by Brassey's. He is currently Professor of Aerospace Policy at The University of Birmingham.

Alan Stephens is the Royal Australian Air Force historian. The author of many books and articles on security, air power and military history, he has been a principal adviser on foreign affairs and defence in the Australian Federal Parliament and a pilot in the RAAF, where he primarily flew bomber aircraft.

Frederick L Frostic is the former Deputy Assistant Secretary of Defence for Requirements and Plans. He was an Associate Program Director at RAND, leading many studies on the applications of airpower. He retired from the USAF after serving 26 years as a fighter pilot flying F-4s and F-16s. He is a co-author of *The New Calculus: Analyzing Airpower's Role in Joint Theater Campaigns*.

Colonel John A Warden III is a former fighter pilot, his service having included over 250 combat missions, and a distinguished author, strategist and air power theorist. He has served as Commander, 36th Tactical Fighter Wing, Deputy Director for Strategy, Doctrine and Warfighting at HQ USAF, Commandant of the Air Command and Staff College, and Special Assistant to the Vice President of the USA. He is best known for his seminal work on air power, *The Air Campaign*, and for his role as architect of the Persian Gulf air war.

ACKNOWLEDGMENTS

A number of individuals and institutions have formed and nurtured a supportive climate that has resulted in this work. First, I wish to thank each of the authors for taking time from pressing schedules and other duties to contribute their essays. But numerous others in various domestic and overseas locales have had an important role in shaping the thinking that has gone into the work.

First and foremost are old friends from the Air Staff and Secretary's Staff Group: Colonels David Deptula and John Piazza, and Ellen Rose Piazza. Lieutenant General Jay Kelley and the staff and instructors of the Air University at Maxwell AFB – specifically the Air War College, Air Command and Staff College, and the School of Advanced Airpower Studies – have been a constant source of collegiality and insight. Stimulating meetings and discussions with the Directors of Defence Studies for the Royal Air Force, British Army and Royal Navy have been most helpful, particularly Group Captains Neil Taylor and Andrew Lambert, RAF; Colonel Jonathan Bailey, RA; and Captain Christopher Page, RN.

I wish to acknowledge also the contributions of Squadron Leader Sarah Hermon, RAF, Mrs Sue Hutchinson, Mr Adonis Kyriakides and Mr Arthur Williamson, staff researchers of the Royal Air Force Staff College, Bracknell; Drs Philip Sabin and Richard Overy of the Department of War Studies, Kings College, London and Dr David Gates of the Centre for Defence Studies, Aberdeen University. Majors Marius Johansen and Arent Arntzen and their students at the *Luftkrigsskolen* (the Royal Norwegian Air Force air academy) at Trondheim and Lieutenant Colonel Jerome Martin, USAF, and his students at the United States Air Force Academy, Colorado Springs, have furnished useful insights and points of departure.

I have benefited from discussions with Air Chief Marshal Sir Patrick Hine, RAF, the Military Advisor to British Aerospace; Lieutenant General Dato' Seri Abdul Ghani Aziz, Chief of the Royal Malaysian Air Force; Air Commodore Robert Wright, RAF, the Assistant Chief of Staff for Policy and Requirements, Allied Air Forces Northwestern Europe; Colonel Frantisek Padelek, the Executive Chief of the Air Force Department, Czech Republic; Colonel M (SES) Svejgaard, Deputy Chief of Staff, Operations and Policy, HQ Tactical Air Command, Royal Danish Airforce; and Lieutenant Colonel L Kraft van Ermel, Director of Air Studies, Netherlands Defence College. The staff and researchers of the Royal Australian Air Force's Air Power Studies Centre, RAAF

Fairbain, have undertaken notable and influential work in the field of air power analysis, particularly Group Captains Gary Waters and John Harvey, Wing Commanders Mark Lax and Rick Casagrande, and Dr Alan Stephens.

Dr Christopher J Bowie of the Northrop-Grumman corporation, an assiduous student of airpower, furnished important insights on the interplay of stealth and precision attack, and on Iraq's weapons of mass destruction acquistion programmes.

I wish to thank General Bryce Poe II, USAF (ret.) for granting permission to publish my essay on precision; an earlier version had appeared in the journal of the Air Force Historical Foundation, *Air Power History*.

Finally, Drs Diane Putney and Wayne Thompson of the Air Force History and Museums Program have influenced my thinking on air power issues, and Lieutenant Colonel Charles Hunt, USAF, Dr Richard Wolf and Ms Dolores Toni assisted greatly in the preparation of this work.

RICHARD P HALLION
LAUREL, MARYLAND
APRIL 1997

PREFACE

THE CHANGING NATURE
OF AIR WARFARE

by
Air Commodore Andrew G B Vallance OBE MPhil RAF
SPECIAL WEAPONS BRANCH,
SUPREME HEADQUARTERS ALLIED POWERS EUROPE

I t has become something of a truism to say that the strategic outlook is
now far less clear than it was ten years ago. The collapse of the Warsaw
Pact and the disintegration of the Soviet Union introduced changes into
the international order which are still underway and as yet show no signs of
stabilising. History did not end, as some had proclaimed; if anything it was
reborn into an increasingly interdependent world in which regional change
triggered rapid global effects. Nor did conflict end; if anything it increased, at
least in terms of diversity and geographical span. As the clamp imposed by the
old strategic balance was released, long constrained pressures were unleashed,
often with explosive effect.

Today, despite the increased harmony between the major powers and the
now well-established United Nations' prohibition on the use of armed force to
resolve international disputes, conventional wars continue to break out, the
Gulf War being the most prominent recent example. It is arguable that the
outcome of that war reduced the danger of a straightforward invasion of one
state by another to seize territory and population. However, border disputes
continue to exist and some states still aspire to territorial enlargement and/or
military aggrandisement.

We need also to remember that what one state might see as a purely
'internal' affair may not be seen as such by other states. The term 'nation' does
not necessarily equate with that of 'state' and vice versa. A nation (essentially
an ethnic concept) may populate a number of states (a political concept); equally,
a state may contain several nations. In such circumstances, ethnicity/nationhood
may be used by some states as a pretext for absorbing a neighbour (as Iraq
attempted to do with Kuwait), or for a part of a state to break away and join

xiii

another (as in Bosnia) or form a separate nation (as the Tamils seek to do in Sri Lanka). In such cases, the stability and security of neighbouring states is bound to be affected, perhaps to the extent that they feel obliged to intervene (as, for example, Russia has done in Moldova, Chechnya, Georgia, etc.).

The prospect of more 'Kuwaits' cannot be ruled out, but the most likely contingency seems to be more 'Bosnias'. Hence, while the need to be able to wage conventional war will still remain, the relative importance of crisis management and peace support operations – those operations which are conducted to contain or defuse crises and prevent them developing into full-scale conflicts – is set to continue to grow.

What part then can air power play in this confused and complex future world and what changes can we expect in the nature of air warfare? One of the few things that we can discern as we peer into the crystal ball of military utility is that in future – even more than the past virtually – all forms of military action, will be joint (i.e. air–land–sea) in nature. But although the principle of joint action is widely accepted, the issue of 'who supports whom' is becoming increasingly important. The days when aviation forces could be treated as an ancillary arm to the surface forces have long since passed.

Aviation forces have always offered capabilities which in part complement – and in part can substitute for – those of land and sea forces. Today, far more than in the past, air power – the use for military purposes of vehicles operating in or passing through the air – is a multi-Service concept. Air power is not (nor has it ever been) the sole preserve of air forces. The United States Army has for some years possessed more aircraft than any other air force or air arm, while the United States Navy now ranks fifth (in terms of size) in the world's air power league.[1] In both France and Germany, the army has a similar number of aircraft to the air force. Moreover, aviation forces encompass not only 'anything that flies', but also anything that directly affects flying operations (e.g. surface-to-air defences).

But while land, sea and aviation forces are each likely to contribute to future operations, they are unlikely to do so in equal measure. Different strategic and operational situations will demand different force structures, and if planning is to be effective, a clear delineation must be made in any operation between the lead-element (the 'supported force') and subordinate formations (the 'supporting forces'). In the past, the lead-element has often been identified in geographic terms. But in the future this approach will be too narrow, and planners will need increasingly to focus on force-type when identifying the lead-element.

In essence, there are clear indications that aviation forces will increasingly be required to undertake the leading role within a joint force operation. Indeed, air power seems likely to be the first instrument of choice for governments, not only for waging war, but also for preventing it. Two key factors support this assertion.

Firstly, as set-piece scenarios disappear and the geographic span of operations increases, the importance of the basic characteristics which distinguish aviation forces from surface forces is growing. Reinforced by the rapid march of technology, the innate ability of aviation forces to exploit the third dimension, and the consequent reach, speed, flexibility, responsiveness and power of concentration that this confers, offers a spectrum of strategic and operational applications which is well suited to diffuse and rapidly evolving strategic conditions.

Secondly, and for the developed world in particular, the public and politicians alike have become increasingly sensitive to casualties of both friend and foe. Clearly, aviation forces involve the commitment of far fewer 'front-line troops' than either land or sea forces. Furthermore, because far fewer people are put at risk to achieve the same operational result, the scope for sustaining heavy casualties is inevitably far less. Aviation forces do, of course, have great killing power, but they can also effectively disarm an enemy by cutting off his supplies and destroying his heavy equipment. They can also strike at the heart of an enemy's war-making ability by dislocating war-industries, utilities and transport systems. And thanks to precision-guided munitions they can do this with far lower risk of collateral casualties and damage than in previous years. In sum, air power is a humane instrument of force; it can be used to terminate conflicts rapidly and with minimum loss of life to friend and foe alike.

The trends in defence spending and the force structure development of the Western armed forces provide hard evidence that the growing primacy of air power is well-recognised. During the last four decades in particular, and notwithstanding periodic fluctuations, aviation forces have tended to grow as the spectrum of air power roles has expanded. Of key significance, whereas the overall sizes of the world's armies, navies and marine corps have (in general) fallen markedly since the 1960s, their air arms have expanded in both proportional and (in some cases) actual terms.[2] For example, in 1986 the British Army had 163,000 personnel, 1,030 main battle tanks and 323 aircraft. In 1996, these figures had changed to 116,000, 500 and 391 respectively.

This process of growth is still continuing in terms of both quantity and quality. Therefore, there is every sign that air power will be increasingly required to play the leading role in future conflicts. In this context, the Gulf War was of course a watershed. It proved that aviation forces could act as the lead force element and secure an overwhelming military victory with mercifully few casualties. But like most historical 'watersheds', the Gulf War was essentially a manifestation of trends which had for some time been underway and which – sooner or later – would inevitably have emerged.

A key element in these trends has been the rapid development of aerospace technology, which continues to advance with unrivalled dynamism and pace. During the last two decades, parameters such as the range, payload and manoeuvrability of platforms and the lethality, accuracy and reach of their weapons have all increased by several orders of magnitude. To these must be added increases in serviceability and survivability which have produced a dramatic growth in sortie rates and surge potential (the ability to meet a critical need for air power by operating as many of one's aircraft as possible), and now allow air operations to be sustained for far longer periods. Overlaying all of this has been the great expansion in targeting and surveillance capabilities, defence suppression and penetration aids, improved navigational accuracy and night/all-weather capabilities. The net result of this sustained technological sprint has been the development of air power capabilities which – *inter alia* – can now hit and destroy almost any target, anywhere in the world in almost any weather and in all operational conditions.

But clearly it will always be better to avert a war rather than having to wage it; hence the importance of effective crisis management techniques. Observation, detection, signalling, deterrence and coercion (both lethal and non-lethal) have long been key instruments in the air power crisis management repertoire, and much experience has been gained during the last four decades in their use.

Naval forces can also contribute to crisis management by exerting what some naval strategists have termed 'poise', i.e. patrolling close enough to a crisis region either to exert pressure or to intervene. However, by their very nature, crises can degenerate into conflict, often with startling rapidity. And if naval forces are sufficiently close to exert pressure or intervene, they will also be within the range of (potentially hostile) air power. In such circumstances, ships will be critically vulnerable unless protected by strong aviation forces and – even with them – could quickly become far more of a liability than an asset. Thus, naval 'poise' can only be exercised in crisis management situations when naval forces are protected by air power; in contrast, air power crisis management techniques do not rely on naval support.

But every crisis is different and, in this field at least, history has never repeated itself. So a major challenge in the future use of air power in crises will be to understand much more clearly the effects that different air actions can have on different players in different scenarios. Involving as it must some very fine political judgements, this multi-function equation will not be easy to resolve, and clear-cut answers cannot be expected. Nevertheless, it may be possible to prepare a range of flexible templates which could be adapted to meet a wide spectrum of crises. Only through this type of work can we hope to exploit to best effect the vast potential of air power in containing or defusing crises or potential crises.

If crises and conflicts cannot be avoided, then the next best option is to impose some degree of stability in which lasting solutions can be sought. This is the province of peace support operations. Until recently, such operations were seen largely as the preserve of surface forces, particularly land forces, as these alone could be used to mount a permanent physical presence throughout a crisis region. However, recent experience has highlighted the risks and limitations of such permanent physical presences. Putting people on the ground throughout a crisis region is inevitably manpower-intensive, and whether the task of these forces is peacekeeping or conventional deterrence/defence, they can quickly find themselves taking heavy casualties even in skirmishes. Sustaining casualties tends to undermine public support, weaken political resolve and strengthen the pressures for withdrawal. However, because their strategic mobility is relatively poor and their equipment heavy, substantial land forces can be very difficult to extricate, particularly if their withdrawal is opposed by the local population. All this makes the large-scale use of ground forces potentially problematical in peace support operations.

We do not need to look far for examples to support this thesis. Somalia, Rwanda and the long agony of Sarajevo all testify to the limited utility and high risks of mounting a physical presence 'on the ground'. In Somalia, the ability of warlords to inflict casualties on US troops ensured that US involvement would soon end. In Bosnia, although UN ground troops did help to protect the humanitarian effort, they could not prevent the blockage of road convoys nor could they protect UN-designated safe areas against determined attack. More importantly, the commitment of many thousands of UN troops into Bosnia did nothing to resolve the basic impasse. If anything, it increased the complexity of the problem; for the dangers faced by peacekeeping troops quickly made policy a hostage. Shortly after the start of the UN mission, Denmark, Norway and Canada all expressed concern for their troops if NATO used force. As each new nation contributed peacekeeping forces, so they too became conscious of the vulnerability of their troops and reluctant to endorse calls for decisive action.

Only when NATO and the UN agreed to an air campaign was it possible to cut this Gordian Knot. Significantly, it was the United States (a country which had decided not to commit ground troops) which took the lead in pressing for air action. That air campaign (Operation DELIBERATE FORCE, 30 August – 14 September 1995), assisted by some artillery action (most notably from Mount Igman within the close confines of Sarajevo and its environs) unlocked the Bosnian impasse. It offered the Croatian and then the Bosnian armies their first opportunity to engage the Bosnian Serbs on more than equal terms and set the scene for the Dayton Peace Accord. DELIBERATE FORCE combat operations took only 15 days and involved 3,515 sorties, of which 1,045 were support sorties flown outside the combat area. Some 338 individual targets were struck within 48 target complexes.³ Only one French Mirage 2000 aircraft was lost, and its two-man crew (though captured) were subsequently liberated. In contrast, during the 45-month course of its stay in former Yugoslavia, the UN Protection/Peace Force sustained 1,690 casualties from all causes, including 214 killed; of these, some 708 casualties (including 80 killed) were caused by hostile action.

Bosnia was a watershed in the use of air power for peace support but, like the Gulf War watershed, it too was only a manifestation of trends which had long been in progress. British experience with 'air control' in the 1920s, 1930s and 1940s and French experience in Africa in the 1960s and 1970s, both pointed to the growing advantages of using air power in peace support operations, albeit it in relatively straightforward operational and political environments. Advances in technology and technique over the last 20 years allowed air action to be similarly effective in the far more difficult operational and political conditions of Bosnia.

To be sure, air power will not always be a practical option: geography, cover, terrain, force-to-space ratios, density of population etc. may on occasion militate against its use. But the historical trend is unmistakable. Aviation forces are quick and easy to insert and extract, involve less human and material, and therefore political, commitment, and thus offer fewer potential liabilities in a crisis. For these reasons, it seems unavoidable that air power will be required to play an increasing part, not only in future conflict, but also in crisis management and peace support.

Much then is likely to be asked of air power in the years ahead, and perhaps the key challenge facing airmen is to ensure that the doctrines which guide air power employment are sound and allow the full capabilities of aviation forces to be exploited. And here three specific dimensions would seem to hold the key.

Firstly, there is the dimension of technology. It has long been recognised that the interaction between doctrine and technology in aviation forces is far more marked than that in land or sea forces. Doctrine sets out how forces can best be developed and employed, whereas technology determines the extent to which such aspirations can be realised. In the early years of air power, doctrines were based too much on theory and too little on practical experience. They were far ahead of the technology needed to realise them and, thus, often proved invalid when put to the litmus test of war.

Today, that problem is increasingly being turned on its head. Rapid developments in aerospace technology now offer a range of options truly vast in their scale and scope. A glittering jeweller's tray of possibilities lies before air power planners, but with ever-tightening purse strings, it will be more difficult than ever to choose between the different options on offer.

In large part, such choices must be steered by the second key dimension: that of strategy. As capabilities have expanded, strategic options have increased. Prominent amongst these is that of Information Warfare. Information Warfare is designed to reduce the enemy's ability to make timely and well-informed decisions by minimising his information flow, while ensuring that the speed, quality and quantity of the friendly information flow is preserved. At the root of this is John Boyd's 'OODA-loop' concept, in which the speed of the decision cycle of Observation-Orientation-Decision-Action is enhanced for friendly forces and reduced for the enemy. Like a chess player who prevents his opponent from seeing all of the board and who makes three moves to every opposing move, the information warrior seeks to out-think and out-pace his enemy.

Information warfare is by no means restricted to those who enjoy the benefits of high technology, and is likely to have particular appeal to those who are unable to compete in the technology race. Such people may seek to nullify the advantages of advanced systems and exploit any perceived over-reliance on them, and they may choose to do this with unconventional means. So the potential opportunities offered by information warfare have to be linked to the parallel challenges of developing options for coping with enemy initiatives in this field. These latter may include – *interalia* – the use of more systematic delegation, perhaps along the lines of the German *Auftragtaktik* doctrine of mission-orientated orders (delegating decision-making authority and responsibility to the lowest possible level). This sets guidelines for action at different levels, allowing lower-level commanders to exercise their initiative – within the overall framework of a general plan. But whatever actions are taken, they must be based on the realisation that information warfare is a 'can-lose' as well as a 'can-win' business.

Information warfare is unlikely to prove a stand-alone strategic option, particularly when crisis degenerates into conflict. Like electronic warfare, it is essentially a supporting strategy; its role is to supplement rather than to displace force employment strategies. Current debate in the latter field centres on whether air power would best be used in 'parallel operations' or 'asymmetric operations'. Parallel Operations – the brainchild of John Warden and David Deptula – strike at an enemy state's ability to wage war. Their object is to destroy a horizontal cross-section of key target sets on a scale which would overwhelm enemy resources and resilience and cause the enemy state to collapse. Asymmetric Operations focus on using the growing asymmetries in the capabilities of aviation forces and those of the surface forces to destroy the enemy army and navy.

Both of these strategic concepts seek to exploit developments in sortie generation, precision, surveillance and targeting, and each draws a measure of validity from the success of different phases of Operation DESERT STORM.

The essential prerequisite for each strategy is obviously to achieve air superiority; the essential difference between them is how best to exploit that superiority once it has been won.

There are of course echoes from yesteryear in both strategies. Parallel Operations are essentially Douhetist in approach. However, they specifically seek to avoid the very high level of collateral damage and civilian casualties which Douhet saw as inevitable and indeed essential. Asymmetric Operations are a development of Second World War 'tactical air force' concepts, although with the roles reversed between aviation and surface forces.

Each of these air strategies has its own problems, not the least of which is achieving widespread credibility. Advocacy of parallel operations continues to be burdened by previous failures to realise Douhet's prophecies and the problems experienced with 'panacea targeting' during the Second World War and later conflicts. In contrast, the promotion of Asymmetric Operations has to overcome the intellectual baggage produced by millennia of land and sea warfare in which only armies could defeat armies and only navies could defeat navies. It seems probable that Parallel Operations and Asymmetric Operations may well be more complementary than competing in their respective natures. Which of the two proves to be the most effective is likely to vary from situation to situation. And in some situations, a combination of the two may well produce the best results (as indeed it did in the Gulf War).

Criticism of both of these concepts of air strategy often seems based on an unwillingness to accept the scale and scope of technological developments and their impact on the operational balance. In all probability, neither concept will gain widespread acceptance until validated by the litmus test of war. And even if and when that happens there will still be doubters who will argue that this was not proof, merely a one-off anomaly. Inevitably, there will be a general preference for staying with well-known and well-tried concepts, even though such concepts may cost more and yield less. As Liddell Hart ruefully remarked 'The only thing more difficult than getting a new idea into the military mind is to get an old one out.'[4]

But whatever the choice of strategic direction and doctrinal guidance, each and all are likely to be underpinned by the third key dimension: organisation. At the core, this issue seems likely to revolve around how unity of air action can be promoted. As that distinguished airman Marshal of the Royal Air Force the Lord Tedder pointed out, 'The old fable of the bundle of faggots compared with individual sticks is abundantly clear. Its strength lies in unity.'[5] Indeed, unity of development and employment and unified control at the highest practical level have always been fundamental to air power effectiveness.

With the growing diversity and interdependence of air power roles, unity is becoming ever more critical. Operational effectiveness now demands the highest possible level of cohesion not only between the various types of combat forces (for example, there are critical interactions between airfield attack, fighter sweep, escort, suppression of enemy air defence etc.) but also between the combat support forces that act as essential force multipliers (such as tankers, air-to-air and air-to-ground surveillance, electronic support and counter-measures). No less important is the cross-telling and integration of information, not only to build recognised air and ground pictures, but also to integrate surface-to-air, air-to-air, and air-to-surface action.

The growing use of stealth technology in all of its many forms may at first sight seem to moderate the need for unified action. Thus far, stealth aircraft have operated in a largely independent fashion. However, historical experience suggests that it is more likely that advances in stealth will trigger advances in counter-stealth. Moreover, radar-stealth is most useful at night, and the need to operate in daytime and to make electronic transmissions will inevitably introduce compromises in stealth operations. Hence, as is the case with electronic countermeasures and the offence/defence balance, the relative effectiveness of stealth and counter-stealth may swing like a pendulum as one initiative is countered by another. Time does not stand still, but air unity will continue to be the key to air power.

At the micro level this depends on issues such as ensuring the cohesion of force packages. These airborne battle groups deploy a spectrum of combat and combat support capabilities to enable them to penetrate enemy defences and achieve the desired operational effect with minimal loss. But if different types of aviation forces are to fight together, they must also train together; this is a prerequisite if they are to become a cohesive force and not just a collection of different air elements which meet for the first time *en route* to a target. The need to train together suggests a need for co-location; that in turn suggests moving away from single-type wings (currently the world-wide norm for air forces) and towards composite wings (the current norm for deployed naval aviation).

At the macro level, fostering unity is likely to centre around developing the greatest possible organisational integration. Two issues are involved in this complex and emotive area: *ownership* (i.e., which service operates which aircraft) and *command and control*. In theory, which service owns which system is in operational terms unimportant, providing that command and control arrangements ensure integrated and unified action. But in practice, dividing aviation forces between several services inevitably complicates C^2 arrangements and often leads to turf disputes which erode (sometimes seriously) operational effectiveness. In his book *It Doesn't Take a Hero*, General H Norman Schwarzkopf of DESERT STORM fame describes an incident during the 1983

US invasion of Grenada, when he had to threaten a US Marine Corps colonel with court martial before the colonel agreed to task Marine Corps helicopters to carry US Army troops.[6]

The more capable the air system and the greater the spectrum of operations in which it can usefully participate, the more serious this problem becomes. Exercising effective tasking control over highly capable aircraft – such as fighter-bombers and attack helicopters – can be particularly difficult if they are owned by different services. As the distinguished British soldier Field Marshal the Viscount Slim emphatically stated, 'Private armies, . . . [like] private air forces, are expensive, wasteful and unnecessary.'[7] And the fundamental difficulty in dividing aviation forces between different armed services is that it does tend to lead to private air forces. Abolishing air forces and dividing air assets between navies and armies (and marine corps?) would only exacerbate this problem. We know from the Second World War the disastrous consequences and heightened rivalry that such an expedient would inevitably cause. As Richard Hallion has pointed out, had the British not formed an independent air service, and instead kept their air assets divided between their army and navy, there would have been no Battle of Britain in 1940: the Royal Flying Corps would have been destroyed in France with the rest of the British Army; there would have been nothing to oppose a subsequent German invasion and no alternative but surrender. For further confirmation, we need only to look at the Japanese, who fought in the Second World War with their aviation forces divided between their army and the navy. After a strong initial showing, Japan soon lost the initiative and proved unable to formulate cohesive strategies for air power employment or even force development. Aircraft development and production became chaotic; and navy and army air operations became totally disjointed, to the extent that Japan soon lost control of her own airspace even though her enemies were hundreds of miles from her shores. When the atomic-armed Boeing B-29 Superfortress *Enola Gay* appeared over Hiroshima on 6 August 1945, it did so alone and completely unopposed.

The air is a distinct and indivisible environment. This, when combined with the speed of events in air warfare, means that what happens in one section of airspace has inevitable and rapid consequences for what happens in the rest; unlike land areas and far more than seaspace, airspace is three-dimensional and cannot be compartmentalised. Thus, history and logic are in accord: the fundamental condition for success in air war is to unify all air assets in a single air service. Setting aside the operational arguments, the economic advantages in favour of such a step are compelling. Only the very biggest of nations can afford the luxury of maintaining separate training, maintenance, repair and logistic organisations for three or four different aviation forces. Even the very biggest nation should be reluctant to sacrifice the economies and benefits that such unification would bring. In all cases, efficient administration demands that air power supporting capabilities are unified, a process which is already underway in Great Britain and other states. The unification of air power support elements is the first step on the road which leads inevitably to the unification of air power operational elements.

In sum, the nature of air warfare and air power employment in this diffuse, increasingly interdependent and ever more complex world, is changing quickly. Rapidly developing capabilities are bringing with them growing responsibilities and obligations. Radical new thinking will be required if these challenges are to be met and mastered. That of course is the purpose of this book, and the following chapters explore in depth the evolving air power contribution to security, peace and stability in the still-developing new world order.

NOTES

1. Aircraft held by air forces/air arms: US Army, 7,588; US Air Force, 5,800; Chinese Air Force, 4,970; Russian Air Force, 2,150; US Navy, 1,935. Source: IISS, *Military Balance* 1995/96 (OUP, Oxford, 1995).

2. Sources: IISS, *Military Balance* 1985/86 (Brassey's, London, 1985) and *Military Balance* 1995/96. It should be noted that in qualitative terms, the increase in the air power vs. the land power of the British Army was even greater.

3. Allied Forces Southern Europe Fact Sheet 'Operation Deliberate Force' dated 6 November 1995.

4. Liddell Hart, Sir Basil, *Thoughts on War* (Faber & Faber, London, 1943), p. 112.

5. Tedder, Marshal of the Royal Air Force, the Lord, *Air Power in War,* (HMSO, 1948), p. 45.

6. Schwarzkopf, General H Norman, *It Doesn't Take a Hero,* (Bantam Press, London, 1943), p. 254.

7. Slim, Field Marshal the Viscount, *Defeat Into Victory,* (Corgi Press, 1971) p. 465.

The views expressed are those of the author and do not necessarily reflect the polices either of the UK MOD or of NATO.

INTRODUCTION

AIR POWER PAST, PRESENT AND FUTURE

by

Richard P Hallion

THE AIR FORCE HISTORIAN,
HQ USAF, WASHINGTON, DC

T here are many fine museums of military aviation, museums that showcase the development of aircraft and missiles; the dedication and bravery of aviators and support personnel; and the influence that air power has had upon conflict in the 20th Century. These museums share, to a great degree, a remarkable quality of sameness whether, for example, one is visiting the Air Force Museum in Dayton, the Royal Air Force Museum in Hendon, the Naval Aviation Museum at Pensacola, the *Musée de l'Air* in Paris or the Czech aviation museum at Prague-Kbely. They are replete with a variety of artefacts: aircraft, missiles, weapons, engines, instruments, flying equipment, maps, documents, photographs; in short, all the necessary accoutrements of military flight. The specialist visitor goes to them to see particular vehicles or exhibits that cannot be seen elsewhere – for example, the only surviving North American XB-70A Valkyrie at the Air Force Museum, the last Hawker Typhoon at Hendon, or the last-of-its-kind Avia B-534 biplane at Kbely.

Ironically, two of the most interesting artefacts in the history of military air power are located not in aviation museums, but in other institutions. One is a section of sculptural relief in the British Museum; the second is a chair in a conference room at Ramstein Air Base, Germany. They are separated by over 2,800 years, spanning an epoch in human history from the dream of flight through to the devastating effectiveness of air attack in the Second World War, from nearly the earliest phase of Indo-European civilisation to the era of spaceflight and global communication.

1

The first is one of several reliefs from the ancient palace at Nimrud, of the time of the Assyrian king Ashurnasirpal, approximately 865–860 BC. In these, Ashurnasirpal is shown going into battle on a chariot, supported by a god on a flying disk who shoots arrows at enemy infantry; exulting in victory over his foes while the flying disk god hovers protectively overhead; and presiding over his kingdom while being guarded by winged deities and other flying beings. Air power, in short, is shown as a virtually miraculous force and necessary attribute in both peace and war: the gods are in the air, holding in thrall the mortals on the ground. These Assyrian works, from the pre-history of flight, speak to the dream and promise of air power for offence, defence and as a protective force ensuring regional stability and domestic well-being. One cannot but wonder that if Saddam Hussein had been more cognisant of his own national history, he might not have been quite so cavalier in his attitude towards air power on the eve of the Gulf War; for it was General Schwarzkopf who enjoyed the Ashurnasirpal air power advantage, not this petty tyrant of the Tigris who invoked the great era of Assyrian and Babylonian expansionism.

The second is a chair – not surprisingly a large plush chair – used by the late *Reichsmarschall* of the Third Reich, Hermann Wilhelm Göring. It is one of a set of chairs appropriated by the United States Army Air Forces from the ruins of one of his headquarters meeting rooms. Today a registered artefact in the Air Force History and Museums Program, it resides in a conference room at the logistics centre at Headquarters, United States Air Forces in Europe, Ramstein Air Base, Germany. Göring's chair teaches a sobering lesson about air power, and one of the important reasons it does so is precisely because it was the chair occupied by the head of the Luftwaffe. A reasonably successful fighter pilot in the First World War, Göring failed to adapt to changing times. He proved so inept as a pre-war and wartime leader of his own service that one frustrated fighter commander boldly and sarcastically asked for a squadron of Spitfires to replace his unit's increasingly unsatisfactory Messerschmitts, and two of his generals – one the commander of all bomber forces, the other charged with responsibility for the Luftwaffe's technical development – took their own lives. The dozens, then hundreds, and finally thousands of bombers that pounded Germany's industrial centres and cities into rubble discredited his boast to Hitler that no Allied aircraft would ever overfly the Reich. No member of the Nazi team bears greater responsibility than Göring for ensuring – fortunately – that the 'Thousand Year Reich' fell short of Hitler's prediction by 988 years. Göring's chair teaches that if you do not understand air power, if you do not use it creatively and to good effect, if you do not appreciate the damage that an enemy can cause to you by the insightful use of air power, then the time can – and likely will – come when the enemy air commander is cosily ensconced in your headquarters, sitting in your chair, making out his after-action report, musing

2

about your missed opportunities and failures, and probably sipping your cognac as he does so.

It is in the spirit of these two artefacts that this book of essays is offered for, as young as it is, air power without vision runs the risk of becoming a museum of outmoded technology exemplifying outmoded ideas. There has been a veritable explosion of writing on air power and its uses since the late 1980s, particularly, after the Gulf War. Much of this writing falls into two camps: screeds that state (usually defensively) that nothing has really changed, and that warfare today must still be decided by such traditional means as large-scale surface action by land warfare forces; and enthusiastic accounts that argue that air power has created a new and revolutionary period in warfare. The writings in this work fall between these two views but, unapologetically and unabashedly, are more on the latter than the former side. Undoubtedly air power *has* revolutionised warfare in this century, from the time of the First Battle of the Marne, through the Battle of Britain, Normandy, then on to the Gulf and, today, Bosnia.

Despite the obvious changes that have occurred in diverse technologies and capabilities, there can be little doubt that the roles and missions first established by air power in the First World War or (in the case of air mobility) immediately after, are even more relevant today than they were when first formulated. No matter how the world has changed, any nation that considers itself an 'air power' has to be concerned with fulfilling four dominant challenges:

- *ensuring air superiority* (i.e., denying an enemy access to one's airspace and, even better, to his own);

- *furnishing mobility* (including troop transport and supply, humanitarian airlift and combat insertion of forces);

- *air-to-surface attack* (virtually synonymous in the modern era with precision attack);

- *furnishing awareness* (through aerial reconnaissance, surveillance, signals, intelligence and the like).

Obviously not every air force is equipped to do these in the same ways: the F-16 of a NATO nation may well be an older MiG-21 for another service; the U-2R of the United States may be an over-40-year-old Canberra in a Third World air force; the P-3 Orion of a Norway or Australia may be a Britten-Norman Islander or a Grumman S-2 Tracker in another, smaller service. Perhaps the greatest difference is in the ability of larger nations (and, more recently, more prosperous smaller ones) to exploit the space domain. Space is now so critical to Western military operations for communications, weather, navigation, intelligence, and cueing ground-based defensive systems to incoming threats, that it is impossible to conceptualise undertaking them without space support. Such will certainly become true (witness the GPS revolution, as one example) for smaller nations in the near future as well, particularly as smaller satellite launch systems proliferate.

Though air power is employed in both warfare and peacetime applications, it is, of course, in air warfare across the spectrum of conflict that it is most critical, for a nation's survival might quite literally hang in the balance. While this is somewhat less significant since the end of the Cold War, it is of continuing importance to smaller nations locked in regional rivalries. Further, the pattern of 20th Century conflict has, sadly, been one where no situation of relative peace and security has remained so for long. It may be anticipated that, early in the next century, new regional alliances and reinvigorated older ones will rise to challenge the existing hegemony, even for larger and now-secure nations. Relative terms such as 'superiority', 'supremacy', 'dominance', etc. often cause their own confusion in the minds of defence planners and students of warfare. Therefore, it is useful to define and examine what might be considered an 'Air Warfare Spectrum' which, even allowing for the tremendous changes that have accompanied the end of the bi-polar confrontation of the Cold War, can be seen as a relevant means of understanding both air warfare and the various verbal nuances that accompany it:

Air Subordination		Air Parity	Air Dominance	
(greater)	*(lesser)*		*(lesser)*	*(greater)*
Air Paralysis	Air Inferiority	Air Parity	Air Superiority	Air Supremacy

One can argue that, whether talking about air or (future) space operations, that there are three 'states of nature' in air warfare: *air subordination, air parity* and *air dominance*. There are five 'case relationships' that, in effect, form a spectrum of conditions reflecting these three states. These five are *air paralysis, air inferiority, air parity, air superiority* and *air supremacy*. Aside from *Parity*, which is an obvious condition, the states of nature in air warfare may be defined as follows. *Dominance* is the condition attained by the possession of, first, superiority and, ultimately, supremacy, for, in both cases, the enemy is dancing to the air attacker's tune and is not free to pursue his own initiatives. The 'mirror-image' of this is *Subordination*, which is what a nation faces if it suffers, first, inferiority, followed by paralysis. The spectrum of effects may be defined as:

4

- *Air Paralysis.* A nation is unable to undertake offensive military action of any significance because it is controlled by enemy air forces; there is no hope of victory. The enemy has Air Supremacy.

- *Air Inferiority.* A nation can undertake limited offensive military action possessing some potential significance, but only by taking the enemy's air activity into consideration; enemy air power forces the emphasis of most operations to switch from offensive to defensive warfare; there is little hope of victory. The enemy has Air Superiority.

- *Air Parity.* Both sides can secure, when they choose, *localised* air superiority over a portion of a front or theatre, even at the same time; neither can possess superiority over an *entire* front or theatre; either side may secure victory. Both sides operate in conditions of relative parity.

- *Air Superiority.* A nation can exert its power over a foe with minimal air losses of its own, and without serious concern about the enemy's ability to contest for control of the air with its own air forces; the enemy can only undertake limited offensive action in return, and must devote the bulk of its activity to defensive warfare; there is a high expectation of victory. The enemy experiences Air Inferiority.

- *Air Supremacy.* A nation can control a foe with essentially no air losses of its own and without need to concern itself about the enemy's air intentions; the enemy cannot undertake any offensive operations, and few if any defensive ones; if these conditions exist across an entire theatre, then victory is virtually assured aside from *Deus ex machina* third-party interventions. The enemy experiences Air Paralysis.

While such a spectrum is offered in hopes that it can frame a view of what air power both has brought and now brings to conflict, it is also worth quickly reviewing what air power has meant in its transformation of traditional war. The 20th Century has been a century of transformations and the technological and scientific explosions of this century – characterised by flight, atomic energy and the electronic revolution – have created swirling fallouts every bit as unsettling as the profound social and political changes that have occurred. In this century, which started amid a deceptive climate of good feeling and general harmony that disintegrated after the assassination of the Archduke Ferdinand in Sarajevo, Europe and Asia witnessed the rise of destructive societies that imposed appalling misery on their own populations and those of nations and peoples they chose to subjugate. The level of cruelty, exploitation, and criminality – depravity in the case of Nazi Germany and Imperial Japan is not too strong a word – echoed the worst of the Dark Ages or the brutality of ancient Assyria.

The new revolution in flight was at once allied with and imposed against this new era of barbarism. Air power began the Nazi attacks on Poland, Scandinavia, the Low Countries and Russia; air power began the Allied counterthrust that left Hitler a shaking mumbling wreck in a Berlin bunker with a pistol in his hand. Air power began the Japanese assault on China, as cities burned under Japanese bombers; it began the war in the Pacific, as American battleships at Pearl Harbor shuddered and sank under waves of Japanese dive bombers and torpedo planes. It began the decline of the Japanese empire as American dive bombers sank Japanese carriers at Coral Sea and Midway. It fulfilled the apocalyptic prophecies of advocates such as Douhet, Trenchard, and Mitchell as twin atomic mushrooms rose over Hiroshima and Nagasaki. Those ominous clouds sent a signal that, in the era of air power and atomic weapons, a nation that ignored its aerial defence did so at its own peril.

In the postwar years, during the long watch of the Cold War, Western air power offset the aggressiveness of the Soviet Union and its client states, maintained a relative balance of power, and contributed to international stability and harmony. Misused for much of the Vietnam War, it was used with such effectiveness in 1972 as to manoeuvre North Vietnam into a hard-won peace – subsequently thrown away by questionable political decision-making. Air power played the principal role in preserving the independence of Israel and in tempering the regional ambitions of Saddam Hussein. When, at the end of the century, the focus of the world again turned to Sarajevo, it was air power – against the expectations of many critics – that proved critical in establishing a shaky peace in the Balkans.

Though initially born solely of the need for battlefield awareness through aerial reconnaissance, air power rapidly achieved primacy over more traditional two-dimensional surface forms of warfare via direct attack. Even as early as the non-precision weapon era of the Second World War (and, in a limited way, in some selected cases from the First World War as well), examples exist of campaigns materially aided or spearheaded by air attack. The key to this was achieving air superiority. With air superiority, all manner of military operations are possible. Without it, one is too busy fighting off an enemy air force to be able to undertake much of significance on the ground, with the exception of limited insurgencies (and even here the balance is shifting rapidly in favour of the air power-equipped combatant).

Less than 40 years after the Wright brothers first flew at Kitty Hawk, Great Britain secured its national salvation through air power in the climatic

Battle of Britain in August–September 1940. At a time when Britain's land power forces were virtually nonexistent, when its naval forces were harried and fighting for their own survival, it fell to the Royal Air Force to impose itself between Britain and a triumphant Luftwaffe flushed with victories over opponents from the Baltic to the North Cape and to the French heartland. As fighters decimated German air attackers, bombers attacked naval craft preparing for an invasion of southern England, forcing Germany to scatter them in ports and anchorages up and down the continental coastline. Unable to secure air superiority over England, Hitler was forced to give up his invasion plans. It is interesting to imagine what might have happened in 1940 if, instead of a Royal Air Force, Great Britain had still possessed a Royal Flying Corps appended to the British Army. Given the history of the French campaign, it is likely that any such 'RFC' would have been thrown away in penny packets on futile efforts to stem the German tide in France and Belgium. If so, when Hitler's Messerschmitts appeared over southern England, they might have faced older Gloster Gladiator biplanes, instead of encountering more modern Vickers-Supermarine Spitfires and Hawker Hurricanes. After a short and vicious air war, Britain, then, would likely have shared the terrible fate of her continental neighbours. As it was, the triumph of the RAF in the Battle of Britain marked not only a triumph for a free Britain and a triumph for air power, but an important and validating triumph for the notion of strong and independent air forces possessing equal status with their older sister services.

The victory of the 'Few' set the stage for the subsequent pounding of Nazi Germany by British and American aircraft that weakened it to the point where, in 1944, Allied forces could storm the Normandy coast. When General Dwight Eisenhower stated (late in June 1944, as he and his son John surveyed the build-up on the Normandy beaches for the breakout from the beachhead), 'Without air supremacy I wouldn't be here', it was both an affirmation of the obvious and an acknowledgement that war, as humanity had known it for thousands of years, had forever changed. Not quite 50 years later, another coalition secured air supremacy, enabling ground forces to liberate Kuwait and impose the will of the United Nations upon Iraq with minimal casualties and losses. Control of the air was, is and will remain, first and foremost, the most important of all air power missions.

To understand what it means when a nation loses or does not possess air superiority, one only need review the historical record. During the Second World War, when armies faced air attack and were unable to rely upon their own air forces to defend them, they were pinned in place, denied mobility and denied the freedom to undertake strategic manoeuvre by long-range air attack. This was true of the French and British in 1940 and the Germans in 1944. By 1944, deep in captured territory on both the Eastern and Western Fronts, for example,

7

German road signs warned truck convoys not to use roads by day, from fear of Allied fighter-bombers; the threat of air attack alone was robbing German planners of the ability to use half of their available time. At sea, increasingly deadly aerial attack took a heavy toll of both Allied and Axis shipping. In the Pacific campaign, as agreed by a postwar Joint Army-Navy Assessment Committee (JANAC), American aircraft directly or indirectly caused 47 per cent of Japan's shipping losses (submarines claimed 48 per cent). (Of this air power total, 56 per cent of sinkings were by land-based aircraft and 42 per cent by carrier-based ones.) Wars since that time have largely confirmed these trends, from the various Arab–Israeli struggles, to the Falklands and on to the Gulf. Today, with the ability to project highly effective precision weapons capable of striking a target accurately from up to hundreds of miles away (thousands, in the case of missiles), the primacy of air power has extended to virtual dominance as well.

One aspect of air power often neglected is that of air transport and air mobility. As early as 1929, the Royal Air Force used an emergency airlift to transport women and children to safety in India from Kabul, Afghanistan, then besieged by rebel forces; 87 years earlier, a desperate retreat from Kabul in similar circumstances had ended in bloody disaster at Gandamack when Afghan rebels overran and butchered the column. From the start of the Spanish Civil War, air mobility proved to be of crucial importance. Francisco Franco would have been unable to undertake his revolt without the support of German and Italian troop carriers that flew his forces from North Africa to Spain. During the Second World War, air mobility enabled great airborne invasions and resupply activities, from the 'Hump' across northern Burma to the Rhine crossing. After the war, the dual-nature of air transport permitted humanitarian food-drop operations that fed starving populations. In 1948–49, when the Soviet Union isolated Berlin, airlift enabled the Allies to circumvent the land blockade and prevent a seizure of the former German capital: the first great triumph of the West in what would become known as the Cold War. The advent of the high-capacity jet transport revolutionised air mobility even further; Israel, for example, largely owed its survival in the 1973 war to long-range resupply of critical materials and weapons by Lockheed C-5 Galaxy transports. The subsequent introduction of aerial refuelling for air transports, reflecting lessons learned from the Israeli experience, made air transport truly global in nature. DESERT SHIELD/DESERT STORM marked this full-up maturation of modern airlift capabilities; air-refuelled transports constituted the only means of delivering personnel and supplies into the theatre within hours over global distances. Throughout the crisis, an average of one jet airlifter arrived every 11 minutes. Since that most recent conflict, the airlifters of the NATO nations, in concert with other countries, have turned from supporting war to supporting peace, with widespread humanitarian operations on a continuing basis into well over 90 per cent of the world's nations.

Air power now confronts an uncertain and unstable world. The predictability associated with the Cold War, with the superpower rivalry that built a bi-polar world of client states, is gone. Instead of a single unifying threat to global stability, there are multiple threats reflecting regional rivalries; resurgent nationalism; growing ethnic and religious unrest; internal instabilities; medical emergencies and food supply crises; economic dislocations; and various forms of civil unrest, from the narcotics trade through to varied forms of terrorism. In all of these, air power is called upon to play a role: surveillance, enforcement of United Nations' resolutions, deterrence, mobility, food and medical relief, and, if necessary, direct attack, including defeating regional aggressors. Though old areas of tension such as the Middle East and the Korean Peninsula remain likely flashpoints, new crisis areas have largely supplanted these as the focus of interest. If multiple generations of airmen earned their wings and then flexed them attuned to the demands of potential nuclear war in a NATO–Warsaw Pact environment, then their successors, the airmen of today, do so more cognisant that their theatre may be a Haiti, a Somalia or a Bosnia. Symbolically, the television image of crisis air power in the 1990s is more often a transport such as a C-130, rather than the B-52 or V-bomber of the Cold War.

The joining of the aerospace revolution with the electronics revolution has generated a profound synergy that has greatly increased the influence of both. Today, the capabilities of air and space systems ensure routine global access by both military and commercial aircraft. Tomorrow this may extend to the routine exploitation of space by both manned and unmanned systems as well. What form future air power systems will take is itself a challenging question, for even for smaller nations, technologies exist that can generate new air and space vehicles having significantly different qualities and capabilities from those of the present day. Indeed, the technology is available – if economics permits – to move rapidly beyond exclusively manned aircraft. If for no other reason than economic necessity, air forces in the future will have to incorporate more unmanned air vehicles (UAVs) into their inventories. Stealth has already established itself as a necessary attribute of advanced precision strike systems, and will shortly – if the Lockheed-Martin F-22 enters service – become a feature of the air superiority arena as well. The precision weapon revolution will continue to proliferate, blurring further the distinction between the 'throwaway' weapon and the UAV. Aircraft will increasingly become like ships: vehicles capable of decades of service, with updated systems few might even have imagined when those same aircraft first entered service. They will act as platforms for sophisticated UAV/precision weapon combinations for a variety

9

of roles, giving new life to the old term 'battleplane'. Electronic combat and the ability to acquire information and exploit it for military use (and, conversely, the ability to engage in information warfare against any level of opponent) will be even more critical in the next century than they are now. New weapons – particularly directed energy weapons such as lasers – will both threaten and enhance the ability of air forces to conduct operations against a foe.

Nor can one take comfort that these advances will be the sole province of wise and responsible nations. Potential opponents, regional aggressors and, even, certain categories of state and sub-state terrorists will possess increasingly sophisticated weapons (through longer-range nuclear-, biological- and/or chemical-tipped ballistic and cruise missiles) and be able to use forms of air power projection and influence (including both exploiting space and even threatening its denial to others), enhancing the threat posed by nuclear, biological, and chemical weapons and thus holding at risk populations far distant from their own. Responsible large and small nations alike must be prepared to confront this future, in which air power can be expected to play the predominant – indeed pre-eminent – part in ensuring both stability and security.

This largely technological vision of the future still demands that air power application and exploitation be rooted firmly in doctrine and understanding. Doctrine is of great importance to an air force (or, for that matter, to any military service), but there is a constant challenge in ensuring that the doctrine is as relevant, dynamic and flexible as the field of military aviation itself. An air force without doctrine is always uncertain about what it is doing and why it is doing it. An air force with outdated doctrine can, in effect, imprison itself, intrinsically limiting its ability to project air power. Such has, in fact, happened many times. Germany's subordination of its air service in the First World War (and its air force in the Second) to the needs and perspective of the German army, coupled with a failure in both wars to fully appreciate the inherently offensive nature of air power led to its losing both air wars. The mistaken interwar years doctrine that unescorted bombers could always penetrate enemy air defences even in the face of intercepting fighters cost virtually all combatant nations – including the United States – dearly. In Vietnam, the United States Air Force discovered that the years of the Cold War had generated a nuclear warfare straightjacket upon its doctrinal development, leading to costly rediscovery of lessons lost from the Second World War and Korea. Even in the Gulf War, the activities of air force planners – from the 'Black Hole' in Riyadh to the Checkmate planning and assessment operation in the Pentagon – reflected more accurately an informal unspoken doctrine rather than the official pronouncements of the Air Force doctrine manual.

Nor are such examples limited to air forces; when NATO armies arrived in Bosnia they reflected, for the most part, their Cold War-inherited training and emphasis upon large-scale manoeuvre warfare. Instead, they found themselves operating in a static base camp environment unsuitable, in most respects, for heavy mechanised vehicle operations and without even the means to adequately house themselves. Imprisoned by a land-warfare manoeuvre mindset that minimised the potential contribution of organic army aviation forces, they set as their first major task – which took a surprising two weeks to accomplish – the putting of a single, highly vulnerable bridge across a river so that tanks and other armoured vehicles could cross to the other side, even though the subsequent presence resulted in little use of such heavy mechanised vehicles. Such episodes clearly indicate that doctrine must be realistic and, above all, flexible enough to be applied to varying circumstances, and understood and appreciated by all levels of a service.

For all of these many reasons, it is good that the authors of this work have pooled their considerable skills to produce a series of provocative essays on various aspects of air power thought and utilisation. There has been no attempt to produce or impose upon the reader a single unifying 'generic' view of air power. Likewise, this book does not claim to represent the official position of the United States Air Force, the Royal Air Force, the Royal Australian Air Force or any other governmental agency, company or body. It is, instead, a collection of individual views and opinions by a diverse group of practitioners who work in the air power field. It has been produced as an exercise in dialogue: to promote discussion and debate, and to trigger further analysis and thought as the world's airmen fly boldly – and confidently – from one century into the next.

1

DOCTRINE, TECHNOLOGY AND AIR WARFARE

by
Lieutenant Colonel Barry D Watts, USAF (ret.)
DIRECTOR, NORTHROP GRUMMAN
ANALYSIS CENTER, ARLINGTON, VIRGINIA

As an institution, the military largely discourages independent thought and critical inquiry. This is an unfortunate, self-defeating contradiction for a profession whose *raison d'être* is closely tied to outwitting adversaries and grappling with uncertainty.[1]

This paper aims at illuminating some of the more basic relationships between doctrine, technology and war, via selected historical vignettes used to shed light on these relationships.[2] Nevertheless, the discussion will not be exclusively historical or backward looking. The deeper, more enduring linkages between doctrine, technology, and war also suggest certain bounds on how much the conduct of war can be expected to change in the decades ahead – even if the *hypothesis* of an emerging revolution in military affairs is borne out in the decades ahead. These boundaries or limits, presumably, should be of interest to anyone concerned with either air power or joint doctrine.

Why concentrate on the more basic relationships between doctrine, technology, and war – particularly at a time when so much about war seems subject to imminent change? The answer stems from a point repeatedly emphasised by Albert Wohlstetter: namely, to avoid confusing ourselves 'about matters of great importance for national security'.[3] Today, as during the opening years of the nuclear age, we are confronted with the likelihood of significant changes in the weapons of war arising from a panoply of technological advances, especially those bearing on the gathering, processing, dissemination and rapid exploitation of ever more precise, detailed and comprehensive information. Precision weapons, advanced surveillance platforms, and even low observability can be viewed as technologically driven variations on this overarching theme.

Such changes in the prevailing means of war inevitably entail changes in other aspects of military societies. In the words of the historian Elting Morison:

> Military organizations are societies built around and upon the prevailing weapons systems. Intuitively and quite correctly the military man feels that a change in his weapon portends a change in the arrangements of his society.[4]

Confronted by such far-reaching and potentially uncontrollable changes, it is easy to lose sight of fundamentals, to lapse into the belief that little or nothing we have learned from past wars is likely to apply in the future. At best, the impression that everything about war is in flux is exaggeration. At worst, it leads us to confuse ourselves.

The discussion that follows aims first and foremost at avoiding such confusion. Of particular importance is to distinguish those aspects of future war that are likely to change from those that are not. Toward this end, we will examine, in turn, doctrine and air warfare; technology and air warfare; and doctrine and technology. The result, hopefully, will be at least a few propositions on which we can risk hanging our 'doctrinal hats' even in a period of considerable technological change. In addition, by concentrating on the first-order or fundamental relations in each area, there is also the possibility that the outlines of a more objective, empirically based kind of doctrine may become visible.

DOCTRINE AND AIR WARFARE

The relation between doctrine and war seems as good a place to start as any. Are there any enduring linkages between doctrine and combat outcomes? Or, to put the point more bluntly, does doctrine matter?

There is, of course, a popular tradition in the US Air Force that doctrine does not count for much. In the first heady flush of combat, so goes one variant of this popular view, the dry doctrinal tomes written by staff 'pinheads' are jettisoned and 'innovative' free-wheeling 'operators' begin making it up as they go along in response to the pressing needs of the moment. My own reading of military history is that this view, however popular in many quarters of the Air Force, is misguided at best and nonsense at worse. Two illustrative cases in point follow, one a negative lesson and the other a more positive one in terms of doctrinal soundness.

The first example concerns the so-called doctrine of bomber invincibility that grew up among bomber proponents at Maxwell Field, Alabama, in the 1930s during the heyday of the Air Corps Tactical School (ACTS).[5] In the visionary and oft-quoted words of ACTS graduate and instructor Kenneth L Walker, 'A well planned and well conducted bombardment attack, once launched, cannot be stopped.'[6] Over time, this view was incorporated into ACTS texts. In April 1930, the revised ACTS text *The Air Force* boldly asserted that 'a defensive formation of bombardment airplanes properly flown, can accomplish its mission unsupported by friendly pursuit, when opposed by no more than twice its number of hostile pursuit'.[7] Five years later, the school's bombardment text noted that 'escorting fighters will neither be provided nor requested unless experience proves that bombardment is unable to penetrate . . . resistance [from enemy pursuit] alone'.[8] In short, the doctrinal thesis that American bomber advocates developed during the 1930s was that well-flown, well-led bomber formations could, even in daylight, penetrate enemy defences *without escort* by friendly fighters and accurately bomb targets from high altitude without suffering unacceptable losses.[9]

Did this doctrinal belief have consequences for American bomber operations during the Second World War? The US Eighth Bomber Command under (then Brigadier) General Ira Eaker flew its first bombing mission from the United Kingdom on 17 August 1942. This initial test of daylight precision bombing dispatched 12 B-17s to Rouen in German-occupied France; these dozen American bombers were shepherded to the target and back by over a hundred Spitfires.[10] That same month the Air Staff's Air War Plans Division began updating its August 1941 estimate (AWPD-1) of the Army Air Forces' munitions requirements for defeating Germany. The fundamental view expressed in AWPD-42 was that 'the heavy bomber formation was self-defending and thus escort was not required'.[11] The crucial point for present purposes is that this optimism concerning the defensive abilities of *unescorted* American bomber formations was embraced by General Eaker in England.[12] As he wrote to General H H 'Hap' Arnold in Washington on 20 October 1942:

> You have probably been asked whether it is feasible to bomb objectives in Germany by daylight without fighter cover. I am absolutely convinced that the following measures are sound. . . . *Three hundred heavy bombers* can attack any target in Germany by daylight *with less than four per cent losses.* A smaller number of bombers will naturally suffer heavier losses.[Emphasis added.][13]

In late 1942, of course, Eighth Bomber Command did not have the planes or bomber crews to test this brave proposition. Not until the beginning of October 1943, almost a year later, was General Eaker in a position to dispatch three hundred or more heavy bombers against targets in Germany over the course of a series of missions. Since the more 'vital' of these targets lay beyond the range of any long-range fighter then available, fighter escort all the way to the target and back was not possible.[14]

By the time General Eaker was in a position to test bomber invincibility, he was under considerable pressure. From Washington, General Arnold pressed Eaker to prove the viability of daylight, precision bombing; in England, British airmen like Arthur 'Bomber' Harris still hoped that American airmen would abandon daylight bombing of 'panacea' targets, as both the German and British air forces had already done, and join the Royal Air Force in area attacks at night.[15] Confronted with such pressures, Eighth Air Force mounted a series of six deep-penetration missions against German targets during the 13 days spanning 2–14 October, 1943. The results are well known. Including those bombers written off, these six deep-penetration missions cost Eighth Bomber Command 198 heavy bombers – roughly 37 per cent of the command's average 'fully operational' bomber strength in combat units during October. Ignoring wounded and dead airmen in aircraft that survived the trip back to England, 166 crews totalling 1,651 American airmen went 'missing in action' over enemy territory – nearly 40 per cent of the command's average effective combat-crew strength that month.[16] Eighth's overall loss rate as a percentage of the 2,014 heavy-bomber sorties dispatched against German targets for the missions of 2, 4, 8, 9, 10, and 14 October, 1943 was 9.8 per cent, more than double the 4 per cent upper limit that Eighth Air Force leaders had believed putting up 300 or more bombers at a time would guarantee. Worse, the losses per mission escalated dramatically over the course of these 13 days as the Germans reacted to the American daylight, deep-penetration raids. On the final mission to the ball-bearing plants at Schweinfurt – better known to the bomber crews who flew it as 'Black Thursday' – German defensive measures included large-scale use for the first time of rockets fired from beyond the bombers' effective machine-gun range to break up formations; the concentration of fighter attacks on one bomb group at a time; and aggressively pressing home head-on fighter attacks from '12 o'clock high'.[17] The upshot was 60 B-17s missing in action on Black Thursday alone.

Such aircraft and crew losses constituted levels of attrition that Eighth Bomber Command could not sustain. While Luftwaffe fighters opposing the raids of 2–14 October, 1943 also sustained severe losses,[18] American hopes of conducting unescorted, daylight bombing of German targets ended in what the official history of the Army Air Forces in the Second World War rightly termed the 'autumn crisis' of October 1943.[19] For the next two and a half months, the 'Mighty Eighth' suspended 'deep-penetration bombing missions into Germany during clear weather'.[20] As Eighth Air Force tacticians under Major General Orvil A Anderson wrote in July 1945:

> These deep bomber penetrations beyond fighter escort range represented a
> bold attempt by the Eighth Air Force to establish that heavily-armed bombers

could fly deep into enemy territory with only the protection of their own defensive fire-power. The losses on some of these missions tended to prove the opposite, if the bombers were opposed by an alert and desperate enemy.[21]

Not until adequate numbers of P-38 and P-51 fighters, properly equipped with external drop-tanks, became available in December 1943 in sufficient numbers for deep escort did it become practical for Eighth Air Force 'to renew the systematic bombing under visual conditions of targets deep in Germany'.[22]

The saga of bomber invincibility is, obviously, not a happy doctrinal story. American airmen got at least one vital aspect of their prewar bombardment doctrine wrong, and they paid a heavy price for that mistake in both men and machines when the test of combat arrived in the skies over northern Europe. Depressing as this story may be, though, it establishes a clear, concrete linkage between doctrinal precepts and combat outcomes. It illustrates an occasion on which prewar doctrine mattered very much insofar as it failed to take into account the operational challenges that a determined, resourceful opponent could pose for unescorted bomber formations.

That said, can we also point to happier examples in which prewar doctrinal precepts were not only validated by the test of combat, but appear to have been crucial in producing positive results? A recent case can be seen in the thinking behind the offensive air campaign that the air forces of the US-led coalition conducted against Iraq from 17 January to 28 February, 1991. At the core of this air campaign – both as planned and as executed – was a bold 'vision of air power' as the 'essential element' in all but the fourth and final phase of a theatre war.[23] In the opening three phases, air power alone attacked strategic target systems deep in Iraq, achieved and maintained air superiority, and prepared the battlefield. (These opening three 'phases' overlapped in execution although the relative weight of effort accorded to each varied considerably during the war's first 39 days.) Only during the final 100 hours of offensive operations by Coalition ground forces did air power function mainly in a supporting role.

In the aggregate at least, the results achieved by the DESERT STORM air campaign constituted the basis of one of the most lopsided military campaigns in modern military history. At an astonishingly low price in friendly lives (less than 250 Coalition members died from enemy action during DESERT SHIELD and DESERT STORM), Iraq's air force and integrated air defences were destroyed, disrupted, or lost to Iran; Iraqi ground forces were ejected from Kuwait and over 70 per cent of their heavy equipment (tanks, artillery, and armoured personnel carriers) destroyed; and Iraq's ability to threaten other states in the Persian Gulf was greatly reduced (even though significant elements of Iraq's Republican Guard escaped destruction as did the majority of Iraq's nuclear-weapons program).[24] Granted, air power fell short of achieving victory

17

on its own as some of the American airmen involved in both planning and execution had privately hoped. For a variety of reasons, a multi-corps ground offensive still proved necessary after 39 days of Coalition air operations. Nevertheless, the lion's share of the credit for the Coalition's overall military success at so small a cost in friendly lives and treasure must go to the air campaign.

What were the origins of the conceptual ingredients underlying the DESERT STORM air campaign? Among other things, the air campaign emphasised: the notion of an enemy state as a 'system of systems'; the direct use of air power to achieve national objectives through the judicious selection of 'strategic target categories' containing enemy 'centres of gravity'; the functional disruption of target systems (as opposed to the physical destruction of individual target elements); precision munitions, especially laser-guided bombs which, when delivered from platforms like the F-111F and F-117, permitted precision attacks to be carried out at night on an operational scale ('parallel' operations); and the F-117s stealth, which offered a capability to attack strategic targets from the opening moments of the war without first achieving traditional air superiority.[25]

Where did these ideas and concepts come from? If we set aside various historical antecedents that, in many cases, reach back to the Air Corps Tactical School, the answer is that they came largely (though not entirely) from the prewar thinking about offensive air campaigns of a small handful of individuals. Key among those individuals in terms of the role their ideas subsequently played in the planning and execution of the DESERT STORM air campaign were two Air Force officers: Colonel John A Warden III and (then) Lieutenant Colonel David A Deptula. The history of their involvement, as well as that of many others, has been documented extensively since the Persian Gulf War in Air Force-sponsored reports and histories, as well as in numerous articles and books by scholars, journalists, and military participants in the Persian Gulf War.[26] This history need not be recounted beyond a few basic points bearing on the relations between doctrine and war. First, the INSTANT THUNDER campaign plan developed by Warden's Checkmate group in August 1990, which was more a concept for an offensive air option against Iraq than a series of detailed air tasking orders, did provide the 'conceptual base and overall blueprint' from which (then) Brigadier General Buster Glosson's Special Planning Group in Riyadh (known as 'the Black Hole') and, later, Central Command Air Forces (CENTAF) worked to fashion the detailed operations plan for the DESERT STORM air campaign executed in 1991.[27] Although two target categories (Republican Guard forces and surface-to-air missiles) were added before the war to the 11 Warden's group originally picked, and while a 14th (consisting of a half-dozen breaching targets) was added during DESERT STORM, INSTANT

THUNDER'S categories and their relative priority (as a percentage of total targets) persisted into the opening days of the air campaign. Thus, 'the first days of the air campaign plan were remarkably similar to those proposed five months before by INSTANT THUNDER planners'.[28]

Second, INSTANT THUNDER represented 'a radical revision' in the way both air and theatre planners had come to view the proper application of air power by the late 1980s.[29] Consider the alternative concept developed by Tactical Air Command (TAC) planners in early August 1990, with its emphasis on demonstrating resolve, incremental escalation, and concentrating air strikes on Iraqi ground forces then occupying Kuwait.[30] TAC's campaign concept was not only light years apart from Warden's conceptually, but in fact represented the mainstream of doctrinal thought within the Air Force at the time Iraq invaded Kuwait. As Colonel Edward Mann later concluded: if air power 'zealots' such as Warden and Deptula 'had not inserted themselves in the planning process, the offensive air campaign plan likely would have developed in concert with the plans for ground operations during November 1990'; that is, air power would have been subordinated directly to the manoeuvre and perspective of corps-level ground forces.[31] After the war, retired Major General Perry Smith reached much the same conclusion. While stressing that by the eve of DESERT STORM many in the Air Force had come to accept the wisdom of the INSTANT THUNDER concept, in August 1990 all too many senior officers, having become prisoners during the 1980s of a tactical air-power 'paradigm', opposed Warden's concept with a 'narrow-minded, anti-intellectual, and, at times, mean spirited' group think.[32]

What do these brief observations suggest about the brief relationship between doctrine and war in the case of the Gulf War? Given the unprecedented degree of success that the Warden-Deptula campaign concept subsequently achieved in the only meaningful test – actual combat – it is hardly plausible to argue that the approach chosen was misguided or wrong. Note, too, very different air campaigns from the one executed were possible, as the TAC alternative confirms.[33] The most intriguing implication for doctrine and war, however, is that key ideas underlying the DESERT STORM air campaign – parallel warfare, the enemy state as a 'system of systems', the emphasis on precision and stealth, the conscious goal of seeking functional disruption of whole target systems, etc. – were neither officially sanctioned at the time nor even mainstream doctrinal thinking within the Air Force. In other words, while imaginative doctrinal ideas underwrote operational success in January–February 1991 every bit as much as the flawed doctrine of bomber invincibility underwrote tactical defeat in October 1943, the notions that count in wartime need not be recorded in official prewar doctrinal publications. Why? Because the conduct of actual campaigns can, as happened in DESERT STORM, be shaped by the unofficial,

19

unsanctioned doctrinal concepts of a handful of individuals.

The suggestion that Warden and Deptula's ideas about air campaigns were not officially sanctioned at the time Iraq invaded Kuwait should not be misconstrued as implying that these officers had no encouragement from senior Air Force officers. While a student at the National War College during the 1985–86 academic year, Warden wrote a research paper entitled *The Air Campaign*, which sought 'to come to grips with the very complex philosophy and theory associated with air war at the operational level'.[34] In no small part due to Major General Perry Smith's enthusiasm for the paper, it was published by National Defense University Press in 1988 with (then retired) Air Force General Charles Donnelly's endorsement that a 'book of this type has been needed for a long time'.[35] Subsequently, when (then) Lieutenant General Michael Dugan became deputy chief of staff for plans and operations on the Air Staff (XO), he had not only read Warden's book but was sufficiently impressed to recommend it to all officers in XO, as well as to create a special deputy directorate for war–fighting concepts (XOXW) on the Air Staff and install Warden as its head.[36] It was his position as XOXW that, when Iraq overran Kuwait in August 1990, presented Warden with an unprecedented, once-in-a-lifetime opportunity to put his ideas about air campaigns into practice. Further, much as had the authors of AWPD-1 in August 1941, Warden and his like-minded colleagues seized the opportunity and made the most of it.

Deptula received similar 'top cover' and support from senior officers. In early 1988, when Warden became XOXW, Deptula was a major in the Air Staff's doctrine division. Deptula's first major project in the doctrine shop was to write a response to the position espoused in a recent issue of *Military Review* to the effect that the best thing to do with air power is to hand its control over to the corps commander. This project forced Deptula to begin thinking seriously about the design and conduct of offensive air campaigns. With the help of others in the doctrine shop, including the military historian Williamson Murray, Deptula produced a paper that General Dugan liked so much that he had it published in *Military Review* under his own name.[37]

One implication of this history is that serious doctrinal thinking can prepare one to seize opportunities when they occur, as happened with both AWPD-1 and INSTANT THUNDER. Another is that support from senior officers can also be crucial in providing access to opportunities to put one's ideas into practice. Next, it should be stressed that neither Warden's nor Deptula's thinking about offensive air campaigns was complete, much less published, the day Iraq invaded Kuwait. Warden's notion of a modern state being composed of five concentric 'rings' or 'centres of gravity', with the target systems in each ring being increasingly less important or decisive as you move outward from the centre ring, is nowhere to be found in *The Air Campaign*, although he had been discussing the concept in early 1990.[38] Similarly, Deptula's concept of the 'master attack plan' or 'MAP' as a means of structuring or organising the daily air tasking order (ATO) was not invented until September 1990.[39]

There is one final relation between doctrine and war that merits mention. Accepting unpublished, unsanctioned ideas held by a few individuals as 'doctrine' broadens the concept well beyond the most customary usage of what is written in official manuals or accepted as institutional practice. On this more expansive understanding, the doctrinal notions that affect combat outcomes, whether positively or negatively, encompass informal as well as formal precepts. Doctrine in this broader sense can include the past notions, new concepts, prior experiences, and 'lessons learned' that individuals take to war with them about how best to conduct operations along with the contents of official publications such as *Air Force Manual 1-1*.

This expansive view of doctrine has an important corollary. Because no one goes to war with a blank mind – with John Locke's *tabula rasa* ('blank slate') – informal doctrine is inescapable. In this sense, the oft-heard refrain that doctrine is irrelevant is not only wrong, but professionally irresponsible. Like it or not, in time of war doctrine counts, and we ignore it at our peril.[40]

TECHNOLOGY AND AIR WARFARE

What about the relations between technology and war? From the standpoint of air power, the most important linkage to confront is the degree to which superior technology and weaponry can be the *guarantor* of combat success. The hypothesis that technically superior hardware *often* or *always* guarantees success in combat can be described as 'technological determinism'.

Has a tendency toward technological determinism been a characteristic of the US Air Force? Thoughtful students of the institution have certainly acknowledged its strong, enduring commitment to the pursuit of advanced technology. In 1986 David MacIsaac began his survey of air power theory for the new edition of *Makers of Modern Strategy* with the observation that, in a field with no lack of theorists, the effects of technology and the deeds of practitioners had played greater roles than ideas; he ended the essay with the speculation that 'today's primary air power theorist may be technology itself'.[41] In a similar vein, Carl Builder, a long time RAND analyst and participant in Project Air Force, wrote in 1994: 'The Air Force has long worshipped at the altar of technology . . . This is the catechism: If the Air Force is to have a future of expanding horizons, it will come only from understanding, nurturing, and applying technology'.[42]

The reasons this catechism has taken such deep root in the US Air Force are not hard to unearth. To begin with, Army Air Forces leaders had experiences during the Second World War that strongly reinforced the need for technical superiority. The most obvious case, of course, was the development of the atomic bomb. Its employment from B-29s not only ended the war in the Pacific but, for a time, quieted further debate about the efficacy of strategic bombing and the need for an independent American air force. Another wartime experience that underscored the importance of technological superiority in the minds of Army Air Forces leaders was the appearance, in July 1944, of German jets, particularly the Me-262. The fear of senior American air commanders in Europe at the time was that planes like the Me-262, if fielded in sufficient numbers, could 'force an end to the American strategic bombing campaign'.[43]

Such wartime experiences, however, are not the only reasons the US Air Force has been prone to technological determinism. To touch on some of the deeper reasons, armies and navies have been around since ancient times. Air forces, by comparison, emerged less than a century ago and owe their very existence to the technological developments that made heavier-than-air flight possible. The modern airman is, therefore, beholden to and dependent upon advanced technology to a degree that soldiers and sailors historically were not (even if many of them, including tank drivers, submariners, naval aviators, are today as dependent on technology as Air Force fighter and bomber crews).[44] Another reason for the US Air Force's tireless pursuit of ever more advanced technology has been its ahistorical character. As a faculty member of the Air War College recently observed, the inclination of many in the Air Force officer corps to reject the relevance of history goes far to explain the Services's fixation 'on technology as the key to the future'.[45] If the past is viewed as unworthy of serious study, then what else is there for a 'high-tech' institution beyond pursuing technology?

It is a short step from this sort of institutional concern with technological superiority to outright technological determinism, and more than a few in and around the Air Force have teetered on the brink of such determinism, if not embraced it. Consider, for instance, the following statement published in the predecessor to *Airpower Journal* by a senior Air Staff colonel in 1983: 'From ancient times when the Bronze Age superseded the copper only to fall to the iron, technological superiority has most often provided the margin for victory.'[46] Or take (then retired) General T R Milton's assertion in a 1986 issue of *Air Force Magazine* that 'The entire short history of air warfare confirms that victory follows the most technically advanced adversary rather than the most heavily armed.'[47]

One could protest that these statements stop a hair short of full-blown technological determinism, even if they do come very close. Also, they were both written a decade or more ago, and one could object that they may not reflect current Air Force thinking. For those inclined to make such objections, it may be useful to consider Air Force Colonel Jeff Barnett's conclusion, published in early 1996, that technological advances in information, command and control, penetration, and (non-nuclear) precision are 'underwriting a new aerospace approach to future war'.[48] Or, even more to the point, consider the charter that authors of the *New World Vistas* attributed to the Air Force secretary and chief of staff. The Air Force Scientific Advisory Board's understanding of its charter was 'to identify those technologies that will guarantee the air and space superiority of the United States in the 21st century': a formulation that does appear to embrace technological determinism.[49] Granted, the 29 November 1994 memorandum that directed the Scientific Advisory Board to undertake the *New World Vistas* project does not itself explicitly embrace this outlook. Instead, the 1994 memorandum merely notes, strongly confirming Builder's assessment, that a 'high technology orientation' has always been a 'fundamental part of Air Force culture'.[50] Nor is it surprising that the Air Force's scientific advisory board would give pre-eminent importance to technological superiority. Still, it seems fair to conclude that something quite close to technological determinism resonates deeply within the Air Force's institutional psyche and world view.

Is it in fact true, though, that superior technology *guarantees* combat success, either in the large or in the small scale of conflict? To answer the question in the large, we need look no further than to the protracted air war that US forces waged in South-East Asia from 1965–73. In this case, which side, the US or its North Vietnamese foe, was technically superior in the air? This question is often difficult to answer in specific historical cases. In this particular instance, however, it is not. Which of two sides, after all, had:

- fighters with state-of-the-art radars and beyond-visual-range (BVR) air-to-air missiles;[51]

- a large fleet of in-flight refuelling tankers with which to extend the reach of its combat aircraft;

- as many as 200 B-52 heavy bombers;

- large numbers of laser-guided bombs;

- anti-radiation missiles; or

- airborne surveillance platforms?

The answer in every case is the United States. Besides enjoying a heavy numerical preponderance in the air, the US land- and sea-based air forces possessed across-the-board, pervasive technological superiority over their smaller North Vietnamese adversary. Further, so numerically and technically superior were US air forces that the North Vietnamese were never able to sustain a serious challenge to American control of the air, not even in the upper 'route packages' where most of the air-to-air combat between the two sides occurred. ('Route packages' are geographical areas dividing zones of responsibility for air attacks.) True, excepting the Navy in 1972–73, American fighters did not enjoy the highly favourable air-to-air exchange ratios in South-East Asia achieved earlier in Korea's 'MiG Alley' or later during DESERT STORM. There was even a period in early 1968 when the North Vietnamese briefly achieved near parity in air-to-air kills against Air Force and Navy fighters operating over North Vietnam. Nonetheless, American control of the air was never seriously in doubt. Even in the spring of 1968, US airmen operated large strike programmes daily in North Vietnamese airspace, whereas North Vietnamese fighters did not once disrupt a US refuelling track, much less attack an American main operating base. Yet, despite across-the-board technical superiority and control of the air, the United States lost the Vietnam War. At the end of the conflict in 1975, North Vietnamese forces overran and occupied South Vietnam. In the large, therefore, this historical case demonstrates that neither technical superiority nor even control of the air necessarily guarantees ultimate victory.

To pre-empt one possible misinterpretation of this conclusion, it should not be presumed that the Vietnam War in the large was air power's alone to win or lose. To suggest that American air power could have produced overall victory given the strategic circumstances in which the war was fought independent of what happened on the ground inside and adjacent to South Vietnam would surely be hubris on the part of airmen. Short of the nuclear devastation of North Vietnam – hardly a viable option for a western democracy like the United States midway through the Cold War – it is open to question whether ultimate victory was attainable for the American military as a whole. As Andrew Krepinevich argued in 1986, even an outright invasion of North Vietnam might well have failed to produce strategic success.[52] Certainly, occupation of the Hanoi-Haiphong region would have bought South Vietnam more time to become a viable nation able to defend itself, but invasion and occupation would have almost certainly been more costly in American lives while leaving the North Vietnamese with the option of guerrilla warfare in the north aimed at waiting for the US to tire or else to experience a military disaster as traumatic as the French defeat at Dien Bien Phu in 1954.[53] As Mark Clodfelter, Ronald Spector and others have argued, for the United States the Vietnam War was an optional conflict fought for limited objectives, whereas for the North Vietnamese communists it was a total war of national survival.[54] The North Vietnamese 'were prepared to accept limitless casualties' while Americans were not.[55] Given these facts, the stalemate that emerged on the battlefield during 1968 favoured

24

North Vietnam in the long term.[56] Consequently, it remains open to doubt whether 'a plausible facsimile of victory was attainable' for the United States.[57]

What about technological superiority in the small? Can superior technology at least guarantee success at the lowest tactical level of individual engagements? Again the answer is 'No'. The best evidence comes from historical and test data on air-to-air engagements. To start with historical combat data, combat experience going at least back to the Second World War suggests that surprise in the form of the unseen attacker has been pivotal in three-quarters or more of the kills. For example, P-38 pilot Lieutenant Colonel Mark Hubbard stressed that, in his experience over northern Europe with the US Eighth Air Force, *'90% of all fighters shot down never saw the guy who hit them'.*[58] Similarly, the German Bf 109 pilot Erich Hartmann, whose 352 kills during that war made him the top scorer of all time, stated that he was sure that 80 per cent of his victims never knew he was there before he opened fire.[59]

Neither the shift to jet fighters for air superiority during the Korean War nor the development of infra-red and radar-guided air-to-air missiles in time for US involvement in Vietnam appear to have changed the basic pattern observed by Hubbard and Hartmann. US fighter crews experienced some 600 air-to-air engagements in South-East Asia from April 1965 to January 1973. These engagements produced some 190 kills against 75 US losses.[60] Detailed engagement reconstructions revealed that around 80 per cent of all aircrews downed – friendly as well as enemy – either were unaware of the attack, or else did not become aware in time to take adequate defensive action.[61] What historical air combat experience reveals, therefore, is that upwards of 80 per cent of the time, those shot down were *unaware* that they were under attack until they either were hit or did not have time to react. A lapse or breakdown in what fighter pilots have come to term 'situational awareness' – meaning 'the perception of the whole picture, not only location but also likely future activity, both friendly and enemy' [62] – has, by a large margin, been the cause of the majority of losses in actual air-to-air combat. Indeed, the ability of human participants to develop and maintain superior situation awareness has been the driver in engagement outcomes at least four times more often than technological advantages in aircraft, avionics or armament.

The implications of this actual combat experience have been strongly confirmed by large-scale tests designed to produce statistically meaningful data about air combat. In 1977, the bulk of two major air-to-air tests were flown on an instrumented air combat manoeuvring range north of Nellis Air Force Base, Nevada: the Air Intercept Missile Evaluation (AIMVAL) and the Air Combat Evaluation (ACEVAL). These tests pitted 'Blue Force' McDonnell Douglas F-15 Eagles and Grumman F-14 Tomcats against 'Red Force' Northrop F-5E Tiger IIs, chosen to simulate the Soviet-built Mikoyan MiG-21 'Fishbed'; Cubic

Corporation's air combat manoeuvring instrumentation (ACMI) system provided a combat area some 40 nautical miles in diameter as well as real time data on the engagements.[63] The Blue fighters were 'armed' with guns, short-range infra-red (IR) missiles and the medium-range, radar-guided AIM-7F Sparrow missiles; Red ordnance, by contrast, was limited to guns and IR missiles. AIMVAL sought to assess the operational utility of five existing and proposed IR missile systems.[64] ACEVAL explored the factors affecting engagement outcomes when multiple aircraft are involved, with force size, force ratio and initial ground-controlled-intercept (GCI) condition (Red advantage, neutral, or Blue advantage) as the primary test variables.[65] To give a feel for the scale of these tests, AIMVAL's test matrix included Blue-versus-Red force ratios of 1-v-1 (one F-15 or F-14 versus one F-5E), 1-v-2, 2-v-2 and 2-v-4, and called for 540 valid engagements involving 1,800 sorties.[66] ACEVAL's test matrix added 2-v-1, 4-v-2, and 4-v-4 trials to the four force ratios used in AIMVAL and required a total of 360 valid engagements involving 1,488 sorties.[67]

The results of AIMVAL/ACEVAL were highly controversial at the time. At the core of the debate was the fact that 'superior' Blue fighters, avionics, and missiles had not dominated nearly as much as had been expected (except in certain 'test bins' such as isolated 1-v-1 trials). Not widely noted in 1977–78 was the disconnect between these expectations and past historical experience. If superior Blue technology had proven as dominant in AIMVAL/ACEVAL as many expected, then these tests would have also revealed the irrelevance of past combat experience, especially its implication that situation awareness explained why pilots were shot down in air combat four times out of five. So dramatic a break with combat experience would have been a watershed. However, by 1979 more thoughtful reflection on AIMVAL/ACEVAL began to suggest that it was not quite time to reject previous air combat history. As Lieutenant Colonel 'Shad' Dvorchak wrote in a special 1979 issue of the *Tactical Analysis Bulletin*, in AIMVAL incremental hardware advantages had tended to wash out in the long run as opponents adapted; similarly, in ACEVAL human interactions had been five times as influential on outcomes as test variables like force ratio or the initial GCI condition.[68]

Nevertheless, it was still possible to argue in 1980 that technological dominance of engagement outcomes would materialise in the future. Throughout AIMVAL and ACEVAL, visual identification prior to firing had been a mandatory rule of engagement and the only radar missile allowed had been the AIM-7F Sparrow.[69] It was easy to conclude that these constraints had biased both tests against effective BVR (beyond visual range) employment.

The issue of whether widespread use of BVR missiles would finally enable technology to dominate engagement outcomes was settled by the Advanced

Medium Range Air-to-Air Missile (AMRAAM) Operational Utility Evaluation (OUE). Conducted in McDonnell Douglas flight simulators starting in 1981, this test gave Blue fighters the medium-range, radar-guided AMRAAM and half the non-excursion trials were run with BVR rules of engagement. The AMRAAM OUE test matrix called for over 1,200 engagements involving around 10,000 simulator sorties.[70] Instead of a small cadre of specially selected aircrew, AMRAAM OUE participants were drawn from operational units in the US. Scenarios included fighter-sweep situations (2-v-2 and 2-v-4) as well as trials in which the Blue fighters faced Red fighters escorting strike aircraft (2-v-4 + 4, 2-v-2 + 6, and 4-v-4 + 4). About half the trials were excursions from the standard sweep and combat air patrol scenarios.

The natural expectation was that in the BVR trials at least, Blue hardware advantages would drive engagement outcomes. Actual test results, however, proved otherwise. As in both historical combat experience and AIMVAL/ ACEVAL, situation awareness proved to be 'the single most important factor affecting engagement outcomes'.[71] For both sides, being aware of adversary weapons envelopes and keeping outside them to avoid being 'shot down', while trying to manoeuvre adversaries into their own weapons envelopes, proved as important and dominant as it had been in ACEVAL.

To avoid misinterpretation, the *statistical* dominance of AMRAAM OUE engagement outcomes by situation awareness should not be construed as implying that hardware – including aircraft performance, avionics and missile capabilities – counted for nothing. To the contrary, superior Blue hardware conferred building blocks or baseline elements of advantage that the Red side had to work hard to overcome and, in the aggregate, Blue hardware advantages were reflected in superior Blue exchange ratios. To put the point somewhat more vividly, Blue's hardware advantages conferred tactical options and possibilities not unlike being able to manoeuvre in three dimensions while the adversary is limited to only two. Statistically, though, the outcome of any given engagement depended on very small differences here or there across a large set of interrelated human and hardware factors, and the dominant of these factors, by far, was situation awareness. Thus, what has been termed technological determinism is no more viable in the small than in the large. Indeed, the combined data from combat experience and large tests such as the AMRAAM OUE provide *compelling* refutation of technological determinism in at least one technologically intensive area of air warfare.

What does this result suggest about the relations between technology and war? Clearly, the connections between technology and war are neither simple nor straightforward. Yes, superior technology is important, especially for a western democracy concerned to minimise the sacrifices its sons and daughters may have to make in future wars. General Hap Arnold's observation in

27

November 1944 that the United States will 'continue to fight mechanical rather than manpower wars' because Americans find personnel losses so distasteful is, if anything, even more valid today than it was then.[72] Still, superior technology does not and cannot guarantee success, either in the large or in the small. The successful application of military hardware in the pursuit of political objectives requires more than technological superiority. As General Charles Donnelly wrote in the introduction to John Warden's *The Air Campaign*, 'It is possible for an air force to have absolutely superior forces – numerically and qualitatively – and lose not only the air war but the entire war.'[73] Whether Air Force officers view this proposition as common sense, a doctrinal precept, or a generalisation about 20th Century warfare that is well supported empirically, it needs to be kept constantly in mind as a counterweight to the institution's legitimate pursuit of technological superiority. While there remains an element of truth to the thesis that superior weapons *favour* victory, they do not, and cannot, guarantee it.[74]

DOCTRINE AND TECHNOLOGY: THE VITAL INTERPLAY

What about doctrine and technology? What are some of the elementary relations between doctrinal precepts and hardware that may help to minimise confusion as we try to think about the future of war in the post-Cold War era? One elementary point that has, at least occasionally, been neglected in the Air Force's enthusiasm for advanced technology is the gap between *technical feasibility* and *operational utility*. That a given capability is technically feasible does not always mean that it is operationally useful in the demanding world of actual combat. The limited number of BVR missile kills attained by American and Israeli fighter crews from the early 1960s to the early 1980s offers an illuminating case in point.

The advent of radar-guided missiles for air-to-air combat with sufficient range to be fired BVR on a fighter, and a powerful enough radar to exploit such a missile, dates from the early 1960s when the initial US Navy variants of the McDonnell (subsequently McDonnell Douglas) F-4 Phantom II, equipped with the AIM-7 Sparrow III missile[75] and the AN/APQ-72 radar, entered operational service. Since the Marine Corps had embraced the F-4 from the outset, and because Robert McNamara imposed the Phantom II on the Air Force in 1962,[76] all three Services were re-equipping their fighter, interceptor and attack squadrons with either F-4Cs (the Air Force variant) or F-4Bs (the Navy-Marine model) by the eve of American military involvement in Vietnam. By the eve of the Yom Kippur War in October 1973, the Israeli Air Force (IAF) also had F-4s and Sparrows. Beginning in late 1969, the first F-4Es were exported to Israel[77] and, by October 1973, the IAF had acquired nearly 130 Sparrow-equipped Phantom IIs.[78] As a result, over the course of the Vietnam War American air forces were increasingly equipped with fighters able to employ BVR missiles in aerial combat, and the IAF had this capability in both 1973 and 1982.

The salient fact about the technical capability to fire from beyond visual range was simply this: it was very seldom exploited successfully in actual air combat either by American aircrews in South-East Asia during 1965–73 or by Israeli aircrews in the Middle East during the conflicts of 1973 and 1982. From the beginning of Operation ROLLING THUNDER in March 1965 to the end of US air operations against North Vietnam in January 1973, only two BVR kills were officially recorded out of a reported 597 Sparrow firings.[79] The Yom Kippur War of 6–24 October 1973 was a much shorter conflict, but the air-to-air combat was intense. During the 18 days of fighting, the Israeli Air Force claimed to have downed some 265 Egyptian and 130 Syrian planes.[80] Yet, despite the large amount of air-to-air combat, Israeli F-4s fired only 12 AIM-7 Sparrows in anger and claimed but a single BVR kill.[81] The seven days of intense air combat associated with Israel's June 1982 invasion of Lebanon tell a similar story. By the time Operation PEACE FOR GALILEE began, the Israelis had added General Dynamics (subsequently Lockheed Martin) F-16A Fighting Falcons and Sparrow-equipped F-15A Eagles to their inventory. During the major air battles between Israeli and Syrian fighters that occurred over the Bekaa in June 1982, the IAF split air superiority duties between their F-15s and F-16s, the latter being armed only with an internal gun and short-range, infra-red missiles. While the Israelis are thought to have downed 80 Syrian MiG-21 'Fishbeds', MiG-23 'Floggers', and Sukhoi Su-20 'Fitters' (plus five helicopters), only 23 AIM-7s were fired and, as in October 1973, only a single BVR kill was claimed.[82] In sum, out of some 632 combat firings of radar-guided missiles from 1965 to 1982 by US and Israeli aircrews, *only four* beyond-visual-range kills were officially recorded.

Attempts to achieve BVR shots by American and Israeli aircrews during this period appear to have been similarly limited. Only about 10 per cent of the 632 firings occurred at distances beyond five nautical miles.[83]

Why was the exploitation of the technical capability to fire from beyond visual range so rare? Why were there not considerably more BVR shots and kills? The reasons that the AIM-7 had so little success as a BVR weapon throughout this period were many and complex.[84] The overriding constraint, however, was not a technical one but a matter of compelling human preference. American and Israeli fighter pilots were, understandably, reluctant to shoot BVR unless they could be highly confident, if not virtually certain, that the target on the radar scope would not turn out to be a friendly aircraft. This natural reluctance to risk air-to-air fratricide was often reinforced by stringent rules of engagement that required positive target identification prior to firing.[85] Consequently, BVR kills were, for the most part, feasible only under very carefully controlled conditions in which special equipment for identifying friend from foe was available and accompanying procedural safeguards (rules of engagement) could be satisfied under actual combat conditions.

Not until the Persian Gulf War of 17 January to 28 February 1991 did the marriage of equipment, including by this time Boeing E-3B Sentry Airborne Warning and Control System (AWACS) aircraft, and operational circumstances permit a significant portion of the engagements that resulted in air-to-air 'kills' made by Coalition aircraft (15 out of 38) to begin with BVR shots.[86] But as impressive as this performance was, a razor-thin margin between successful 'kills' of enemy aircraft and the tragedy of fratricide remains a stubbornly persistent feature of modern air warfare. Missiles of all sorts—air-to-air, surface-to-air, and air-to-surface—have grown ever more reliable and lethal. Yet combatants must still make split-second shoot/no-shoot decisions in order to be effective and, under the extraordinary pressures of combat environments, those decisions remain open to fatal error. The tragic downing of two US Blackhawk helicopters by a pair of US F-15Cs in the 'no-fly zone' over northern Iraq on 14 April 1994, which resulted in the deaths of all 26 people on board the Blackhawks, goes far to illustrate the difficulties of reliably separating friend from foe even in visual engagements, much less at beyond visual range.

The historical reluctance of American and Israeli fighter crews to risk BVR shots in actual combat can, of course, be viewed as a technological problem in the sense that ongoing advances in sensors and information systems ought to provide improved means of identifying both friends and foes. The Joint Tactical Information Distribution System (JTIDS), which has been recently declared operational on one squadron of US Air Force F-15s, represents a step in this direction within the realm of air-to-air combat. US Army efforts since the 1991 Persian Gulf War to begin digitising future battlefields constitutes another. Given the increasing reliability and lethality of air-to-air, air-to-surface and surface-to-surface precision weaponry, the imperative for US forces to be able to separate friends from foes with very high reliability in real time is clear, and there is every reason to expect that technological advances can provide significant improvements in American technical capabilities to do so.

Nonetheless, the great reluctance of US and Israeli fighter crews to exploit their technical ability to take BVR shots from 1965 to 1982 illustrates the power of national values and Service cultures to constrain military operations regardless of fielded capabilities. Prior to DESERT STORM, the Joint Forces Air Component Commander, Lieutenant General Charles Horner, imposed stringent rules of engagement for BVR shots that very few Coalition fighters could satisfy on their own.[87] He also made it crystal clear before and during the conflict that he would not tolerate Blue-on-Blue fratricide in the air. The resulting constraint was fundamentally a *doctrinal* one. As in South-East Asia and the Middle East during 1965–82, this doctrinal constraint limited the capability of friendly forces to fully exploit the technical capabilities of available equipment, and rightly so. Technical feasibility, as people are prone to forget in the pursuit of superior weapons, is not the same as operational utility.

The other side of this proposition is that doctrinal myopia can also *prevent* the full exploitation of technically superior weaponry. A good illustration is provided by the very different results that laser-guided bombs (LGBs) are perceived to have achieved in South-East Asia compared with the Persian Gulf War. In Vietnam, LGBs were a historical footnote, mostly of interest to Fighter Weapons School instructors tasked with teaching others how to employ them. In DESERT STORM, by contrast, the combination of precision weapons and, in the case of the F-117, stealth, has been widely billed as tantamount to a revolution in warfare. As Colonel John Warden has argued, DESERT STORM was 'revolutionary' in the 'sense of the very few number of bombs that were required to achieve an enormous amount of very, very focused, precise destruction'.[88] How might this apparent discrepancy be explained?

Air Force interest in laser-guided bombs dates from 1958 when the Limited War Committee of the Woods Hole Summer Study Group began exploring whether monochromatic or single-frequency laser light could be used for guidance. In 1960, researchers demonstrated a practical method for generating and projecting laser light. Development work on laser guidance began soon thereafter.

The Air Force's first laser-guided bomb programme was started in 1965, and the initial combat experiments with 750-pound (Mark 117) Paveway I LGBs were carried out during the spring of 1968 by F-4s from the 8th Tactical Fighter Wing (TFW) in southernmost North Vietnam (Route Package I).[89] By September 1968, combat experience indicated that about half of the 2,000-pound (Mark 84) LGBs could be expected to hit within 20 feet of the aiming point.[90]

This early success with LGBs led to their growing combat use until the end of large-scale American combat involvement in the Vietnam War in early 1973. Perhaps the most famous accomplishments of 'smart' bombs during this period were the dropping of the Thanh Hoa and Paul Doumer bridges in the spring of 1972 as part of Operation LINEBACKER I (April–October 1972).[91] While precision targets other than bridges were also attacked with LGBs during LINEBACKER I, including thermal power plants, the bulk of the employment to the end of the Vietnam War appears to have been against choke points, especially bridges. For example, between 6 April and the end of June 1972, laser bombers from the 8th TFW alone were credited with destroying 106 bridges.[92] In this sense, the operational concept, or employment doctrine, for LGBs did not differ greatly from that underlying the use of radio-controlled

Razon and Tarzon bombs against bridges during the Korean War.[93]

This fact probably goes far to explain why the advent of LGBs in South-East Asia was viewed by most observers as, at best, a tactical advance. The tactical utility of these weapons during the final years of the war in hitting point targets was clear. Individual bridges that had survived repeated attacks during ROLLING THUNDER (and cost a number of losses to North Vietnamese ground-based air defences in the process) were dropped in 1972 by one or two strikes by laser bombers.[94] Yet, for all their tactical success, LGBs were not widely perceived during the decade after Vietnam to have signalled any major breakthrough or profound change in aerial warfare. Postwar surveys of US air operations in South-East Asia not only offered little premonition of the much larger role that precision weapons would play in DESERT STORM,[95] but largely failed to anticipate the post-DESERT STORM view that 'Precision air weapons have redefined the meaning of mass.'[96]

Why was the potential of precision air munitions so hard for airmen to foresee during the late 1970s and early 1980s? Part of the answer undoubtedly lies in the operational limitations exhibited by Vietnam-era precision weapons such as the Paveway I LGBs. They had to be released so as to fall into the relatively small cone over the aim point within which the seeker could detect reflected laser illumination, which constrained delivery tactics. Further, in the vast majority of cases, the aircrew in the designating aircraft had to rely on 'Mark I eyeballs' to see the aim point in order to illuminate it, which largely limited laser bombing to daylight hours during periods of relatively good visibility.[97] After the Vietnam War, as American airmen began thinking anew about conventional air operations in central Europe, this particular feature of LGBs seemed especially limiting given the low ceilings and limited visibility typical over Germany and the Low Countries during certain portions of the year.

Of course, between 1973 and 1991 improvements were made to laser-guided bombs and the associated designation equipment needed to illuminate aim points. Although the Paveway II kits slightly increased the cone-shaped volume or 'basket' over the target into which an LGB had to be dropped by the releasing aircraft for the bomb to 'see' the laser illumination, the Paveway III low-level laser-guided bomb (LLLGB) expanded release baskets greatly by adding an autopilot that would enable the bomb to fly itself into the basket.[98] The other major upgrade to Vietnam-era laser-bombing capabilities was the introduction during the 1980s of Pave Tack, an infra-red imaging targeting pod initially deployed on the F-111F. By mounting the sensor in a rotating turret, Pave Tack enabled the laser spot to be kept on the aim point through a wide range of aircraft manoeuvres, and the ability to look to the rear permitted imaging to be maintained to weapons impact.[99] In addition, infra-red imaging permitted precision attacks to be conducted at night.

On the one hand, these improvements in US laser-bombing capabilities from 1973 to 1991 were far from trivial. They gradually began to overcome some of the more glaring limitations of the LGBs employed during the Vietnam War. On the other hand, they hardly seem tantamount to a revolutionary advance in warfare, not even when the stealth of the F-117 is taken into account. After all, even by DESERT STORM standards, the quantities of laser-guided bombs expended during the final years of the Vietnam War were large. The total number of LGBs dropped by US forces in South-East Asia during fiscal years 1970–73 was 27, 507 kits, with roughly another 1,000 expended in prior years for a total of 28,508.[100] This total of 28,508 LGBs expended in South-East Asia is three times greater than the 9,342 dropped by US air forces during 43 days in January and February 1991. Even if one adds the roughly 1,200 laser-guided munitions known to have been dropped by British, French and Saudi aircraft, the Coalition total for laser-guided bombs and missiles probably does not exceed 11,000 weapons.[101] Yet it is DESERT STORM that marks the real 'coming of age' of precision bombardment in most people's minds, including that of John Warden, one of the conceptual architects of the Coalition air campaign.

Is Warden mistaken? This author thinks not, but the reason lies more in differences in concepts and doctrine from Vietnam to DESERT STORM rather than in technological improvements. The Gulf War was the first campaign in history in which precision-guided munitions (PGMs) in general, and LGBs in particular, directly influenced effectiveness at the operational and strategic levels of a theatre conflict. One obvious example is the success of LGBs in destroying Iraqi aircraft in hardened shelters, thereby precipitating efforts to move the most capable Iraqi aircraft to 'sanctuary' in Iran. Another example is the success of LGBs during the second half of DESERT STORM in separating Iraqi armoured crews from their vehicles in the Kuwait theatre of operations, thereby doing much to ensure that Coalition casualties would be unprecedentedly low when Coalition ground forces engaged Iraqi Republican Guard units such as the Tawakalna mechanised and Madinah armoured divisions. Yet another (and even more fundamental) example is the conscious use of precision and stealth to enable Coalition air planners to pursue functional effects against a number of target systems more or less in parallel. The decision to use precision and stealth to permit the parallel attack of multiple target systems from the opening minutes of the campaign was a fundamental conceptual change from the one-target-system-at-a-time approach generally used in the Second World War, Korea and Vietnam. By contrast, the use of LGBs in South-East Asia was largely a tactical matter. Unguided weapons had enjoyed scant success in dropping heavily defended bridges without the expenditure of inordinate numbers of sorties; in the case of the Thanh Hoa, even hundreds of sorties and a number of aircraft losses had failed to eliminate the target on any permanent basis. LGBs provided a means of doing so with much increased efficiency, but that greater efficiency did not exert any obvious operational or strategic impact on the overall outcome of the conflict. Hence, there is a legitimate sense in which precision-guided bombs, especially LGBs, came of age in 1991, and the difference lay first and foremost in a doctrinal change.

Doctrine, then, may not only constrain the operational utility of technically feasible capabilities for the very best of reasons, as in the case of BVR missiles; it can also hobble technically useful ones, as in the case of LGBs. To generalise only slightly, the trick is to get a better 'fit' than the opponent between hardware, doctrine and operational concepts and, to make things work in the real world, appropriate organisational adaptations. One of the best examples in this century of one side getting the 'fit' far closer to 'right' than its opponents is surely the Germans' campaign against France and the Low Countries in May 1940. The Allies, it turns out, possessed a numerical edge of approximately 1.3:1 in tanks, and many of their armoured vehicles possessed superior protection and armament to the Germans' tanks.[102] Moreover, at the outset of the May 1940 campaign, the Allies had force-ratio advantages of around 1.2:1 in manpower, a slight edge in divisions (1.03:1) and, from Luxembourg to the Swiss border, the French had completed the Maginot Line; only in total aircraft and anti-aircraft artillery did the Allies face substantial disadvantages at the theatre level.[103] In the end, however, these qualitative and quantitative advantages failed to save the western Allies from one of the most stunning military defeats in modern military history. In a nutshell, the Germans had evolved sound concepts for mobile, combined-arms warfare and had trained their combined-arms units to execute their operational doctrine. They had, in short, achieved a much better 'fit' between military hardware, concepts and doctrine, and organisational arrangements.

The larger lesson is clear. *Technology is important, but so is doctrine.* Even more important is a harmonious fit between the two. Developing a better fit than the adversary involves, as Andy Marshall has repeatedly emphasised since 1989, doctrine development and organisational adaptation as well as technological progress.

IMPLICATIONS FOR THE FUTURE

The widely discussed hypothesis of an emerging 'revolution in military affairs' suggests that much about war may change in the decades ahead. It seems fairly clear that, in the not-too-distant future, US surveillance systems are going to be able to collect and disseminate in 'near-real time' vastly more information relevant to military operations than US commanders, operators and planners have had in the past. Concurrently, the fielding in quantity of all-weather precision weapons with affordable per-round costs, notably the Joint Direct Attack Munition (JDAM) now estimated at less than $20,000 per kit, means that in the years ahead it will become possible to shift to largely precision strike campaigns. Indeed, it seems difficult to imagine why the US would choose to conduct a major air campaign after 2010 in which, as in DESERT STORM, more than 90 per cent of the air-to-surface and surface-to-surface weapons employed are 'dumb' unguided rounds. If one adds to these modest and foreseeable changes in the means of combat nothing more than the appearance of first-generation, remotely piloted strike platforms, it is not difficult to anticipate major changes in both Air Force doctrine and warfighting organisations.

As our exploration of the relationship between doctrine, technology and war indicates, though, the central problem the US military needs to solve in such a period of change does not lie in technological development *per se.* Instead, the key to the future probably lies in the intellectual task of getting a better 'fit' between advanced hardware, concepts and doctrine, and organisations than the opponent. While one clearly prefers to have superior technology if at all possible, the most pressing problem in coping with the kinds of changes likely to lie ahead 'is to be the first, to be the best in the intellectual task' of 'developing appropriate concepts of operation, making the organisational changes, and creating the doctrine and practices that fully exploit the available technologies'.[104] For the youngest of America's military services, the intellectual flexibility and openness to criticism demanded by this task may be particularly challenging. As Perry Smith recently observed, while there are signs that the Air Force may be growing beyond some of its former tendencies toward doctrinal rigidity, 'group think, parochialism, and anti-intellectualism', the youngest Service still 'lacks a journal of the quality of the *Marine Corps Gazette*, where tough-minded criticism is encouraged and published on a regular basis'.[105] Hence, if the main task of the next one or two decades really is predominantely an intellectual one, then it will be important for the Air Force to transcend the doctrinal rigidities of its youth. The choice, of course, is up to the Air Force's officer corps and, within the metaphor of the *Blitzkrieg* of May 1940, one would definitely hope that they choose to think more like the Germans than like the western Allies.

The thrust of this essay has been to try to place the intellectual challenges of future war in a broader context by recalling fundamental relations between doctrine, technology and war – relations that, arguably, have withstood the test of time throughout the 20th Century, if not longer. To reiterate the main points: doctrine really does count; getting doctrine wrong or adhering too stubbornly to outdated doctrine can lead to military disaster; doctrine encompasses more than what is written in official manuals; superior technology in and of itself does not, and cannot, guarantee military success, either in the large or in the small scale of conflict; technical feasibility is not equivalent to operational utility, indeed doctrine rooted in societal values may rightly constrain the employment of fielded capabilities; and finally, old doctrine seldom makes the most of new hardware, as the case of LGBs so aptly illustrates.

At this stage, a reasonable speculation would appear to be that these sorts of conclusions, if understood in historical context, may begin to sketch the outlines of a more empirically rigorous foundation for future doctrine than doctrine has generally enjoyed in the past. The issue of the long-term future of Clausewitzian friction offers an illuminating example of how such a foundation may help us to avoid confusing ourselves in an era of considerable change. (Clausewitzian friction is the problem of unanticipated difficulties or circumstances not necessarily immediately evident to planners before a conflict, but which act to inhibit the commander's freedom to execute his plan of action.) Some US military officers who have begun to grapple with the prospective changes in warfighting that may lie ahead have begun to argue that foreseeable advances in surveillance and information technologies will sufficiently lift 'the fog of war' to enable future American commanders to 'see and understand everything on a battlefield'.[106] Advances in sensor technologies and information systems may (or will) enable the side exploiting them more effectively to eliminate its 'fog of war' while turning the opponent's into a 'wall of ignorance'.[107]

Implicit in this view is the presumption that 'knowing everything that is going on' in a volume of battlespace is a problem that technological advances will eventually solve once and for all.[108] However, driving one's own friction to zero while, simultaneously, rendering the enemy's effectively infinite is not, at its core, a technical problem. In the first place, even in an 'information-rich' environment, there is only so much that any human can absorb, digest, and act upon in a given period of time. The greater the stress, the more data will be ignored, noise mistaken for information and information misconstrued, and the greater will be the prospects for confusion, disorientation and surprise. Second, the spatial and, especially, temporal distribution of information relevant to decisions in war means that some key pieces will be inaccessible at any given time and place, just as in market economies or biological evolution. Third, the ubiquity of nonlinear systems that exhibit extreme sensitivity to the smallest differences in initial or later conditions, when coupled with unavoidable discrepancies between the reality of those conditions our best approximations of them, reveal fundamental limits to prediction, no matter how much information and processing power technological advances may one day place in human hands.[109] In short, friction reinterpreted in modern terms gives every indication of reflecting *structural* features of human cognition and combat processes. If so, then technological progress may be able to manipulate friction, but certainly not eliminate its potential to dominate combat outcomes.

The deeper point of this example is, of course, that there are aspects of war that technology is unlikely to affect other than on the margin, and doctrine needs to be fully, constantly cognisant of these more enduring, structural aspects of war and combat processes. As Eliot Cohen has observed: 'The simple and brutal fact remains that force works by destroying and killing.'[110] Similarly, Colin Gray has recently produced a whole list of things about war that are unlikely to change in the years ahead, including the central role of geopolitical conflict in international politics and the absence of change in human nature.[111] These are things that the writers of future doctrine ought not to neglect.

Nevertheless, doctrine should neither be cast in stone nor viewed as if it has been. We should approach it as a 'work in progress', always open to modification or revision on the basis of evidence from the only test that matters: actual combat. Again, the architects of AWPD-1 and the DESERT STORM air campaign were able to seize once-in-a-lifetime opportunities because they had grappled with doctrine long enough and hard enough to be prepared to do so. That requirement did not end with the Gulf War or even with DELIBERATE FORCE in Bosnia.

NOTES

1   Gregory D Foster, 'Reading, Writing, and the Mind of the Strategist', *Joint Force Quarterly*, Spring 1996, p. 112.

2   The views expressed in this paper are the author's. They do not represent the views of the Air War College, the Air University, the United States Air Force, the Department of Defense or the Northrop Grumman Corporation. This paper was originally presented at the annual air and space doctrinal symposium, Maxwell AFB, Montgomery, Alabama, 1 May 1996.

3   James Digby and J J Martin, 'On Not Confusing Ourselves: Contributions of the Wohlstetters to US Strategy and Strategic Thought', *On Not Confusing Ourselves: Essays on National Security Strategy in Honor of Albert & Roberta Wohlstetter*, ed. Andrew W Marshall, J J Martin, and Henry S Rowen (Boulder, Colorado: Westview, 1991), p. 3. See also Andrew W Marshall, 'Strategy as a Profession for Future Generations', *On Not Confusing Ourselves*, p. 306.

4   Elting E Morison, *Men, Machines, and Modern Times* (Cambridge, Massachusetts: MIT Press, 1966), p. 36.

5   The author owes a great intellectual debt to Thomas Fabyanic for the discussion of interwar Army Air Corps doctrine in this section.

6   Major General Haywood S Hansell, Jr., *The Air Plan That Defeated Hitler* (Atlanta, Georgia: Higgins-McArthur/Longino and Porter, 1972), p. 15.

7   Quoted in Robert Frank Futrell, *Ideas, Concepts, Doctrine*, Vol. I, *Basic Thinking in the United States Air Force 1907–1960* (Maxwell AFB, Alabama: Air University Press, December 1989) p. 64.

8   Quoted in Lieutenant Colonel Thomas A Fabyanic, 'Strategic Air Attack in the United States Air Force: A Case Study', Air War College Report No. 5899, April 1976, p. 31. The cited passage from the 1935 bombardment text referred specifically to the case in which opposing fighters were 'assumed to possess an overwhelming superiority in all factors influencing air combat' (*ibid.*).

9   Geoffrey Perret, *Winged Victory: The Army Air Forces in World War II* (New York: Random House, 1993), p. 28; Fabyanic, 'Strategic Air Attack in the United States Air Force', p. 30; and David MacIsaac, 'Voices from the Central Blue: The Air Power Theorists', *Makers of Modern Strategy: from Machiavelli to the Nuclear Age*, ed. by Peter Paret with Gordon A Craig and Felix Gilbert (Princeton, New Jersey: Princeton University Press, 1986), p. 634.

10 Perret, *Winged Victory*, p. 246; Roger A Freeman with Alan Crouchman and Vic Maslen, *Mighty Eighth War Diary* (New York & London: Jane's, 1981), p. 9.

11 Fabyanic, 'Strategic Air Attack in the United States Air Force', p. 65.

12 Not everyone embraced the doctrine of invincibility. For example, in August 1941 then Lieutenant Colonel Clayton Bissell's comments on AWPD-1 stressed the need for an escort fighter (Miscellaneous papers for AWPD-1, Air Force Historical Research Center, Maxwell AFB, Alabama, 145.82-1, Part 3, p. 1). Similarly, in September 1942, General Carl A Spaatz also expressed concerns over Eighth Air Force's ability to conduct daylight bombing in the face of German air superiority (Fabyanic, 'Strategic Air Attack in the United States Air Force', pp. 69–70).

13 Quoted in Bernard Boylan, 'Development of the Long-Range Escort Fighter', USAF Historical Study No. 136, Air University, Maxwell AFB, Alabama, September 1955, pp. 68 and 265.

14 At this stage of the war, Eighth's escort fighters could only penetrate about 160 miles into enemy territory; by comparison, Schweinfurt involved a

penetration of some 320 miles (Major General William E Kepner, *Eighth Air Force Tactical Development: August 1942–May 1945* (England: Eighth Air Force and Army Air Forces Evaluation Board, 9 July 1945), p. 116).

15 James Parton, *'Air Force Spoken Here': General Ira Eaker and the Command of the Air* (Bethesda, Maryland: Adler & Adler, 1986), pp. 188–200, 222, 279, 311, and 316–320.

16 Freeman, *Mighty Eighth War Diary*, pp. 120–133; Wesley F Craven and James L Cate, *The Army Air Forces in World War II*, Vol. II, *Europe: Torch to Pointblank, August 1942 to December 1943* (Chicago: University of Chicago, 1949), pp. 849–850; and, 'Statistical Summary of Eighth Air Force Operations: European Theater, 17 August 1942–8 May 1945', Air Force History Office 520.308A, p. 14. To dispatch the 'magical 300 heavies', Eighth needed at least 800 bombers in theatre (Parton, *'Air Force Spoken Here'*, pp. 290–291). The average number of bombers assigned to Eighth in October 1943 was 1,000, of which 763 were 'on hand' in tactical units, and only 535 of the 'on hand' heavies were 'fully operational' ('Statistical Summary of Eighth Air Force Operations,' p. 14).

17 Craven and Cate, *The Army Air Forces in World War II*, Vol. II, p. 699. Line bomber crews who participated in unescorted, deep-penetration missions like the second American attack on the ball-bearing plants at Schweinfurt have tended to remain puzzled and bitter right down to the present day. See, for example, Elmer Bendiner, *The Fall of Fortresses: A Personal Account of the Most Daring – and Deadly – American Air Battles of World War II* (New York, New York: Putnam, 1980), pp. 227–239; also George C Kuhl, *Wrong Place! Wrong Time! The 305th Bomb Group & the 2nd Schweinfurt Raid: October 14, 1943* (Atglen, Pennsylvania: Schiffer, 1993), pp. 247–250. For Eaker's side of the argument as articulated by a member of his wartime staff in England, see Parton, *'Air Force Spoken Here'*, pp. 327–328. Parton's assessment specifically challenges the conclusions drawn by Arthur B Ferguson in Chapter 21 ('The Autumn Crisis'), Volume II, of Craven and Cate's *The Army Air Forces in World War II*.

18 Williamson Murray, *Strategy for Defeat: The Luftwaffe 1933–1945* (Maxwell Air Force Base, Alabama: Air University Press, 1983), p. 226.

19 Craven and Cate, *The Army Air Forces in World War II*, Vol. II, p. 707.

20 Richard G Davis, *Carl A. Spaatz and the Air War In Europe* (Washington, DC: Center for Air Force History, 1993), p. 287.

21 Kepner, *Eighth Air Force Tactical Development*, p. 116.

22 Craven and Cate, *The Army Air Forces in World War II*, Vol. II, p. 717.
For details of the range improvements provided by the P-38s and,
especially, the P-51s, see Davis, *Carl A. Spaatz and the Air War In Europe*,
pp. 362–363.

23 Alexander S Cochran, Lawrence M Greenberg, Kurt R Guthe, Wayne W
Thompson, and Michael J Eisenstadt, *Part I: Planning in Gulf War Air
Power Survey*, Vol. I, *Planning and Command and Control* (Washington,
DC: US Government Printing Office, 1993), pp. 223 and 230.

24 Department of Defense, *Conduct of the Persian Gulf War Pursuant to
Title V of the Persian Gulf Conflict Supplemental Authorization and
Personnel Benefits Act of 1991 (Public Law 102–25)* (Washington, DC:
Government Printing Office, April 1992), pp. 313–317; Thomas A Keaney
and Eliot A Cohen, *Revolution in Warfare? Air Power in the Persian Gulf*
(Annapolis, Maryland: Naval Institute Press, 1995), pp. 67–69, 72, 92–
93, and 102–103; and Central Intelligence Agency, Office of Imagery
Analysis, 'Operation Desert Storm: A Snapshot of the Battlefield', IA 93-
10022, September 1993.

25 For an informed and clear account of the ideas and concepts underlying
the DESERT STORM air campaign, see Colonel David A Deptula, 'Firing
for Effect: Change in the Nature of Warfare', paper presented at the Air
National Guard long-range planning conference, Reno, Nevada, 3
November 1994; in August 1995, the Aerospace Education Foundation
published a version of Deptula's essay as part of its Defense and Airpower
Series.

26 See, for example: Cochran, *et al.*, *Part I: Planning in Gulf War Air Power
Survey*, Vol. I, *Planning and Command and Control*; Colonel Richard T
Reynolds, *Heart of the Storm: The Genesis of the Air Campaign against
Iraq* (Maxwell AFB, Alabama: Air University Press, January 1995); and,
for context bearing on the development of the DESERT STORM air
campaign from two well-informed observers, see Daniel T Kuehl, *Airpower
Journal*, Spring 1996, pp. 121–123, and Perry Smith, 'Translating
Airpower Theory to Practice', Marine Corps Gazette, November 1995,
pp. 78–80.

27 Cochran, *et al.*, Part I: *Planning in Gulf War Air Power Survey*, Vol. I,
Planning and Command and Control, p. 226; Reynolds, *Heart of the Storm*,
pp. 133–134.

28 Reynolds, *Heart of the Storm*, p. 232.

29   *Ibid.*, p. 229.

30   *Ibid.*, pp. 39–45.

31   Colonel Edward C Mann III, *Thunder and Lightning: Desert Storm and the Airpower Debates* (Maxwell AFB, Alabama: Air University Press, April 1995), pp. 177 and 179.

32   Major General Perry M Smith, USAF (ret.), 'Translating Airpower Theory to Practice', *Marine Corps Gazette*, November 1995, p. 79. General Smith, though retired by August 1990, was not a completely disinterested observer concerning the planning of DESERT STORM air campaign. As head of the National War College, he had pushed for early publication of Warden's *The Air Campaign* by the National Defense University's press. Additionally, in 1970 General Smith, then a young officer, had published a book 'about the doctrinal rigidity of the Army Air Corps from 1936 to 1943' that had incurred the personal wrath of the sitting Air Force chief of staff, General Jack Ryan (*ibid.*, p. 80).

33   After the Gulf War, the present author did encounter one Air Force intelligence officer who had served in Riyadh with CENTAF during DESERT STORM and who argued vehemently that any dozen or so Air Force officers would have selected more or less the same campaign concept as was actually executed. This viewpoint seemed to be predicated on the notion that air campaigns are *uniquely* determined by political objectives and target lists. Given the latitude with which the military has always been able to interpret objectives, the present author has never been able to see the logic of the view that objectives and targets dictate one and only one campaign concept.

34   Colonel John A Warden III, *'The Air Campaign'*, February 1986, p. vi.

35   Colonel John A Warden III, *The Air Campaign: Planning for Combat* (Washington, DC: National Defense University Press, 1988), p. xxiii.

36   Lieutenant General Michael J Dugan, *'The Air Campaign'*, memorandum to 'All Officers DCS Plan & Operations', 15 November 1988; John A Warden, interview notes taken by Thomas A Keaney and Barry D Watts, Executive Office Building, Washington, DC, 21 February 1992, p. 1.

37   General Michael J Dugan, 'Air Power: Concentration, Responsiveness and the Operational Art', *Military Review*, July 1989, pp. 12–21.

38   Barry D Watts, personal notes from conversation with John Warden, 26 January 1990. Lieutenant Colonel Charles Westenhoff recalled in 1996 that Warden presented a paper on the five rings at a symposium of the

Military Operations Research Society in the spring of 1990 or possibly earlier. However, the proceedings of the symposium were not published until after the Gulf War.

[39] David Deptula, marginalia on draft of Chapter 7, Gulf War Air Power Survey 'Effects and Effectiveness' Report, 11 December 1992.

[40] Ed Mann's argument in *Thunder and Lightning* is that, because the generic Air Force officer would rather have root canal work than read about air power doctrine, the institution has repeatedly disarmed itself intellectually by ignoring the 'whys' of air power and concentrating instead on the 'hows' of flying and fighting (Kuehl, *Airpower Journal*, Spring 1996, p. 122).

[41] David MacIsaac, 'Voices from the Central Blue: The Air Power Theorists', *Makers of Modern Strategy from Machiavelli to the Nuclear Age*, ed. Peter Paret (Princeton, New Jersey: Princeton University Press, 1986), pp. 624 and 647.

[42] Carl H Builder, *The Icarus Syndrome: The Role of Air Power Theory in the Evolution and Fate of the US Air Force* (New Brunswick and London: Transaction Publishers, 1994), p. 155.

[43] Lieutenant Colonel Donald R Baucom, 'The Coming of the German Jets', *Air Force Magazine*, August 1987, p. 90. See also, Lieutenant General Carl Spaatz, 'Enemy Jet-Propelled Fighters', memorandum to General Arnold, 23 July 1944, Spaatz Papers, Box 50, Folder marked 'Aircraft Development – Jet Propelled', Library of Congress.

[44] As Perry Smith pointed out in 1970, perhaps the closest parallel to the special bond between American aviators and their planes is that between cavalry officers and their horses. (Perry McCoy Smith, *The Air Force Plans for Peace: 1943–1945* (Baltimore and London: Johns Hopkins Press, 1970), p. 18.

[45] Alexander S Cochran, 'Service Perspectives on the Present and Future: A Minority View on the Wild Blue Yonder', unpublished paper, Conference on Interservice Rivalry and the American Armed Services, Monterey, California, 6 March 1996, p. 5.

[46] Colonel Alan L Gropman, 'Analysis by Hyperbole', *Air University Quarterly Review*, September–October 1983, p. 91.

[47] General T R Milton, 'Forecasting for Security', *Air Force Magazine*, August 1986, p. 99.

[48] Colonel Jeffrey R Barnett, *Future War: An Assessment of Aerospace*

Campaigns in 2010 (Maxwell AFB, Alabama: Air University Press, January 1996), p. xx.

[49] Dr Gene H McCall and Major General John A Corder ,USAF, (ret.), *New World Vistas: Air and Space Power for the 21st Century*, Summary Volume (Washington, DC: Department of the Air Force, December 1995), p. 3.

[50] See McCall and Corder, *New World Vistas*, Summary Volume, pp. A-3 and A-4.

[51] As Tony Mason has rightly noted, the American F-4 was superior to Soviet-produced contemporary aircraft (Air Vice-Marshal Tony Mason, *Air Power: A Centennial Appraisal* (London & Washington, DC: Brassey's, 1994), p. 78).

[52] Andrew F Krepinevich, Jr., *The Army and Vietnam* (Baltimore and London: Johns Hopkins University Press, 1986), pp. 261–264.

[53] Bernard B Fall, *Street Without Joy* (New York: Schocken Books, 1961), pp. 105–106, 285, 302–303, 312–329.

[54] Mark Clodfelter, *The Limits of Air Power: The American Bombing of North Vietnam* (New York: The Free Press, 1989), pp. ix–xi, 134–146, and 194–202; Ronald D Spector, *After Tet: The Bloodiest Year in Vietnam* (New York: The Free Press, 1993), p. 314; Colin S Gray, 'On Strategic Performance', *Joint Force Quarterly*, Winter 1995–96, p. 30.

[55] Stanley Karnow, *Vietnam: A History* (New York: Viking Press, 1983), pp. 17–18.

[56] Spector, *After Tet: The Bloodiest Year in Vietnam*, pp. 311–313 and 315.

[57] Gray, 'On Strategic Performance', p. 31.

[58] Mark E Hubbard in Major General William E Kepner, 'The Long Reach: Deep Fighter Escort Tactics', Eighth Fighter Command, 29 May 1944, p. 10.

[59] Raymond F Toliver and Trevor J Constable, *The Blond Knight of Germany* (New York: Doubleday, 1970), p. 173.

[60] *Armed Forces Journal International*, May 1974, p. 30; R Frank Futrell, William H Greenhalgh, Carl Grubb, Gerard E Hasselwander, Robert F Jakob and Charles A Ravenstein, *Aces and Aerial Victories: The United States Air Force in Southeast Asia 1965–1973* (Washington, DC: Office of Air Force History and Air University, 1976), p. 157. The US Air Force was credited with 135 fighter kills (plus two more by B-52 tail gunners)

for 60 losses; the US Navy and Marine Corps fighters scored 55 kills for 15 losses.

61   *Project Red Baron III: Air-to-Air Encounters in Southeast Asia* (Cameron Station, Virginia: Defense Documentation Center, June 1974), Vol. I, *Executive Summary*, p. 24. As of the summer of 1975, instructors at the US Navy Fighter Weapons School (Topgun) were briefing that 55–60 per cent of the American crews downed in South-East Asia did not see their attacker until after they were hit, and another 25 per cent saw the bogey before weapons impact but not in time to do anything about it (Barry D Watts, personal notes, Topgun Class 04-75, 24 June 1975 lecture). Israeli experience in 1982 revealed a similar pattern. Israeli F-16 pilots, who accounted for about half of Israel's kills in 1982, reported that, excluding gun kills, 60 per cent of their victims did not react prior to weapons impact (Colonel James Burton, 'Letting Combat Results Shape the Next Air-to-Air Missile', unclassified briefing, January 1985, Slide 6).

62   Veda, 'The Influence of 'Operational Factors' (U),' briefing slides, 14 February 1985, unclassified slide '(U) Definitions (Continued)'.

63   Clarence A Robinson, Jr., 'Fighter, Missile Gains Pressed', *Aviation Week and Space Technology*, 4 April 1977, p. 12.

64   Lieutenant Colonel R E Guild, 'AIMVAL Analysis', Headquarters US Air Force, Studies and Analysis, briefing, 25 February 1978, Slide 3 ('Test Objectives'). For details on the five IR missile concepts tested on F-15s and F-14s during AIMVAL, see Clarence A Robinson, Jr., 'Aerial Combat Test to Advance', *Aviation Week and Space Technology*, 25 April 1977, pp. 28–30.

65   Colonel E J Griffith, 'ACEVAL: Origin, Description, Results, Applicability', briefing, undated, Slide 2 ('ACEVAL'). Griffith was the Blue Force commander.

66   Guild, 'AIMVAL Analysis', Slide 6 ('Test Trial Matrix for AIMVAL').

67   Griffith, 'ACEVAL: Origin, Description, Results, Applicability', Slide 8 ('Test Matrix').

68   Lieutenant Colonel S R Dvorchak, 'Getting It On in the All-Aspect Arena (U)', *Tactical Analysis Bulletin*, Vol. 79–2 (special), 25 July 1979, pp. 3–4 and 18.

69   Guild, 'AIMVAL Analysis', Slide 7 ('Summary Observations – Test Environment'); Griffith, 'ACEVAL: Origin, Description, Results, Applicability', Slide 3 ('Test Design') and Slide 7 ('Test Hardware').

70   Veda, 'AMRAAM OUE Lessons Learned Briefing (U)', Dayton, Ohio, 11 April 1984, Slide 9 ('(U) AMRAAM OUE Test Matrix').

71   S R 'Shad' Dvorchak, 'On the Measurement of Fog', briefing to the Military Operations Research Society, June 1986, Slide 7 ('Foggy Variables Are Important'). The source of this conclusion was Veda's 'AMRAAM OUE Lessons Learned Briefing (U)', SECRET, 3 August 1983, Slide 41 ('(U) Overall Comments'). This slide was later declassified.

72   Theodore von Karman, *Toward New Horizons* (Washington, DC: Army Air Forces Scientific Advisory Group, 15 December 1945), p. v.

73   See Warden, *The Air Campaign*, p. xxv.

74   I B Holley, Jr., *Ideas and Weapons* (Washington, DC: US Government Printing Office, 1983), pp. 13 and 19.

75   Note that the Sparrow III missile first saw operational service on the US Navy's McDonnell F3H-2 Demon, never very successful due primarily to engine problems.

76   Alain C Enthoven and K Wayne Smith, *How Much Is Enough? Shaping the Defense Program, 1961–1969* (New York: Harper and Row, 1971), p. 263; also, René Francillon, *McDonnell F-4D* (Arlington, Texas: Aerofax, Inc., 1985), pp. 1–2.

77   *Born in Battle: Israel's Air Force*, Issue 2, Eshel-Dramit, 1978, p. 47.

78   Nadav Safran, *Israel: The Embattled Ally* (Cambridge, Massachusetts, and London: Belnap Press, 1978), p. 275; also, Mason, *Air Power: A Centennial Appraisal*, p. 78.

79   Colonel James G Burton, 'Letting Combat Results Shape the Next Air-to-Air Missile', unclassified briefing, January 1985, Slides 3 and 5. US fighters are credited with downing 190 North Vietnamese aircraft in aerial combat from April 1965 to January 1973 (R Frank Futrell, William H Greenhalgh, Carl Grubb, Gerald E Hasselwander, Robert F Jakob, and Charles A Ravenstein, *Aces and Aerial Victories: The United States Air Force in Southeast Asia 1965–1973* (Washington, DC: Office of Air Force History and Air University, 1976), p. 157; *Armed Forces Journal International*, May 1974, p. 30.

80   Zeev Schiff, 'The Israeli Air Force', *Air Force Magazine*, August 1976, p. 37.

81   Burton, 'Letting Combat Results Shape the Next Air-to-Air Missile', Slides 3 and 5.

[82]   Victor Flintham, *Air Wars and Aircraft: A Detailed Record of Air Combat, 1945 to the Present* (New York: Facts on File, 1990), p. 70; Burton, 'Letting Combat Results Shape the Next Air-to-Air Missile', Slides 3 and 5.

[83]   Burton, 'Letting Combat Results Shape the Next Air-to-Air Missile', Slide 5.

[84]   The limitations of the early Sparrow IIIs for fighter-versus-fighter combat were common knowledge in the US F-4 community by 1967. The AIM-7Cs and AIM-7Ds used during most of the ROLLING THUNDER period proved far less reliable in actual combat conditions than the engineers had predicted; and, not until the AIM-7E-2 version appeared in 1968 did the Sparrow III achieve a minimum-range capability compatible with close-in dogfights. The Vietnam-era versions of the missile, with their vacuum-tube electronics and hand-soldered wiring, proved particularly hard to maintain under the stress of regular launches and recoveries aboard aircraft carriers.

[85]   Burton, 'Letting Combat Results Shape the Next Air-to-Air Missile', Slide 9.

[86]   During the Gulf War 41 air-to-air victories were officially credited to Coalition fighters. Since three of these kills involved Iraqi pilots flying into the ground after being engaged, there were 38 kills credited to Coalition air-to-air missiles (36) or guns (2). Of these 38 kills, 24 (just over 63 per cent) were achieved with the radar-guided AIM-7M (Major Lewis D Hill, Doris Cook, and Aron Pinker, *Part I: A Statistical Compendium in Gulf War Air Power Survey*, Vol. V, *A Statistical Compendium and Chronology* (Washington, DC: US Government Printing Office, 1993), Table 206, Coalition Air-to-Air Kill Matrix). In 15 of these 24 AIM-7M kills, the engagements opened with BVR shots (Barry D Watts and Thomas A Keaney, *Part II: Effects and Effectiveness in Gulf War Air Power Survey*, Vol. II, *Operations and Effects and Effectiveness* (Washington, DC: US Government Printing Office, 1993), p. 113). Ten of these BVR engagements occurred during daylight and five at night. Also, there were some occasions on which the initial BVR shot missed and the kill was achieved by a subsequent missile fired after the pilot visually acquired the bogey.

[87]   Watts and Keaney, *Part II: Effects and Effectiveness in Gulf War Air Power Survey*, Vol. II, *Operations and Effects and Effectiveness*, pp. 122–123.

[88]   Thomas Friedman, *et al.*, 'Can Bombing Win a War?', NOVA Show #2002, 19 January 1993 (air date), *Journal Graphics*, p. 1.

89   David R Mets, *The Quest for a Surgical Strike Capability: The United States Air Force and Laser Guided Bombs* (Eglin Air Force Base, Florida: Office of History, Armament Division, Air Force Systems Command, 1987), pp. 62–64.

90   *Ibid.*, p. 67. That half of the LGBs can be expected to land within 20 feet of their aim points means that the weapon has a circular error probable (CEP) of 20 feet.

91   Colonel Delbert Corum, *et al.*, 'The Tale of Two Bridges', *The Tale of Two Bridges and the Battle for the Skies over North Vietnam*, ed. Major A J C Lavalle (Washington, DC: US Government Printing Office, 1976), pp. 79–92.

92   Mets, *The Quest for a Surgical Strike Capability*, p. 87.

93   *Ibid.*, pp. 26–31.

94   In May 1972, four flights of F-4s dropped one span of the Thanh Hoa bridge and inflicted other critical damage on the bridge with LGBs. Prior to that time the Thanh Hoa bridge had survived 871 sorties; over the course of these earlier sorties, 11 US aircraft had been lost to North Vietnamese air defences (Kenneth P Werrell, 'Linebacker II: The Decisive Use of Air Power?', *Air University Review*, January–March 1987, p. 51).

95   See, for example, General William W Momyer, USAF (ret.), *Air Power in the Three Wars (WW II, Korea, Vietnam)*, eds. Lieutenant Colonel A J C Lavalle and Major James C Gaston (Washington, DC: US Government Printing Office, 1978), pp. 149–150, 236, 241, and 328.

96   Colonel Phillip S Meilinger, 'Ten Propositions Regarding Airpower', *Airpower Journal*, Spring 1996, pp. 63–65. See also Barnett, *Future War: An Assessment of Aerospace Campaigns in 2010*, pp. 10–12. For an earlier version of this thesis, see Lieutenant Colonel Edward Mann, 'One Target, One Bomb: Is the Principle of Mass Dead?', *Airpower Journal*, Spring 1993, pp. 35–43.

97   Slant-range visibility was the main obstacle to LGB employment in the Vietnam War. During the 11 days of B-52 strikes against North Vietnam in late December 1972 (LINEBACKER II), there was only one period of about eight hours in which the weather was good enough for LGB employment (Oral history interview with General John W Vogt, conducted by Robert M Kipp, 22 August 1975, K105.5-210, p. 8). Targets attacked with LGBs during this brief period were the 'Hanoi power plan, railroad classification yard, and radio station' (Momyer, *Air Power in Three Wars*,

p. 241). However very little night LGB employment took place in South-East Asia either. The rare exceptions involved laser designation by Pave Nail OV10s or AC-130 gunships.

[98] Mets, *The Quest for a Surgical Strike Capability*, pp. 66 and 109–111.

[99] Mets, *The Quest for a Surgical Strike Capability*, p. 106. Tactically, the Pave Knife pods employed during LINEBACKER were a forerunner to Pave Tack insofar as both enabled a single aircraft to illuminate a target with laser energy and deliver a bomb against it.

[100] Headquarters US Air Force, Management Information Division, *United States Air Force Statistical Digest: Fiscal Year 1973*, 31 July 1974, Table 34, p. 86; *United States Air Force Statistical Digest: Fiscal Year 1974*, 15 April 1975, Table 37, p. 73.

[101] Keaney and Cohen, *Revolution in Warfare? Air Power in the Persian Gulf*, p. 171.

[102] French tanks were considered superior to any of the German panzers (Douglas Porch, 'Why Did France Fall?', *The Quarterly Journal of Military History*, Spring 1990, p. 33). Similarly, the British Matilda had stronger armour than the German tanks and the 37mm gun on the German Mark III was inferior to the British two-pounder (F W von Mellenthin, *Panzer Battles: A Study of the Employment of Armor in the Second World War*, trans. H Betzler (Norman, Oklahoma: University of Oklahoma Press, 1956), p. 12. On the other hand, the operational ranges and turret sizes of the panzers used in May 1940 favoured the Germans.

[103] Phillip A Karber, Grant Whitley, Mark Herman, and Douglas Komer, 'Assessing the Correlation of Forces: France 1940', BDM Corporation, BDM/W-79-560-TR, June 1979, pp. 2–3; also, Trevor N Dupuy, *Understanding War: History and Theory of Combat* (New York: Paragon House, 1987), pp. 93–94. While the Germans had a substantial edge in total combat aircraft in May 1940, the opposing sides were nearly equal in single-/twin-engine fighters (ignoring British fighter strength retained in England).

[104] Andrew W Marshall, 'Some Thoughts on Military Revolutions', OSD/ Net Assessment, 27 July 1993, p. 2; and Andrew W Marshall, statement before the Senate Armed Services Committee, Subcommittee on Acquisition Technology, 5 May 1995, p. 1.

[105] Smith, 'Translating Airpower Theory to Practice', *Marine Corps Gazette*, November 1995, p. 80.

[106] '[Admiral William A] Owens Says Technology May Lift "Fog of War":
Breakthroughs Could Give Forces Total Command of Future Battlefield',
Inside the Navy, 23 January 1995, p. 3. See also Admiral William A Owens,
Dominant Battlespace Knowledge: The Winning Edge, ed. Stuart E
Johnson and Martin C Libicki (Washington, DC: National Defense
University Press, October 1995), pp. 14–15; and Owens, 'System-Of-
Systems: US' Emerging Dominant Battlefield Awareness Promises To
Dissipate the "Fog of War"', *Armed Forces Journal International*, January
1996, p. 47. The meaning initially associated with Admiral Owens' notion
of Dominant Battlefield Awareness was that, by connecting largely existing
sensors and shooters together via appropriate information and command-
and-control systems, it should be possible to detect, track and classify
most (or all) of the militarily relevant objects moving on land, the surface
of the ocean, through the air, or in space within a cube of battlespace
some 200 nautical miles each side.

[107] Lieutenant Colonel Ed Felker, 'Information Warfare: A View of the Future',
A Command Perspective: Joint Warfighting Center's Newsletter,
September 1995, p. 18.

[108] Larry Lynn, 'Battlefield Dominance and ARPA Focus', Advanced
Research Projects Agency (ARPA) memorandum, 29 June 1995, p. 2.

[109] For a more extended development of these three points, see Barry D Watts,
'Clausewitzian Friction and Future War', McNair Paper 52 (Washington
DC: National Defense University Press, October 1996), pp. 105–132

[110] Eliot A Cohen, 'The Mystique of US Air Power', *Foreign Affairs*, January/
February 1994, p. 122.

[111] Colin S Gray, 'The Changing Nature of Warfare?', *Naval War College
Review*, Spring 1996, p. 17.

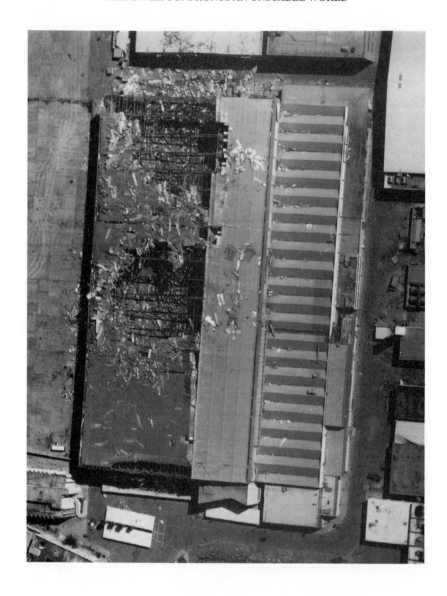

2

AIR TARGETING STRATEGIES: AN OVERVIEW

by
Colonel Phillip S Meilinger, USAF
PROFESSOR OF STRATEGY
US NAVAL WAR COLLEGE

G iulio Douhet, the noted Italian air theorist, stated in 1921 that the aeroplane was an inherently strategic weapon.[1] By that he meant it was the nature of armies and navies to fight at the tactical level of war – force against force – but air power, because of its ability to operate in the third dimension, could bypass this counterforce battle and operate directly against what he termed the 'vital centres' of an enemy nation. Those centres were the industrial, political, economic and population loci that allowed a country to function. This ability to operate routinely with strategic effects, seemingly unique to air power, has been emphasised by other air power thinkers and leaders in the years since. However, the targets suggested by air power theorists to be struck or neutralised have differed significantly. Today's political and military leaders should understand these various air targeting strategies, and the differences between them, for they collectively define the boundaries of strategic air power thought, and they clarify the connection between the air weapon and its role in war. Moreover, understanding these formative concepts opens the way to a more balanced and flexible grasp of air strategy and the factors that go into its determination.

SURFACE POWER, AIR POWER, AND THE STRATEGIC DIMENSION OF WARFARE

The era between the Thirty Years' War and the French Revolution (1648–1789) is generally referred to as the age of 'limited war'. During that period warfare was constrained both in its purpose and its application. Armies were relatively small, highly trained and expensive. They were not, therefore, often risked in battle. But if a decisive battle was fought, the consequences for the loser were generally catastrophic. Although another army could be raised, it would take time – two to three years were usually required to train a soldier – and money. In the midst of war those were dear commodities. However, with the advent of a virulent nationalism symbolised by the French Revolution, the situation changed. Armies were now relatively cheap. Virtually all men were eligible for service, and because enthusiasm was seen as a partial substitute for martial traditions, it took little time and only slightly more effort to raise and train them. As a consequence, the decisiveness of war began to alter.[2] This did not happen immediately, however. In fact, one of Napoleon's great assets early in his military career was that he and he alone was playing by the new rules of mass armies.

Between 1804 and 1815 Napoleon conscripted three million men for his armies, an astounding figure for that age. When he invaded Russia in 1812 the *Grande Armée* numbered 630,000 – nearly three times the size of the Russian army, traditionally the largest in Europe.[3] As a result, whereas Napoleon's troops were to some extent expendable, those of his adversaries were not. Once Prussia, Austria and Russia began to copy the model of France, however, decisiveness became far harder to achieve. By the time of the First World War a century later, the growth of mass armies – combined with new administrative capacities to manage them – and new technologies that made war far more deadly, meant that it was possible for a country to lose a host of armies and not suffer defeat, or victory.

Psychologists tell us that the most traumatic event of a person's life is his birth. If so, then the birth of air power was doubly traumatic, because it occurred in concert with the First World War. That war smashed empires, spawned dictatorships, caused the deaths of at least ten million people and had a profound effect on the conduct of war. The loss of a generation of European men, as well as over one hundred thousand Americans, convinced military leaders that tactics and strategy had to be altered. Radical solutions were therefore given greater consideration than would ordinarily have been the case. This is important, because it was due to this demand for alternatives that airmen had such a receptive audience. Moreover, farsighted and original thinkers like J F C Fuller and B H Liddell Hart speculated as to the accuracy and viability of a new theory of war centering on air power, which gave the airmen a credibility they might not otherwise have had. Fuller, for example, described the horrific effects of air attack: 'Picture, if you can, what the result will be: London for several days will be one vast raving Bedlam, the hospitals will be stormed, traffic will cease, the homeless will shriek for help, the city will be in pandemonium. What of the government at Westminster? It will be swept away by an avalanche of terror.'[4] Liddell Hart was similarly effusive, and in words that could have been written by any airman proclaimed: 'Aircraft enables us *to jump over* the army which shields the enemy government, industry, and people, and *so strike direct and immediately at the seat of the opposing will and policy.*' (Emphasis in the original.)[5] Clearly, it was not just aviators who saw dramatic possibilities in the military aircraft. Nonetheless, the path to a coherent theory of strategic air power was steep and rocky. This is partly due to the fact that air warfare is fundamentally different from surface warfare.

Over the past several centuries surface warfare has evolved rather evenly, sometimes speeding up or slowing down, depending on the stimuli of technology, leadership, economics, geography, etc. As a consequence of this evolution, there are centuries-old theories dealing with firepower, manoeuvre, shock effect, defence versus offence, logistics, administration, technology, leadership and C3 (command, control and communications), as well as other precepts and principles that discuss the relationship between all of these issues and their effect on land and sea warfare. In reality, however, these amount to little more than a constant rearrangement of certain basic, static parts. Because of this, the soldier and sailor seldom find anything truly new in the practice of their profession, but instead are able to pick and choose examples and theories from over dozens of centuries, in scores of countries and during hundreds of battles to make a point or propose a 'new' doctrine. Thus, the operational techniques and tactics of 'Great Captains' such as Alexander, Frederick, Napoleon, Guderian and Schwarzkopf are surprisingly similar in their purpose and execution. With air power it was different. Given the newness of their weapon, airmen were not so fortunate in being able to look backward for a rich lode of experience they could mine, and thus they had to invent – largely and literally from thin air – a new theory of warfare that involved new strategies as well as new methods of war. Their most fundamental goal was to search for a way to win wars without sustaining the horrendous losses of the First World War.

For many airmen, air power was an intrinsically strategic weapon in ways that traditional surface forces were not: the centres of gravity of an enemy country were, theoretically, always within range of aircraft.[6] These centres of gravity – the political, economic, industrial, cultural and population concentrations that allowed a country to function – had long been the ultimate goal of armed forces. (In my view a country can have more than one centre of gravity. I will discuss that issue below.) Because they were generally well behind the frontier and heavily defended by armies and fortresses, however, it was extremely difficult to reach them. As a consequence, war became a contest between armed forces; the losers in battle exposed their country's centres of gravity to the victor. Usually, actual destruction or even occupation was unnecessary: with the interior of the country exposed and vulnerable, the government sued for peace. Small wonder that military theorists over the centuries equated the enemy army with the main centre of gravity, because when the army fell (or in some cases the navy, as at Salamis in 480 BC and Copenhagen in 1801), so did resistance. As noted, however, the First World War demonstrated that such attritional contests had become far too bloody – for both sides – to serve as a rational instrument of policy.

Even so, there were some who realised that surface warfare was not nearly so simple, but was a very complicated undertaking. Clausewitz stated that war was the most complex of human endeavours because virtually every aspect of the physical, intellectual and psychological natures of man were involved. He was certainly correct. But it is nonetheless true that despite the numbing intricacies of surface warfare, the complexities of air warfare are far greater. For when all is said and done, the surface commander's task can often be reduced to the simple aphorism noted above: find and destroy the enemy army or fleet. The air strategist has no such singular focus: an enemy's entire country lies open to attack. Thus, air power offered a potential solution to surface attrition warfare, while at the same time introducing a new set of problems. If the enemy army or navy was no longer the main target, then what was? Obviously, it was now incumbent upon airmen to become far more familiar with the inner workings of an enemy nation than had ever been the case previously. But knowing that a country depended on its railroads, canal system, political leaders, steel mills, coal mines, electrical power grid, arable land, fishing industry, telephone system, chemical factories, etc. was interesting, but of limited practical value. Certainly, not all of these targets could be struck or neutralised. Which centres of gravity were the *most* important? Selecting targets became the essence of air strategy. There was a major caveat, however: simply because something could be targeted did not mean it was valuable, and a thing that was valuable was not necessarily targetable. Thus, when perceptive air planners noted that a systematic destruction of target sets did not automatically equate to victory, and that there were intangible factors such as religion, nationalism, tradition and culture that were no less important in holding a country together during war than were its physical attributes, the problem became daunting indeed. As time has passed, this problem has become more, not less, complex. Today there are a host of 'new targets' critical to the proper functioning of a modern state in addition to those already noted: fibre-optic networks, satellite constellations that provide surveillance and communications data, nuclear power plants and their attendant distribution systems, and the new electronic medium, often referred to as 'cyberspace', that plays an increasingly important role in all aspects of a population's personal and professional life. How is a modern airman to sort it all out?

A schematic representation of a modern country illustrates the problem and may also help point to a solution.

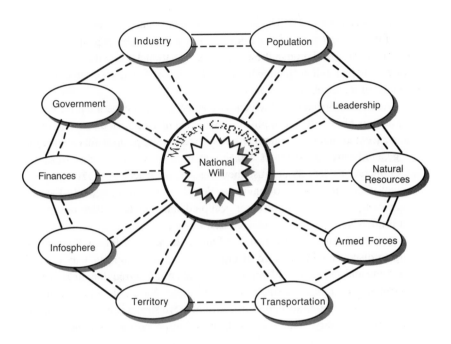

The key to all war is the amorphous and largely unquantifiable factor known as the 'national will'. It occupies the central place in the schematic because it is the most crucial aspect of a country at war. At its most basic, war is psychological. Thus, in the broadest sense, national will is always the key centre of gravity – when 'the country' decides the war is lost, then, and only then, is it truly lost.[7] However, saying that really says very little. The obvious challenge for the strategist is to determine how to shatter or at least crack that collective will. Because it is an aggregate of so many different factors, and because it has no physical form, attacking national will directly is seldom if ever possible. Rather, the manifestations of that will are the things that must be targeted. In a general sense those manifestations can be termed 'military capability'.

This military capability is the sum of the physical attributes of power: land, population, money, natural resources, finance, industry, government, armed forces, transportation and communications networks, etc. When these things have been dissipated or destroyed – when there is no capability left with which to carry on the fight – then the national will either expires or becomes militarily unimportant. Thus, in the schematic presented here, military capability is closely tied to national will – actually fused onto it – to indicate the mutual dependency. By the same token, however, because military capability is at the centre of a nation's being and it is the sum of a country's total physical power, it is extremely difficult to destroy entirely. The key, therefore, is to selectively pierce this hard shell of military capability in one or several places, thereby exposing the soft core of national will. Through these openings the national will can be punctured, prodded, shaped and influenced. In most cases, will collapses under such pressure before capability has been exhausted.[8]

The nodes surrounding the central core of will and capability are the *de facto* centres of gravity, those physical elements of a country that are of great importance and that can be targeted. As noted above, prior to this century it was generally the armed forces and the territory of the enemy that were the foci of operations, largely because they were the most accessible. It was often true that if the enemy army or navy was defeated, or if a strategically-located province or port could be overrun or occupied, a negotiated settlement would soon follow. New capabilities offered new opportunities.

One could argue that the history of air strategy is a history of targeting – trying to discover which centre of gravity is the most important in a given place, time and situation. Although air theorists might agree that air power is an intrinsically strategic weapon, they have generally disagreed, vigorously, over which targets are most appropriate to achieve strategic objectives. What follows is a summary of the various strains of air power targeting theory.

THE EVOLUTION OF TARGETING THEORY

General Giulio Douhet believed that the population was the prime target for an air attack.[9] He viewed the average civilian, especially the urban dweller, as being prone to panic in the face of air assault. The limited experience from the First World War seemed to support that contention. Not only in Italy, but in England and France as well, the bombing strikes of the war, even though sporadic, caused widespread absenteeism and evacuation from the cities.[10] Relatively limited in number and scale though these air strikes were, their psychological effects were disproportionately large. To Douhet, the implications were apparent. By extrapolation he was convinced that dropping a mixture of incendiary, chemical and high explosive bombs on a country's major cities would cause such disruption and devastation that revolt and subsequent surrender were inevitable:

> A complete breakdown of the social structure cannot but take place in a country subjected to this kind of merciless pounding from the air. The time would soon come when, to put an end to horror and suffering, the people themselves, driven by the instinct of self-preservation, would rise up and demand an end to the war – this before their army and navy had time to mobilize at all![11]

56

Utterly pragmatic and a realist, Douhet rejected arguments that air attacks on civilians were illegal or immoral. War itself was immoral, and in the total war he had just witnessed there were no innocents. Offering a paradox common to other air theorists, he maintained that air warfare would be so horrible it would be humanising. Certainly many thousands would die, but many millions died in the old form of war. A short, violent and decisive conflict dominated by air power was much preferable to another world war that might drag on for several years and wipe out an entire generation. Although Douhet's predictions regarding the fragility of a country's vital centres and the weakness of a population's resolve were to prove grossly in error during the Second World War, his basis premise has had an enduring appeal.

Fortunately, Douhet's American and British counterparts saw in air power the hope of targeting things rather than people. In contrast to Douhet, air doctrine in the United States and Britain during the interwar years focused on the enemy's industrial infrastructure, not his population. In this view, the modern state was dependent on mass production of military goods: ships, aircraft, trucks, artillery, ammunition, uniforms, etc. Moreover, most airmen took a broader view and argued that essentials such as electrical power, steel, chemicals and oil were also military targets and actually of greatest importance because they were the essential building blocks for other types of manufactured military goods needed to sustain a war effort.

In America, at the Air Corps Tactical School, this concept was further refined.[12] Hal George, Ken Walker, Don Wilson and others devised a theory that sought industrial bottlenecks: those factories or functions that were integral to the effective operation of the entire system. There is a story told of how one day the School's aircraft were grounded due to a shortage of a particular part used in the propeller pitch mechanisms. The instructors discovered that only one company in Pittsburgh produced these parts, and it had been flooded by recent rains. The aircraft were out of commission until the company was back in operation. The lesson seemed clear: if the objective was to neutralise US air power, it was not necessary to bomb every airfield or shoot down every aircraft. Rather, destroying a single factory in Pittsburgh could produce the same results.[13] Using this admittedly simplistic example, the ACTS instructors began to study industrial networks in an attempt to locate other such bottlenecks. Their doctrinal theory, termed the 'industrial web', envisioned an enemy country as an integrated and mutually supporting system, but one which, like a house of cards, was susceptible to sudden destruction. If the right bottleneck was attacked or neutralised, the entire industrial edifice could come crashing down.[14] It was this doctrine that the Army Air Forces carried into the Second World War.

The Royal Air Force (RAF), led by Marshal of the RAF Sir Hugh Trenchard for the decade after the First World War, took a slightly different approach.

Trenchard had himself witnessed the extreme reaction by the population and their political leaders to the German air attacks on Britain in 1917 and 1918 – it was, after all, these attacks that were the proximate cause for the creation of the RAF. Although not an immediate convert to the idea of strategic bombing, he tended increasingly in that direction in the years between the wars. He argued, as did Douhet, that the psychological effects of bombing outweighed its physical effects. Unlike the Italian, Trenchard did not believe that attacking people directly was the correct strategy to produce that psychological trauma.[15] Such a policy was morally and militarily questionable:

> I emphatically do not advocate indiscriminate bombardment, and I think that air action will be far less indiscriminate and far less brutal and will obtain its end with far fewer casualties than either naval blockade, a naval bombardment, or sieges, or when military formations are hurled against the enemies' strongest points protected by barbed wire and covered by mass artillery and machine guns.[16]

Instead, he advocated a similar theory to the Tactical School: that a country's industrial infrastructure was the appropriate target. He reasoned that the disruption of the normal life of the population – the loss of jobs, wages, services, transportation and goods – would be so profound that the people would demand peace. In short, whereas the Americans wished to bomb industry to destroy capability, Trenchard and the RAF sought to bomb industry so as to destroy the national will. If there was a shortcoming in both these theories it was the tendency to view societies in overly mechanistic terms and the failure to appreciate the amazing resilience of a population that is determined to resist, rebuild and retaliate, despite the amount of destruction visited upon it.

Another RAF officer who grappled with the complexities of air theory between the wars and who took a different tack was Wing Commander John C Slessor.[17] A combat pilot who was wounded in the First World War, Slessor commanded an army co-operation squadron from 1925 to 1928. He then worked on Trenchard's personal staff and in 1931 was assigned to the faculty at the British Army Staff College at Camberley. This broad background, combined with a first-rate mind, produced one of the more original air thinkers prior to the Second World War. His seminal book, *Air Power and Armies*, was based on his lectures at the Staff College and posits a war in which the British Army has been deployed to the Continent. Thus, a joint campaign has already begun, and a separate strategic air campaign is not discussed. Although there is evidence that Slessor was a strategic air advocate and only proposed this scenario because he was teaching army students, the result was a book focusing on air power complementing land forces.

Slessor argued that the enemy army's lines of supply and communication were the key centre of gravity. Significantly, he did not think only in tactical terms on this matter; rather, Slessor maintained that the entire transportation system of the enemy must be disrupted and neutralised. If this were accomplished, not only would the enemy army be unable to offer effective resistance, but the entire country would be paralysed and vulnerable to offensive action. This paralysation would in turn have a decisive effect not only on the enemy nation's capability, but also its will. In essence, Slessor was advocating strategic and operational-level air interdiction. Significantly, during the Second World War RAF leaders, notably Air Chief Marshal Arthur Tedder, pushed strongly for just such an air campaign against Germany in 1944. The 'transportation plan', as it was called, was indeed enormously successful in assuring the success of the Normandy landings by severely restricting the flow of German reinforcements to the lodgement area. In addition, the wholesale destruction of the German rail system in Western Europe had devastating effects on their entire war effort, as Slessor had predicted.

There were also those who took different approaches to strategic air targeting. Although General Billy Mitchell would by the late 1920s fluctuate between a strategy akin to Douhet and one closer to that of the Tactical School, his writings soon after the First World War were quite different. In his early works, *Our Air Force* (1921) and an operational manual he wrote for his flyers in 1922 entitled *The Multi-Motored Bombardment Group*, Mitchell called for the use of air power to destroy the military forces of the enemy, both on land and at sea.[18] In other words, he saw victory occurring in the time-honoured method of the decisive counterforce battle. Only now, aircraft could accomplish the destruction of an enemy army in a far quicker and more efficient fashion. Mitchell saw fleets as even more vulnerable and his bombing tests of 1921 and 1923 that saw aircraft sink several battleships further hardened this belief: 'Neither armies nor navies can exist unless the air is controlled over them.'[19] Although he soon moved away from the view of military forces as the prime target, there were others following him who held similar opinions. As late as 1988 the head of the USAF's Tactical Air Command stated that the mission of his command was to support the army in the destruction of the enemy army. This is not a foolish argument. Indeed, there are some who would claim that it was the tactical air campaign against the Iraqi army in Kuwait, not the strategic air campaign against centres of gravity in Baghdad, that led to Coalition victory in the Persian Gulf War.[20]

It is significant that most of the individuals and theorists mentioned thus far are from the pre-Second World War era. In one sense, the massive and decisive use of air power in that war should have spawned an outburst of new thinking in the years that followed 1945. Surprisingly and unfortunately, that was not the case. The atomic strikes on Japan had a both catalysing and numbing effect on military leaders worldwide. The new weapon appeared to revolutionise warfare in ways that made all prior experience seem obsolete. The atomic and then nuclear ages redefined war. As a consequence, a different group of theorists arose in an attempt to explain the use of military force in this new age. These theorists were not, however, from the military. Rather, a new breed of civilian academic, with little or no experience in war, emerged to define and articulate theories of nuclear war. Since there was virtually no experience with this type of war, civilian academics were seemingly as capable of devising a theory of nuclear air warfare as were uniformed professionals. The ideas they proposed – balance of terror, mutual assured destruction, strategic sufficiency and the like – were elegant and reasoned, and served the West well throughout the Cold War era. Regrettably, however, military airmen all too easily and quickly abandoned the intellectual field to the civilians. At the same time, the military accepted the premise that future wars would involve nuclear weapons. The result was that few airmen in the USA or abroad gave serious thought to the use of conventional air power, especially at the strategic level.

The Vietnam War had many negative effects on both the United States as a whole and the military services in particular. One positive aspect, however, was the growing realisation that nuclear war between the two superpowers was an interesting intellectual exercise, but hardly likely to occur – if only because we were so well prepared to wage it. At the same time tactical air power seemed not to be a war-winning weapon, as Vietnam amply demonstrated. Thus, while air power had become polarised between those who thought only of nuclear holocaust and those who prepared to fight the tactical air battle, world conditions seemed to indicate that neither extreme offered useful and decisive results. The vast middle ground between those two poles had to be recaptured. The revitalisation of strategic conventional thought began with a Fighter Weapons School instructor at Nellis AFB, Nevada, by the name of Colonel John Boyd.

As a fighter pilot in the Korean War, John Boyd was intrigued by the astounding success of the F-86 in air combat with the MiG-15 (a ten-to-one superiority).[21] Upon reflection, he decided that the F-86's advantage was due largely to its hydraulically operated flight controls and adjustable horizontal stabiliser that allowed it to transition from one aerial manoeuvre to another more rapidly than the MiG. After further thought, Boyd began to see the implications of this theory in a broader context. The key to victory was to act more quickly, both mentally and physically, than your opponent. He expressed this concept in a cyclical process he called the OODA Loop (observe-orient-decide-act). As soon as one side acted, it observed the consequences, and the loop began anew. The most important portion of the loop was the orient phase.

Boyd speculated that the increasing complexities of the modern world necessitated an ability to take seemingly isolated facts and ideas from different disciplines and events, deconstruct them to their essential components, and then put them back together in new and unusual ways. He termed this process 'destruction and creation'. It was this process that dominated the 'orient' phase of his OODA Loop.

The significance of Boyd's tactical air theories is that he later hypothesised that this continuously operating cycle was at play not only in a tactical aerial dogfight, but at the higher levels of war as well. In tracing the history of war Boyd saw victory consistently going to the side that could think the most creatively – orienting itself – and then acting quickly on that insight. Although military historians tend to blanch at such a selective use of history, the thesis is an interesting one. Significantly, because of the emphasis on the orientation phase of the loop, in practical terms Boyd was calling for a strategy directed against the mind of the enemy leadership. Although put forward by an airman, these theories encompassed far more than a blueprint for air operations. Warfare in general, indeed life in general, was governed by this process. Nonetheless, because of the OODA Loop's emphasis on speed and the disorienting surprise it inflicts on the enemy, Boyd's theories seem especially applicable to air power, which embodies these two qualities most fully.

Another American airman who has thought deeply on strategic air power, and who also focused on enemy leadership as the key centre of gravity, is Colonel John A. Warden III. Like Boyd a fighter pilot and combat veteran, Warden began a serious and sustained study of air warfare while a student at the National War College in 1986. The thesis he wrote that year was soon published and is still a standard text at Air University.[22] His subsequent assignment in the Pentagon put him in an ideal location when Saddam Hussein invaded Kuwait in the summer of 1990. Putting his theories into practice, Warden was responsible for designing an air campaign that called for strategic attacks against Iraq's centres of gravity.[23] He argued that war is always a combination of physical and psychological factors. However, since the psychological facet is difficult to measure or even identify, the air strategist must focus on the physical manifestations of the enemy. The device he used to illustrate his plan was a target bull's-eye consisting of five concentric rings, with leadership at the centre – the most important centre of gravity while also the most fragile – and armed forces as the outermost ring – the least important but also the most hardened.

Warden likened his Five Rings model to the human body.[24] The innermost ring and key centre of gravity, the enemy leadership, equated to the human brain. Just as the brain was the most important organ of the body – it controlled all movement while also receiving all inputs and was thus irreplaceable – so too was the enemy leader the key to enemy resistance. If the leadership could be killed or captured, then the entire country – the enemy body – would be incapacitated. Warden cited the examples of King Harold's death at Hastings in 1066 and Hitler's in 1945 as evidence that victory could be achieved through this principle. Although these are hardly clinching examples, it is nonetheless apparent that both Boyd and Warden have turned away from the economic emphasis of previous air power theorists. Instead, they focus on the enemy's leadership. However, whereas Boyd seeks to disrupt the *process* of the enemy's leadership, Warden wishes instead to disrupt the *form* of that leadership. The epitome of such an air strategy – for both men – was the Gulf War. Air strikes against the Iraqi communications network, road and rail system, and electrical power grid made it extremely difficult, physically, for Saddam Hussein to control his military forces, but it also induced enormous confusion and uncertainty into his decision-making process. His OODA Loop was expanded dramatically, and its cycle time was slowed accordingly.

Warden went on to argue that the other rings – organic essentials (raw materials and power), infrastructure (industry and transportation), the population and fielded forces – are distractions generally best avoided. These target systems should be attacked only as necessary to expose the leadership ring to offensive action. Warden concluded that this type of 'inside-out' warfare has always been the most effective in theory, but it was the invention of air power that made it routinely possible. In his view, the strategic nature of air power, combined with new technology, can provide the type of rapid and relatively bloodless victories military leaders have sought for centuries. In short, it can lead to strategic paralysis, and this in essence is what airmen have sought for the past seven decades. Warden's theories are controversial, as are those concerning information warfare.

One of the most recent theories regarding modern warfare involves the explosion of information. Seemingly, everyone in the world has, or soon will have, a fax machine, cellular telephone, powerful microcomputer and access to the Internet. (As of mid-1996, the total Internet population was growing at a phenomenal 10 per cent per month; global electronic mail access as measured by electronic mailboxes has exploded, from 400,000 in 1980 to greater than 12 million in 1990, to over 40 million in 1996.)[25] As a result, the accelerating pace of information exchange has become both a tremendous strength and a vulnerability for a modern country. Knowledge, presumably, is power. Whoever controls information flow has a tremendous advantage: 'perfect information' for oneself and imposed ignorance, through either denial or corruption, for an enemy. As one advocate stated succinctly, 'Information is becoming a strategic resource that may prove as valuable and influential in the post-industrial era as capital and labour have been in the industrial age.'[26] To be sure, information, when broadly defined as intelligence, surveillance, reconnaissance, electronic, written and even verbal communications, is not a new phenomenon. However, the explosion in the volume and dissemination of such information made possible by technology such as the microchip, fibre optics and space operations has given new intensity to an old concept. The ability to dominate information is referred to variously as *infowar* or *cyberwar*, and almost presumes a physical entity, sometimes called an *infosphere*, in which information resides or through which it is channelled. This infosphere is thus a potentially very important centre of gravity and one which may have interesting implications for the manner in which air warfare might be conducted.

AIR POWER STRATEGY CONCERNS
FOR TODAY AND TOMORROW

We are now close to possessing the capability to have either *centralised control and centralised execution* – each bomb dropped is designated and approved by the theatre commander or higher; or we can have *decentralised control and decentralised execution* – each bomb drop is determined by the individual pilot. In the Second World War era neither of these were options, *centralised control and decentralised execution* were necessitated by the technology of the time. Only a major headquarters, such as Eighth Air Force in England, had the information and communication facilities available to study all the various intelligence reports, review the photos, maps, charts, etc. and plan an air campaign. The role of the air commander at this headquarters was crucial in determining priorities and weight of effort, because the mass of data required to analyse and make such decisions was so cumbersome and difficult to manipulate. Once the aircraft were airborne, however, the air force commander's job was finished; he could do little but wait for his forces, now controlled by the wing or group commanders actually flying the lead aircraft, to carry out the mission and return to base. Because of the availability of intelligence that is near real-time, and breakthroughs in communications, it will soon be possible for every layer in the chain of command to have virtually instantaneous, accurate information. Thus, an opportunity presents itself to centralise the functions of control and execution in one place. But which end of the spectrum is most appropriate?[27]

Such responsive communications can be viewed as a powerful advantage for the air attacker, because they allow extremely rapid disruption of an enemy's command and control network. If the infowarriors are correct and communication links are the new centre of gravity of a modern state, then a country like the United States is vulnerable in a new and dangerous way. On the other hand, one could just as easily argue that the very proliferation of new communications avenues and methods has made it nearly impossible to wage infowar effectively. The redundancy of the communications network is so profound as to make targeting it impossible. Just as during the Vietnam War there was not a single Ho Chi Minh Trail to be interdicted but rather there were a hundred different trails, so too there may not be an infosphere with a single plug to be pulled – every airman with a computer is a communications network. How can all of them be neutralised?[28] Nonetheless, it must be admitted that countries reliant on rapid mass communications would certainly seem to be at the mercy, theoretically at least, of someone with the knowledge and capability to disrupt that system.

Another 'new' wrinkle in military theory stresses the cultural aspects of conflict. In a sense, the centres of gravity are both the pillars and the appendages of the core: there is a symbiotic relationship between them that is at once both physical and intangible. In addition, these centres of gravity are both strengths and vulnerabilities for a country. This prompted one airman to refer to them not as centres of gravity, which connotes a sense of strength, but as 'national elements of value': vital factors that are important, but may also be quite fragile and brittle.[29] The point is that all centres of gravity are important, but not all are targetable in the traditional meaning of that term. As a consequence, although physical manifestations of power are the most discernible – the easiest to target and the easiest to quantify – the cultural and social aspects of a society are also crucial.

Historian John Keegan has argued that the Clausewitzian model of modern war is flawed, because it presumed conflict occurred between modern nation-states. Moreover, these states were what today would be called 'rational actors' – they made decisions regarding peace and war based on a logical calculus grounded in policy. Admittedly, Clausewitz's term 'policy' (also translated variously as politics or political intercourse) is meant broadly and could include factors such as economics, domestic pressures, irredentism, etc. Nonetheless, Keegan maintained that such factors explained only some motives for war; other societies are far more culturally based. He cited examples of Zulus in Africa, Siberian Cossacks, Eastern Islanders, and Japanese Samurai to demonstrate that some groups made war because it was traditional, a rite of passage to manhood, or a safety valve to release excess energy.[30] In such cultures, what westerners would term the traditional causes of war and peace were largely irrelevant. The significance of this argument is not that small groups of isolated natives have in times past gone to war for reasons we would consider quaint. Rather, if these factors and imperatives are present in some peoples, then in truth they are present in all peoples. In more modern societies, however, these cultural factors are subsumed or overshadowed by the more traditional political imperatives; they are not replaced by them. Thus, all people and countries do things, or do not do things, based on a collection of reasons, some physical and some cultural or psychological. Conceivably, we may not know ourselves what is the dominant factor in our decisions. Yet, the military strategist must be aware that he is dealing with an enemy who is part rational and part irrational, who is motivated by reasons of both policy and of passion.[31] When a modern country is dominated by a world view that is seemingly completely alien from a Clausewitzian perspective, the problem for the air strategist becomes extremely complex.

One could argue, for example, that it is the passionate faith of Islamic fundamentalism that effectively holds modern Iran together, not oil resources or the traditional political bonds of a western country. Rather than the notion that the Iranian state uses religion as a tool of its policy, it would seem that radical Islam uses the state as a tool to achieve its religious goals. Air strategists have a difficult enough time attempting to predict effects and responses when dealing with a 'similar enemy'; when dealing with a 'dissimilar enemy' the problem is greatly magnified. Nevertheless, realising the importance of such seemingly intangible factors as the enemy culture is crucial to military planners. Because something may not have a physical form does not mean it is not important; nor does it mean it is impervious to attack. In such instances the need for psychological warfare operations – the use of propaganda, ruse, deception, disinformation, perhaps even the truth – can be decisive. In the schematic on page 55 these intangible but vital connections are represented by the dotted lines linking the physical centres of gravity to each other and the national core. In some societies – ancient Sparta or modern Israel – these seemingly amorphous threads have the binding force of steel bands.

The task of the air strategist is to make sense of these conflicting targeting theories and concepts and select one, or a combination of several, to translate into a workable plan. This is done by first asking three fundamental questions: what is the goal? how much is it worth to achieve that goal? and what is it worth to the enemy to prevent you from achieving it? These are vital questions and Bismarck's famous dictum, 'Woe to the statesman whose reasons for entering a war are not as clear at the end as at the beginning', is absolutely correct. Once these basic questions are addressed, the air strategist must devise a campaign plan to answer them. This involves transforming broad goals into specific military objectives, identifying the target sets that need to be affected (though not necessarily destroyed) to attain those objectives, and then converting the whole into a co-ordinated operations order that can be implemented by the military forces involved.[32] This last task is no less significant than the first, even if it requires more technical skill than strategic art. What cannot be over-emphasised is that there must be a clear linkage between the targets chosen and the objectives sought. What specifically does the air campaign planner expect the enemy to do if, for example, his power grid is bombed? If the planner's overall objective is to force the enemy to halt an invasion, then how, exactly, will striking the power grid – or munitions factory, or armoured divisions, or intelligence headquarters – contribute towards achieving that objective? In other words, just because a target is destroyed or neutralised does not mean it was important or that one is any closer to gaining a pre-established goal. The air strategist is wise to note that the intellectual process of linking ends and means is crucial, yet too often overlooked.

Perhaps one of the most important factors to remember in this entire discussion of centres of gravity is that society is a living organism that reacts to a myriad of internal and external stimuli. Indeed, all the centres of gravity are connected to each other in my schematic – and in reality, though not, perhaps, in the exact ways implied – to illustrate that an attack on one will have an impact on all the rest. There is a definite symbiotic and synergistic relationship between these various centres. Hence, if one strikes industry, this will have an effect on the overall military capability of a country, which will be transmitted to the national will. In turn, the will may crack or, more likely, a signal will be sent to the leaders to direct more people and resources to rebuild the damaged industries. The organism will react to counter the threat. In short, and this is crucial to note, this schematic depicts a living entity – precisely what a country is – that can act and react to various stimuli, and that can do so in ways that are not necessarily predictable: they move, shift, alter their appearance, defend themselves, panic and/or steel themselves. Indeed, organisms develop scar tissue after they have been injured, sometimes making subsequent injury less severe. As a result, the second attack is, to some extent, hitting a different organism from the first. Correspondingly, the results may also be different. Thus, the tendency to view an enemy country as an inanimate, two-dimensional model is extremely dangerous because it assumes a static, laboratory condition where the experimenter controls all the variables. This is far from the case. Attempting to impose rationality on an enemy society via computer simulations and models is similar to previous attempts by airmen and others to see war as an engineering problem that adheres to certain rules and scientific laws.[33] War, however, can never be completely rational, any more than can be the peoples that wage it.

It is also important to understand that the centres of gravity of one country are not necessarily those of another. In the case of Second World War Japan, for example, sea lanes were vital because Japan required so many raw materials from the Asian mainland or the East Indies. However, sea lanes were useful but not vital to Nazi Germany. Because Hitler controlled most of continental Europe, he was largely self-sufficient in raw materials and was barely affected by the Allied blockade. Similarly, an autocratic country like Nazi Germany may be more dependent on the personality and power of the leader than is a democracy with a balanced government and a clearly established line of

66

succession in the event of the leader's death.

Moreover, not only are centres of gravity often different between countries, but they may change over time within the same country. During the Battle of Britain, for example, the Royal Air Force was perilously short of both pilots and aircraft. Had the Luftwaffe continued to attack the RAF airfields in the autumn of 1940, this key British centre of gravity may have cracked. The following year, however, the RAF was no longer in such dire straits: planes and pilots were now available in sufficient quantities to withstand another Luftwaffe air campaign. By that point, however, the key British centre of gravity had moved into the Atlantic. German U-boats were sinking British shipping at an alarming rate and there was serious concern as to whether or not Britain could long endure. Significantly, this key centre of gravity also changed when the United States entered the war and the massive infusion of shipping capacity alleviated the British plight.

Along these lines, the duration of the war can also have a significant effect on the selection of the appropriate centres of gravity. If the war is expected to be short, either for military or political reasons, it may be wasteful to strike targets such as a chemical factory whose neutralisation could only be felt in the long term, unless one of the military objectives sought was to cripple the enemy's chemical industry for long-term economic or political reasons. Other targets may be preferable. For example, it may be wiser to strike an opponent's élite forces because that may be the most psychologically devastating to the enemy leadership and thus have the greatest immediate impact. In short, it must be remembered that all countries are unique; all wars are unique; and all situations are unique. As a result, unique solutions are similarly demanded, and these solutions are very much time- and situation-dependent.

Remember also that when a state is fighting for its survival the will/ capability equation must shift. In such situations will endures because it must; there is no viable alternative. In these circumstances the only thing that will bring war to a close is the virtual destruction of a country's military capability. Such was the case in Second World War Germany where the Allied policy of 'unconditional surrender' was exploited by the Nazi propaganda apparatus to stiffen resolve, while at the same time the secret police maintained rigid discipline throughout society. Japan, on the other hand, was offered alternatives short of its ultimate death as a state or the ending of its traditional reliance on the emperor. Will was allowed to crack before the capability was exhausted.

THE STRATEGIC HELIX: TOWARDS
MORE EFFECTIVE AIR TARGETING?

If one agrees with the assumptions of this essay that an enemy country is a living organism composed of multiple centres of gravity that act and react with one another and the outside world, then several conclusions follow. First, as air theorists have noted since even before the First World War, air power is an especially effective weapon for affecting those centres of gravity. Most of the vital centres noted above are physical and thus can be directly targeted. Indeed, because they are for the most part immobile and thus vulnerable, they are often especially susceptible to the effects of air power – a power grid, railroad network or factory complex for example. Other types of military force cannot generally act against such targets directly and are limited to operations against fielded forces.[34] Of course, air power can attack those targets as well, and can do so quite effectively. What is important to note is that the reasons for turning to air power in the post-1918 era when anticipating war against an industrial opponent – the desire to avoid bloodshed, the interdependence of modern economies, the perceived vulnerability of strategic centres of gravity and air power's ability to affect them at relatively low risk – have tended to increase over the decades. To be sure, the intangible aspects of a country – its culture, religion and tradition – will be difficult to influence, but that is the case when using all military forces, not just air power.

Determining the key target or group of targets within a country requires careful and accurate measurement of the effects of strategic air attack. This analysis is essential to ensure the results are what were expected, so that adjustment can be made for future operations. This is not a minor consideration. Air intelligence is a relatively new phenomenon. Although information-gathering agencies have existed for centuries, the types of intelligence they sought ran to two extremes. On the one hand, diplomatic insights were sought to determine potential adversaries' foreign policy, the strength of the government, alliance commitment, or the soundness of the economy to withstand a war. On the other hand, it was also necessary to ascertain military information such as the size of the enemy army and navy, the route of march, adequacy of supplies, and rate of fire of the artillery. Although tactical information – the strength, disposition and capability of the enemy air force and air defence network – was also necessary for the air battle, the advent of air warfare demanded a totally new type of intelligence. Detailed economic and industrial information was also now required. Because aircraft could strike military, economic and governmental centres deep within enemy territory, it became necessary to know the precise location and function of such targets. Air warfare required a detailed understanding of the electric power grid, rail and road networks, iron and steel industry, communications network and a host of other such items. This was a fundamentally different type of military intelligence from that of previous eras. As a result, new bureaucracies arose during the Second World War composed of economists, industrialists and engineers, whose main function was to study the make-up and vulnerabilities of an enemy state.[35]

Today, these intelligence agencies form a major portion of the military and their products are vital to the formulation of a viable air campaign plan.

At the same time, however, air leaders quickly realised in the Second World War that understanding how an economic or industrial system *failed* was just as important as how it operated. A procedure was needed to measure the effects of air attacks on a complex, inter-connected and multi-layered system. This is an extremely difficult task because it requires second and third order analyses of complicated networks. For example, it is relatively easy to determine the amount of physical damage an air attack causes to a railroad marshalling yard: the number of buildings or rail cars destroyed, tracks torn up, etc. It is more difficult to measure the effect such damage will have on an entire rail network, given the redundancy of such systems, the availability of repair teams and the ability to route traffic through other yards. It is more difficult still to judge what effect the shortage of materials *not* moved by the destroyed trains will have on the economy as a whole. An illustration of this problem and its complexity is given by one historian who has examined the records of the German railroad bureau in the Second World War. His analysis revealed that the destruction and disruption of German rail traffic severely curtailed the movement of coal throughout the Reich. Coal was the primary fuel for most industrial production and power generation. Therefore, the shortage of coal caused by the disruption of the rail system in turn had a major effect on the production of steel, and this resulted in the decreased output of tanks, ships and heavy artillery.[36] Thus, the overall military capability of the German armed forces was reduced by air strikes against seemingly unrelated targets deep in Germany. Clearly, such analysis requires intimate familiarity with the enemy's economy, as well as keen analytical skills. These are not the only problems.

If John Keegan is correct, and social and cultural factors play a far greater role in war than has hitherto been acknowledged, then the problem of analysis becomes even greater. This difficulty becomes compounded if it is considered that a country may strike a particular target not because of the effect it expects to produce on the enemy, but rather for the effect on its own domestic population. The Doolittle Raid of April 1942 by 16 B-25 bombers launched from an American aircraft carrier against targets in Tokyo was carried out at least as much to bolster American morale after a series of defeats as it was to influence the Japanese leaders or the Japanese economy. Similarly, attacks may be carried out so as to influence a third country. Some revisionists argue, for example, that the atomic bombs were dropped on Hiroshima and Nagasaki not so much to compel Japanese surrender, but to send a political message to the Soviet Union – the bombs were thus primarily an act of deterrence for the future.[37] Similarly, did the air strike on Libya in 1986 in response to the terrorist bombing in Berlin have an equally deterring effect on Syria as it did on Libya? In short, one must remember that warfare consists of living organisms fighting other living organisms while still other living organisms look on and are affected. If such complex and layered motives are indeed at play, the problems of analysis are enormous. It thus becomes necessary for intelligence organisations to focus on making a second leap: from an understanding of industrial and economic processes, to cultural and psychological ones. This will not be easy.

Airmen have been hampered in their attempts to devise practical theories of air power because of the lack of empirical evidence available, especially regarding strategic air power. Before the Second World War there was little evidence available of any kind, and even during that war the use of strategic air power was not convincingly tested, although the Pacific campaign came close. Nor was the application of strategic air power seriously attempted in either Korea or Vietnam. As a consequence, airmen have tended to rely on the force of logic – much like the nuclear theorists of the post-1945 era. In both instances these erudite exercises in formal argumentation have met with understandable scepticism due to the lack of solid empirical evidence. Unsupported opinions, even when passionately argued and elegantly structured, will sway few serious observers.

The Persian Gulf War redressed this situation somewhat. Air power was permitted to conduct a sustained and intense strategic air campaign while major surface operations were held in abeyance. Iraq's communications, transportation system, electrical power network and munitions industry were severely disrupted and in some cases totally halted. Although some will argue over the results of DESERT STORM and their meaning for the future, few can deny that air power played a more significant role in this war than in any other in history. Even so, the authoritative *Gulf War Air Power Survey* did not have access to all information, including Iraqi data, so the story is by no means complete or definitive.[38] Moreover, air theorists need more such evidence in order to formulate a cogent and defensible theory of strategic air power employment.

Unfortunately, the difficulty in measuring strategic-level effects has too often led military planners and pundits to ignore the subject totally and concentrate instead on those things that are easily quantifiable. Martin van Creveld argues that the increasing complexity of modern war has led historians and social scientists armed with computers to concentrate on areas that can be easily measured – the economic, social structure and administrative organisation of war – rather than on the operations themselves.[39] If this trend is true regarding surface operations, which are generally fought at the tactical level of war, the problems of accurately assessing and documenting strategic air warfare are obvious. Specifically, tactical effects are far more visible, obvious and calculable. For example, if one wishes to determine the probability of kill of an infrared Maverick missile fired against a T-72 tank, there are algorithms available that take into account such variables as altitude, distance, attack angle, weather conditions, armour thickness, etc., that will give a highly accurate result. In a wargame scenario, therefore, it is not difficult to ascertain, with a high degree of confidence, the results of air attack by a flight of four aircraft armed with Mavericks against a tank company in open terrain. If, however, one wishes to calculate the effect of air strikes against the logistics base of those tanks, the problem is significantly more difficult and the solution obtained is less precise. Attempting to measure how strategic air attacks against the enemy's oil refineries will impact the operations of that tank unit – although obviously significant – is even more imprecise and uncertain, especially since such effects can only be expected to manifest themselves weeks or even months after the attack. It is an unfortunate fact that measuring the effects of strategic air operations is an insufficiently understood science, if indeed it is a science at all.

Nevertheless, wargaming techniques can, hopefully, be improved, and then they may prove very useful in allowing airmen to test out theories of air power employment in a rapid, neutral and somewhat scientific fashion. In other words, wargames can help fill the void in air power theory left by a lack of readily available empirical evidence produced by war. There are obvious problems with this idea. As noted above, it is extremely difficult to measure the second and third order effects of strategic air attacks. Using computers does little to solve the problem, because there is scant historical data to input that can make such calculations credible. An exception to this dearth of data is the Second World War. The United States Strategic Bombing Survey, appointed by President Roosevelt, collected a mountain of information, statistics, interviews, photographs, graphs, etc. from lengthy studies in Germany and Japan. The product of its labours is enormous and impressive. However, surprisingly few historians and social scientists make use of this research. Although the summary volumes are often cited, the hundreds of more detailed reports on targets and target systems are largely ignored, possibly because of the awkwardness involved in attempting to manage the mass of data.[40] Perhaps someone will soon be able to code this information into a user-friendly computer software programme. Airmen and scholars can then experiment to test hypotheses and gain insights into how economies operate during war using actual data gathered during and immediately after a major air war.

Until it becomes possible to accurately and predictably measure and quantify such macro-level effects, airmen will always be at a disadvantage relative to their surface counterparts. It has been traditional for centuries to measure victory or defeat on land in terms of armies destroyed, soldiers slain and territory captured. Such standards are both quantifiable and widely recognised. It must be remembered, however, that just as the absence of hard statistics does not necessarily mean a theory is wrong, their presence does not confirm that a theory or policy is correct. Americans seem to have a cultural penchant for measuring things, especially in war – bomb tonnage, sortie rates, body counts, tank kills – and this can beguile one into thinking that the mere presence of numbers infers either accuracy or success. If one is measuring the wrong things, however, the statistics are worse than meaningless.

Perhaps the greatest caveat for the air strategist to bear in mind is that few wars are either mono-causal or mono-ending. Just as countries go to war for a complex array of varied, often conflicting, reasons, so too they choose to make peace based on a calculus that is seldom easily identifiable.[41] What precisely was it that caused Saddam Hussein to offer to withdraw from Kuwait in mid-February 1991? A number of possibilities exist: the continuous pounding he had received for four weeks from strategic air attacks; the equally continuous and severe tactical air pummelling meted out to his forces deployed in Kuwait; the fear that a major ground offensive could be launched against his much weakened army, leaving it unable to maintain internal control in Iraq; the threat of an amphibious landing north of Kuwait City that would cut off and isolate his forces if they attempted to retreat; concern for his personal safety after the destruction of several command and control bunkers in the Baghdad area; or the realisation that his attempts to split the Coalition by drawing Israel into the war had failed, leaving no long-term possibility of success against a unified enemy. All of these factors, as well as others, have been proposed by various observers. It is highly unlikely, however, that it will ever be possible to determine exactly what drove Saddam to the negotiating table: perhaps Saddam himself would be unable to answer the question definitively. In truth, given the complexity of war and human nature, it is most likely that all of the factors noted above went into Saddam's decision-making process. And that is perhaps the most valuable lesson for any military strategist: beware the theorist who offers a model of war that purports to give a simple and universally applicable answer to the numbing complications of war. There is seldom one answer, and if there is, it generally varies from one country to the next and from one situation to the next.

In essence, the process that the air strategist uses is what could be termed the 'strategic helix' depicted on page 73.[42] At the beginning of a war, the air planner studies the enemy in detail: his physical, military, economic, psychological and social aspects. From that study he deduces a number of what *may* be the enemy's centres of gravity. The *true* centre of gravity, which is probably hidden from the air planner, is represented by the central pillar in the helix. Uncertain as to which target is most appropriate from the many hundreds available, the air planner designates many for his initial attacks, initiating a series of parallel strategies. As the air war evolves over time, the strategist notes the effects of his air strikes,

72

modifies his targeting scheme and begins, hopefully, to close in on the elusive key centre of gravity – his targeting becomes more appropriate and thus more effective as he moves up the helix. Eventually and ideally, the air strategist uncovers the true centre of gravity and concentrates on reducing it. Theoretically, the more astute the air strategist, the tighter the helix. This is not an easy process. Bearing in mind all the considerations and admonitions already discussed, the theoretical ideal target of the enemy organism will be elusive and shifting. As a war progresses, other targets present themselves that either did not exist previously (the V-1/V-2 rocket sites in North-East Europe that caused a major diversion of air assets in 1944, for example) or were not taken sufficiently seriously early on (the mobile 'Scud' transporter-erector-launchers in 1991). In addition, because there is generally no single key centre of gravity that will cause a catastrophic enemy collapse, the air strategist either gets lucky and quickly hits something truly important or, more likely, attacks all kinds of targets which over time have an accumulative effect. In the Second World War, for example, Germany was so powerful and interdependent that numerous centres of gravity had to be struck, repeatedly, before degradation led to collapse. Nonetheless, the helix may prove useful in demonstrating the highly iterative nature of air strategy, as well as its complexity.

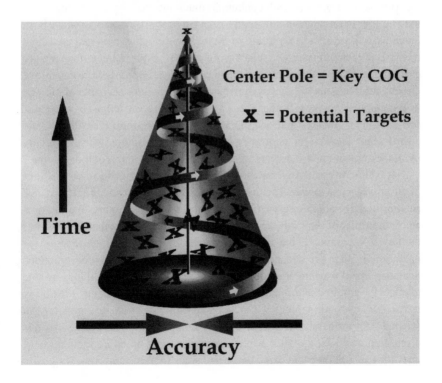

In summary, it has become apparent over the course of the past six decades that air power is playing an increasingly important role in warfare. Surface force commanders realise that their operations are extremely difficult, if not impossible, without the extensive employment of air power. Indeed, the United States Navy has built most of its force structure around air power in the form of the carrier battle groups; the Marines have organised their air-ground task forces around air power; and the Army's 7,000 helicopters constitute an air arm larger even than the United States Air Force. Indeed, perhaps 60 to 70 per cent of the DoD budget is devoted to air power in one form or another.

Few question the ability of air power to be decisive at the tactical and operational levels of war. The issue of its effectiveness at the strategic level of war is, however, a different matter. Airmen have claimed since the first decade of flight that the basic methods and strategies of warmaking have been forever changed because of their new weapon. Without denying for an instant the dominance of air power on the battlefield, they nonetheless argued for its pre-eminence at the strategic level as well. Their arguments for this contention have relied upon their various targeting philosophies. The question as to which strategic targets should have priority in an air campaign is surprisingly complex, and the answer is not at all self-evident. As a result, a whole variety of air theories have sprung up, each containing much internal logic to commend it, but regrettably founded on little hard evidence. In short, air theorists have been much akin to mystics, attempting to divine the thoughts, motives, goals and methods of their adversaries. At best this is a risky business, but airmen require even greater skill in this inexact art than most, since they are more capable of directly affecting the will or psyche of an enemy *and* more capable of missing it. To complicate matters further, these theorists have been, almost by necessity, self-confident, forceful and determined. In preaching their ideas they could afford scant leeway for contrary opinion. Their religions were decidedly monotheistic, and non-believers were to be converted, ignored or overcome.

It is time to move beyond narrow and overly prescriptive interpretations of air power's use in war. The theorists discussed in this essay have provided an enormously valuable service by their impassioned reasoning. We can now enjoy the fruits of their labours. It has become an aphorism that flexibility is the key to air power. That is just as true in the theoretical sense as in the operational. What are needed now are airmen conversant and well-grounded in all aspects of warfare, including the theoretical. Only then will they be able to select the employment concept best suited to the situation at hand. Flexibility is also the key to air strategy. Ultimately, air targeting strategy is an art, not a science. Unfortunately, it is an incredibly complex art. The purpose of this discussion has been to better arm air strategists with an appropriate array of questions so that they can make better decisions in peace and war.

NOTES

1   I would like to thank my colleagues in the School of Advanced Airpower Studies for their comments and suggestions on this essay. Especially helpful have been Lieutenant Colonels Mace Carpenter, Rob Owen and Tom Ehrhard, Major Bruce DeBlois, Drs Hal Winton, Dave Mets, Joe Guilmartin and Phil Sabin (King's College), Group Captain Andy Lambert of the RAF and my old friend Mike Terry.

2   Russell Weigley, *The Age of Battles: The Quest for Decisive Warfare from Breitenfeld to Waterloo* (Bloomington: Indiana University Press, 1991).

3   David G Chandler, *The Campaigns of Napoleon* (NY: Macmillan, 1966), pp.xxix, 333. It should be noted that at the same time he was invading Russia, Napoleon also had over 250,000 troops serving in Spain.

4   Colonel J F C Fuller, *The Reformation of War* (NY: Dutton, 1923), p.150.

5   B H Liddell Hart, *Paris, Or the Future of War* (NY: Dutton, 1925), p.37.

6   A contrary view: in low intensity conflict soldiers can in fact become strategic assets, capable of influencing strategic events, even if by accident. In reality, the idea of a linear 'spectrum of conflict' may be a misnomer. Perhaps the range of wars is better depicted by a horseshoe, because the two extremes often seem quite close together in many ways.

7   An insightful colleague, Lieutenant Colonel Mace Carpenter, noted that in most countries will is a triangle whose three sides are leadership, the people and the military forces. If the will of any of these is broken, the entire structure will likely collapse: the Iraqi army in the Gulf War, the people of France in 1940 and the Japanese leadership in 1945.

8   An exception was Nazi Germany. It was not until the German air forces, armies and navies were largely destroyed, the economy was in shambles and Russian troops had actually entered Berlin that Hitler's successor sued for peace. Given the state of the Reich at that point, his official surrender was almost irrelevant.

9   Douhet's primary work was entitled *Command of the Air* and was first published in 1921, with a revised edition appearing in 1927. In 1942 this essay was combined with three other of his major works, translated by Dino Ferrari, and published as *Command of the Air* (NY: Coward-McCann). This translation was reprinted with a new introduction by the Air Force History Office in 1983. Surprisingly, most of Douhet's writings, including fully one-half of the first edition of *Command of the Air*, have

never been translated into English. The best analysis of Douhet's theories is Bernard Brodie, *Strategy in the Missile Age* (Princeton: Princeton University Press, 1959). See also Colonel Phillip S Meilinger, 'Giulio Douhet and Modern War', *Comparative Strategy*, 12 (Jul–Sep 1993), pp.321–38.

10 Lee Kennett, *A History of Strategic Bombing* (NY: Scribner's, 1982), pp.25–26.

11 *Command of the Air*, 58. Compare this apocalyptic vision to that of J F C Fuller's in 1923 noted above.

12 For the official history see Robert T Finney, 'The History of the Air Corps Tactical School, 1920–1940', Air Force Historical Study No. 100. Maxwell AFB, 1955. (Reprinted by the Centre for Air Force History in 1992.)

13 Thomas H Greer, 'The Development of Air Doctrine in the Army Air Arm, 1917–1941', Air Force Historical Study No. 89. Maxwell AFB, 1955, 81. (Reprinted by the Centre for Air Force History in 1985.) In addition, one historian notes that this period was dominated by the Great Depression, and airmen witnessed each day the collapse of factories across the country, which in turn had a cascading effect on other factories, financial institutions, the labour force, etc. The American economy did indeed look extremely fragile. Stephen L McFarland, *America's Pursuit of Precision Bombing, 1910–1945* (Washington: Smithsonian Institution Press, 1995), p.92.

14 The origins of the industrial web theory can be found as early as the mid-1920s. Major William Sherman, an instructor at the Tactical School, wrote: 'in the majority of industries, it is necessary to destroy certain elements of the industry only, in order to cripple the whole. These elements may be called key plants.' Major William Sherman, *Air Warfare* (NY: Ronald, 1926), p.218. For the developments of the 1930s, see the account by one of the participants, Major General Don Wilson, 'Origins of a Theory of Air Strategy', *Aerospace Historian*, 18 (Spring 1971), pp.19–25.

15 There is not yet available an adequate analysis of Trenchard's theories, but for his biography see Andrew Boyle, *Trenchard: Man of Vision* (London: Collins, 1962).

16 Air Chief Marshal Sir Hugh Trenchard, 'The War Object of an Air Force', 2 May 1928, Public Records Office, London, File AIR 9/8.

17 Like Trenchard, Slessor's ideas have not yet been adequately explored. For his excellent memoirs see Marshal of the RAF John C Slessor, *The*

Central Blue: Recollections and Reflections (London: Cassell, 1956). His most impressive theoretical work is *Air Power and Armies* (Oxford: Oxford University Press, 1936). For an analysis of this work see Colonel Phillip S Meilinger, 'John C. Slessor and the Genesis of Air Interdiction', *Royal United Services Institute Journal*, 140 (Aug 1995), pp.43–48.

18 Brigadier General William L Mitchell, *Our Air Force : The Keystone of National Defense* (NY: Dutton, 1921). Mitchell's most famous book was *Winged Defense* (NY: Putnam, 1925). The best analyses of his work are by Edward Warner in Edward Mead Earle (ed.) *The Makers of Modern Strategy* (Princeton: Princeton University Press, 1941), and Alfred F. Hurley, *Billy Mitchell: Crusader for Air Power*, Revised ed. (Bloomington: Indiana University Press, 1975).

19 *Winged Defense*, p.xv.

20 For an excellent overview of the decisive impact of air power on the Iraqi army, see Fred Frostic, 'Air Campaign Against the Iraqi Army in the Kuwaiti Theater of Operations', RAND Study, 1994. For the effect of air attack against the Iraqi Republican Guard, see Major William A Andrews, 'Air Power against an Army: Challenge and Response in CENTAF's Duel with the Republican Guard', Master's Thesis, School of Advanced Air Power Studies, 1995.

21 John Boyd has never published his theories, but the best description and evaluation of them is by Major David S Fadok, 'John Warden and John Boyd: Air Power's Quest for Strategic Paralysis', Master's Thesis, School of Advanced Air Power Studies (Maxwell AFB: Air University Press, 1994). The US Marine Corps uses Boyd's OODA Loop in its basic doctrine manual to explain the importance of tempo. US Marine Corps, FMFM 1, 'Warfighting', (Mar 1989), p.84.

22 Colonel John A Warden III, *The Air Campaign: Planning for Combat* (Washington: Pergamon, 1989) has had a major impact on Air Force thinking, even though relatively modest in its calls for strategic air power. Indeed, it is illuminating that Warden's book today elicits so little controversy; the ideas he proposed then have now become accepted wisdom. To say the least, however, Warden's ideas took a significant leap with the experience of the Gulf War.

23 For a readable and illuminating account of the air campaign planning story in DESERT STORM, see Colonel Richard T Reynolds, *Heart of the Storm: The Genesis of the Air Campaign Against Iraq* (Maxwell AFB: Air University Press, 1995).

24 Colonel John A Warden III, 'The Enemy as a System', *Airpower Journal* 9 (Spring 1995), pp.40–55. For an analysis of Warden's theories, see Fadok's study cited above, as well as Lewis Ware, 'Ware on Warden: Some Observations of the Enemy as a System', *Airpower Journal* 9 (Winter 1995), pp.40–55.

25 Katie Hafner and Matthew Lyon, 'Talking Headers', *The Washington Post Magazine*, 4 Aug 1996, p.28.

26 John Arquilla and David Ronfeldt, 'Cyberwar is Coming!' *Comparative Strategy* 12 (Apr–Jun 1993), p.143. The whole subject of information warfare has become a cottage industry of late. For good overviews see Alvin and Heidi Toffler, *War and Anti-War: Survival at the Dawn of the 21st Century* (Boston: Little, Brown, 1993), and Winn Schwartau, *Information Warfare: Chaos on the Electronic Superhighway* (NY: Thunder's Mouth Press, 1994).

27 Real-time intelligence from airborne sensors regarding air and ground threats can now be provided to the cockpit. Such cueing for other deep ground targets is not far off. For an excellent treatment see Major William G Chapman, 'Organizational Concepts for the "Sensor-to-Shooter" World: The Impact of Real Time Information on Air Power Targeting', Master's Thesis, School of Advanced Air Power Studies, 1996.

28 For a useful discussion of vulnerabilities (or the lack thereof) to an information society, see George Bugliarello, 'Telecommunications, Politics, Economics, and National Sovereignty: A New Game', *Airpower Journal* 10 (Spring 1996), pp.6–17.

29 Lieutenant Colonel Jason Barlow, *'Strategic Paralysis: An Air Power Theory for the Present'*, Master's Thesis, School of Advanced Air Power Studies (Maxwell AFB: Air University Press, 1993).

30 John Keegan, *A History of Warfare* (NY: Knopf, 1993). For an excellent analysis of how cultural factors apply to air warfare, see Lieutenant Colonel Pat Pentland, 'Centre of Gravity Analysis and Chaos Theory: Or How Societies Form, Function and Fail', Thesis, Air War College, Maxwell AFB, 1993, and Paul M Belbutowski, 'Strategic Implications of Cultures in Conflict', *Parameters* XXVI (Spring 1996), pp.32–42. For a critique of Keegan see Christopher Bassford, 'John Keegan and the Grand Tradition of Thrashing Clausewitz: A Polemic', *War in History* 1 (Nov 1994), pp.319–36.

31 Donald Hagan, *On the Origins of War* (NY: Doubleday, 1995) is a study of several wars since antiquity and concludes that wars are generally fought

for one of three reasons: honour, fear or interest. The first of these, honour, is precisely the type of psychological motivation that is so difficult to predict or calculate. One should also note that what appears irrational to us may be completely rational in our adversary's milieu.

32 For excellent discussions of this process see Lieutenant Colonel Maris 'Buster' McCrabb, 'Air Campaign Planning', *Airpower Journal* 7 (Summer 1993), pp.11–22; and David E Thaler and David A Shlapak, *Perspectives on Theater Air Campaign Planning* (Santa Monica: RAND, 1995).

33 For an important discussion of this problem see Lieutenant Colonel Barry D. Watts, *The Foundations of US Air Doctrine: The Problem of Friction in War* (Maxwell AFB: Air University Press, 1984).

34 It must also be noted that airmen do believe in the decisiveness of the counterforce battle – the one for air superiority. Without air superiority, gained by destroying or neutralising the enemy's air force and ground defences, all other military operations on land, sea and in the air will be extremely difficult.

35 The definitive study of these economic warriors has yet to be written, but for the views of two participants see, for the Americans, W W Rostow, *Pre-Invasion Bombing Strategy* (Austin: University of Texas Press, 1981), and for the British, Solly Zuckerman, *From Apes to Warlords* (NY: Harper & Row, 1978).

36 Alfred C Mierzejewski, *The Collapse of the German War Economy, 1944– 1945* (Chapel Hill: University of North Carolina Press, 1988).

37 For an excellent discussion of these ideas see Major Thomas P Ehrhard, 'Expanding the SAAS Air Power Analysis Framework', Master's Thesis, School of Advanced Air Power Studies, 1995. Of note, although the Doolittle Raid did in fact have an enormous strategic effect – it induced Japan to attack Midway Island – this was not an American intention. Although now widely discredited, for the theory concerning the political motive for dropping the bombs see Gar Alperovitz, *Atomic Diplomacy: Hiroshima and Potsdam; the Use of the Atomic Bomb and the American Confrontation with Soviet Power* (NY: Krieger, 1965). Alperovitz raises an interesting point: if you are doing something for the specific purpose of signaling a third party, do not forget that the *second* party (in this example Japan) pays the price for the signal.

38 Eliot Cohen (ed.) *Gulf War Air Power Survey*, 5 vols. (Washington: Government Printing Office, 1993).

39 Martin van Creveld, 'Thoughts on Military History', *Journal of Contemporary History*, 18 (Oct 1983), p.553.

40 For the summary reports see *The United States Strategic Bombing Surveys: Europe and Pacific* (Maxwell AFB: Air University Press, 1987).

41 The First World War is one of the most complex and oft-debated instances demonstrating the difficulty in determining war causation. The standard work illustrating this example is Dwight E Lee (ed.) *The Outbreak of the First World War: Causes and Responsibilities* (NY: Heath, 1975).

42 I wish to thank Mike Terry for first suggesting the idea of a 'strategic helix' to me in the course of one of our many conversations together.

3

SHATTERING IMPACT: THE PSYCHOLOGY OF AIR ATTACK

by

Group Captain Andrew P N Lambert MPhil RAF

DIRECTOR OF DEFENCE STUDIES,
ROYAL AIR FORCE STAFF COLLEGE

W riting after the horrific slaughter of trench warfare had already seared the military conscience, the South African soldier-statesman Jan Smuts posited a different future for war, one based on the aerial weapon. 'The day may not be far off', he wrote,

> when aerial operations with their devastation of enemy lands and destruction of industrial and populous centres on a vast scale may become the principal operations of war, to which the older forms of military and naval operations may become secondary and subordinate.[1]

And others, of course, went even further. Giulio Douhet, writing in Italy in the aftermath of the war, saw aerial warfare as the new means of combat. Only air power offered the prospect of avoiding the stalemate of the trenches; it would outflank the enemy in the vertical plane, and carry the war directly to his heartland. There, to attack his vitals, to destroy his industry and to drive the populace to sue for peace. Hence air power was an offensive weapon *par excellence* and, used properly, could bring the war to an abrupt and satisfactory conclusion. In this he largely agreed with Hugh 'Boom' Trenchard that 'viewed in its true light, aerial warfare admits of no defence, only offence',[2] and that the strategic bomber offered the potential to foreshorten war by targeting the morale of the civilians.

In Britain, the young RAF found its *raison d'être* in the power of an independent bomber force, supported Stanley Baldwin's *bon mot* that 'the bomber will always get through'. Precisely how the bomber was to be employed was somewhat more difficult to identify. Trenchard had frequently repeated the assertion that the moral effect of bombing was 20 times greater than the material.[3] The effects of the bombing of Shanghai by the Japanese and of Guernica in Spain by the Germans in 1937 seemed to justify these fears, which were further heightened through the medium of the cinema. In March 1939 the threat of a similar aerial 'knock-out blow' against Prague was a factor in forcing the Czechs to concede to Hitler's demands, and similar fears haunted Great Britain. Great Britain – with her huge, densely populated capital so close to the continent – was considered to be extremely vulnerable to air attack.

THE SECOND WORLD WAR EXPERIENCE

Yet these fulsome predictions, and the sentiments that underpinned them, never seemed to match subsequent reality. Despite the dreadful prophecies, strategic bombing using high-explosive bombs did not, by itself, prove to be a war-winning weapon. The strategic bombing doctrine was based too much on theory and not enough on hard practical experience. The capability and invulnerability of the bomber had been grossly exaggerated. Doctrine was far ahead of the technology needed to fulfil it, and civilian populations proved far more resilient to air attack than anyone had foreseen. It is true that the destruction of Warsaw in 1939 and of Rotterdam in 1940 by bombers of the Luftwaffe forced the Polish and Dutch governments to surrender, but only because these cities were already in the front line and their countries largely occupied. When German bombers attacked London, Coventry and other British cities, civilian morale remained firm. Indeed, if anything, the popular perception was that it was strengthened by the experience.

However, the well publicised determination of the British people was not matched by reality. Whilst most of the un-bombed areas of London became ever more dogged, those people who experienced near misses, who witnessed the death of friends and neighbours, who watched their houses destroyed in flames or who themselves were injured, were not reinvigorated. As Professor Janis noted from his postwar analysis, 'It should be noted that these observations on resentment, reported by British social psychologists and psychiatrists, tend to be at variance with the well-publicised conception of high British morale as presented by many journalists during the Battle of Britain.'[4] Since, officially at least, German raids had had such a light effect on morale, it is surprising that the government believed that similar attacks on Germany would undermine German morale.[5] The attraction in continuing the campaign lay more in the opportunity it gave to be seen to 'pay Germany back' and, as the bomber offensive gathered in accuracy and intensity, its effect became ever more acute. As Professor R J Overy has noted, 'A greater diversion of German resources arose through defence against bomb attack itself. By 1944 some two million soldiers and civilians were engaged in ground anti-aircraft defence. This was more than the total employed in the aircraft industry.'[6]

Thus despite its intensity, bombing on its own did not bring the war to a close. Nonetheless, bombing did seriously depress morale. Its main psychological effects were defeatism, fear, hopelessness, fatalism and apathy. As the United States Strategic Bombing Survey (USSBS) reported immediately after the end of the war:

> Bombing did not stiffen morale. The hate and anger it aroused tended to be directed against the Nazi regime which was blamed for beginning air warfare and for being unable to ward off Allied Air Attacks. The reason that poor German civilian morale did not translate itself into action seriously endangering the German war effort . . . was largely due to the terroristic control of the population by the Nazis.[7]

Nor were such effects limited to the Axis powers. Even Winston Churchill, so powerful in belittling German raids, secretly acknowledged their potential. As he wrote after the war, 'Of course, if the [Allied] bombs of 1943 had been applied to the London of 1940 we should have passed into conditions which might have pulverised all human organisation . . . and no one has a right to say that London, which was certainly unconquered, was also unconquerable.'[8]

Nevertheless one little-reported effect of Allied air power was, under the right circumstances, to sap the morale of German soldiers in the field, to undermine their confidence and to create a sense of futility. Interestingly, British military histories do not dwell on this subject, yet German archives are replete with assessments of (Allied) air power's effectiveness. Tactical air power, from its infant beginnings, grew into a highly devastating weapon of destruction, again as noted by the USSBS:

> Prior to 1943, infantry weapons were the leading cause of casualties. Artillery fire was second and aerial bombardment and strafing third. In the latter part of 1943 aerial strafing and bombardment shifted to first position, followed closely by artillery, and during 1944–45 aerial weapons were far ahead of either artillery or infantry weapons as a cause of casualties in the German Armed Forces.[9]

The demoralisation effect of this destruction was not lost on the soldier. Nor was the hopelessness of the situation lost on Field Marshal Erwin Rommel, who wrote famously that: 'Anyone who has to fight, even with the most modern weapons, against an enemy in complete control of the air fights like a savage against modern European troops, under the same handicap, and with the same chance of success.'[10] Later, at the time of Normandy, he complained: 'The enemy's air superiority has a very grave effect on our movements. There's simply no answer to it.'[11] Even Field Marshal von Kluge, Supreme Commander West, writing to Hitler on 22 July 1944, warned that:

> The psychological effect of such a mass of bombs coming down with all the power of elemental nature upon the fighting troops, especially the infantry, is a factor which has to be given particularly serious consideration . . . the moment is fast approaching when this overtaxed front line is bound to break.[12]

Examples of the demoralising effect are legion; perhaps the most pungent is that provided by General Leutnant Fritz Bayerlein, Commander of the *Panzer-Lehr* Division, whose division was attacked by aircraft in preparation for the American offensive across France:

> The long duration of the bombing, without any possibility for opposition, created depressions and a feeling of helplessness, weakness and inferiority. Therefore the morale attitude of a great number of men grew so bad that they, feeling the uselessness of fighting, surrendered, deserted to the enemy or escaped to the rear. . . . Only particularly strong nerved and brave men could endure this strain.[13]

Humans will endure much pain when there is even a faint prospect of victory, but once defeat is inevitable pain is only endured under compulsion or in desperation. Two extracts from the time are notable, the first because of its helplessness and the second because it shows the mindset if soldiers are pushed too far: 'German soldiers had begun to complain that they would soon be told "to fight fighter-bombers with pocket knives"'; and 'Since all was lost, and there was nothing to return to, he should fight the hated enemy to the death in revenge or despair.'[14] Despite the mastery of tactical air power, several factors explain why the *Wehrmacht* did not just give up. Nazi coercion certainly played a part, but there were a number of respites: first, Allied tactical aircraft rarely flew at night; second, against massed anti-aircraft fire in the battle area aircraft losses could be high; and finally, perhaps of the greatest importance, tactical air operations were often prevented by poor weather (as certainly occurred during the first eight days of the Ardennes offensive[15]).

EXPERIENCE AND LESSONS FROM THE GULF WAR

The circumstances that precipitate cataclysmic demoralisation and the true results that spring from it will always be a matter for debate. But it is interesting to compare the factors that contributed to the *Wehrmacht*'s discomfiture in 1944–45 with those experienced by the Iraqi soldiers in 1991.

Arrayed against the Coalition was a modern, sizeable and battle-tested army and air force. Iraqi forces comprised over 950 combat aircraft, 7,000 anti-aircraft guns, 16,000 Surface to Air Missiles (SAMs), 900,000 troops (including eight Republican Guard Divisions) and 5,700 main battle tanks.[16] The Iraqi Army was well motivated, but its experience of combat had both advantages and disadvantages. The Iran/Iraq war of 1980–89 had been intense, with large numbers of casualties on both sides. Under such circumstances, as research on the experience of Israeli forces in the various Middle East wars has already indicated, a number of Iraqi troops could be expected to suffer from either overtly displayed stress or from suppressed stress that might be less visible but no less debilitating. Israeli specialists termed such behaviour Combat Stress Reaction (CSR), and their research indicated that troops manifesting such reactions would be sensitised to subsequent bombardments or attacks that would further weaken and reduce their combat effectiveness. Ba'ath party rule was generally acceptable to most of the population. They enjoyed a higher standard of living than many of their neighbours and religion, though important, was not oppressive or fundamentalist. The people were proud of Iraq's status as a local power; they believed Kuwait was in the wrong over the debt repayment issue and had been 'stealing' oil from the Rumailah oilfield. Support for Saddam Hussein was high and the troops were confident. As the Coalition military chief, General H Norman Schwarzkopf, subsequently noted, Saddam Hussein had confidently predicted that the President of the United States would be defeated if he opposed Iraq's aggression, and he bolstered his prediction by threats to launch a surprise attack on Israel; the Iraqi ruling council (a largely puppet body) predicted 'The Mother of All Battles'. [17]

Propaganda in Iraq was directly controlled by the Ba'ath party, through the Revolutionary Command Council, to Saddam Hussein himself. It combined religiously emotive words, religious symbolism and Arab nationalism with sycophantic praise of Saddam Hussein. Only one source of complaint was evident, and that was in the privileges accorded members of the élite Republican Guard.

Because of bureaucratic delays and local sensitivities, Coalition Psyops did not begin until November 1990, when the first radio broadcasts were made. Leaflet drops commenced in mid-January 1991. The main media of Coalition Psyops were radio broadcasts, loudspeakers and leaflet drops. The relative effectiveness assessed by the US after the war was as follows:[18]

Relative Effectiveness of Coalition Psyops

	Radio Broadcasts	Loudspeaker	Activities Leaflets
Audience Exposure	58%	34%	98%
Persuasiveness	46%	18%	80%
Induced to Surrender	34%	16%	70%

Radio broadcasts were made from high-powered ground transmitters, supported by airborne EC-130 Hercules aircraft. Prisoner of War (POW) debriefs indicated that 58 per cent of the Iraqi forces in the KTO heard the broadcasts and 46 per cent said they had influenced their decision to surrender. Loudspeaker broadcasts were made from ground and helicopter platforms. A postwar US Special Operations Command study concluded that: 'Feedback from EPWs [POWs] was positive, indicating . . . "loudspeaker teams told us where to surrender after the leaflets and radio showed us how"'; and that 'Of a target audience of 300,000 Iraqi troops, an estimated 98% were exposed to the 29 million leaflets dropped in theatre. Many of the 87,000 who surrendered were found clutching leaflets. . ." [19]

Although the Iraqi forces were well motivated at the end of 1990, almost all were to be exposed at some time or another to Coalition Psywar. Propaganda by itself was highly unlikely to be effective, but it is difficult to ascertain Iraqi reaction to Coalition propaganda before the shooting war began. Two points are worth noting. The first is that the Iraqis were certainly not overawed by the Coalition forces arrayed against them. They believed that their own costly equipment and hardened facilities, as well as their weapons of mass destruction, gave them a potent counter to any offensive. The prospect of a major tank battle was viewed with confidence, since a parity in tanks would inflict heavy casualties on the Americans; CNN would then do what was necessary to undermine the will of the American people to continue. Second, the use of 'Scud' missiles against Israel was expected to precipitate an Israeli retaliation, something that would have resulted in the disintegration of the Coalition. For Saddam Hussein, the prospect of defeating the United States, and thereby transforming Iraq into a regional power, appeared good.

Detailed examination of the course of the air and ground war is beyond the scope of this article, but an immediate physical success that translated into a psychological one has been described as follows: '. . . once Allied coalition bombing commenced, the Iraqi broadcasting capability was severely hampered. Iraq's television capability was completely destroyed, and the only radio broadcasts noted were Baghdad Domestic Service and Voice of the Masses – both operating at greatly reduced signal strength.' [20] Under Phase I of the air campaign plan, most of the damage was inflicted on strategic targets deep inside Iraq; however, none of the soldiers would have been unaware of the massive air assault that had passed overhead. Against advanced American technology in the form of conventional cruise missiles and stealth fighters, the Iraqi defences had no answer. Even though Baghdad had seven times the density of defences that Hanoi had during LINEBACKER II, [21] by the end of the opening night's campaign the Iraqi Air Defence Headquarters was out of action, as were three of the four Sector Operations Centres. Moreover, despite a wealth of SAM batteries, few missiles managed to achieve any kills except against drones, and SAMs astride the main ingress routes were either jammed or destroyed by anti-radiation missiles. Without ground control, any Iraqi aircraft that did fly were virtually blind to the raids and had to rely on their own short-range radars. Against them, F-15s, guided by AWACS, achieved easy kills. Any expectation on the Iraqi part that this might be a balanced contest, and that the Iraqis could fight the coalition to a standstill, was shattered. The civilian population was alarmed by the effortless level of destruction; for example, 55 per cent of Iraq's electrical power was destroyed on the first night. As the Coalition's growing air superiority demonstrated, Iraqi forces could do little to prevent Allied aircraft from having free rein across the whole country; they were incapable of preventing aircraft operations and unable to prevent aircraft from attacking targets at will. Even their best efforts seemed impotent. In contrast to the Vietnam War, where aircraft losses had been significant, Coalition losses in the Gulf were measured in fractions of one per cent.

Against this, Saddam Hussein had two options and one ally. His first option was to subject the Coalition and Israel to 'Scud' attacks, just as Hitler had done against London with his V-1 and V-2 almost 50 years previously. Psychologically, this was a powerful move, calculated to undermine Alliance solidarity and to re-motivate the Iraqi people. The reaction was telling. One witness stated:

> I observed from the Scud almost panic among the civilians in Riyadh and I saw an inordinate reaction on the part of the Israelis. We are taught to believe the Israelis are born with a bayonet in their teeth and the Israelis are used to fighting 600 to one and winning. Well, the Scuds just terrified them. [22]

Coalition commanders at the most senior levels had, however, been fully briefed on the risks from the 'Scud', and although a variety of options had been considered, the task of neutralising them fell to the air forces. Considerable air effort was diverted from the prosecution of the strategic aims, but the risk of Israel joining the war was acute, and only just prevented by the deployment of Patriot SAMs to Israel. The effectiveness of these missiles is largely irrelevant; both the Saudis and the Israelis believed in them and their nerves were steeled – stress was thus reduced.

Saddam's second option was to launch a pre-emptive assault on the Saudi coastal town of Khafji. Air and ground planners had been concerned that the obvious husbanding of Iraqi forces might presage what was termed a 'Tet' (in memory of the Tet offensive that surprised the USA in Vietnam, and which had a profound psychological impact upon support for the Vietnam War in America, even though it was, in reality, a terrible defeat for indigenous communist forces in South Vietnam). If there was a clearly defined aim for the attack on Khafji it was probably to unhinge Coalition Arab forces, thereby re-motivating Iraqi forces with a quick and well-trumpeted victory. In the event it did neither, and it attracted unwelcome B-52 attacks on the front-line forces in Southern Kuwait.

Deserted by the Russians, abandoned by almost all Arab nations and only mildly supported by neutral Jordan, Saddam's one loyal ally was the atrocious weather: up to 40 per cent of the Allied missions during the first ten days were aborted through poor weather. However, unlike previous wars where most flying ceased in darkness, the threat to Iraq was equal, if not greater, at night. Only the weather provided any respite against the continuous air attacks. Between 1,000 and 1,500 sorties were launched every day, and the Republican Guards to the west of Basra were attacked by B-52s every three hours. As a psychological weapon, the B-52 impressed soldiers with the number of weapons it could carry, the frequency of its attacks and the damage it created. That said, the level of attrition could have been even higher for, as Coalition air commander Lieutenant General Charles Horner recollected:

> [President Bush] wanted a war that was conducted with minimal loss of life on both sides. . . . I could have loaded the B-52s up with cluster bombs and gone after casualties as in World War II – but we just put in regular 500-pound bombs, knowing that we were going in against dug-in forces and this would not be a good weapon, except for psychological purposes.[23]

Fear of the B-52 was considerably heightened by the warning that the Coalition gave to Iraqi soldiers. Psychologically, this achieved three things: first, it created an expectancy, which the USA then had to ensure was carried out; second, it created a feeling of impotence – there was nothing Iraqis could do to prevent the attack, and the only route to self-preservation was through desertion; and third, the announcement that the raid would take place on an appointed day created a level of anxiety which rose hour by hour as the deadline approached. Specific divisions were targeted by number (to further demoralise Iraqi forces by showing the apparent omniscience of Coalition intelligence) with upwards of a million and a half leaflets being dropped over the front at night so that Iraqis would awake to find them. The leaflets stated which division would be hit, and when. And then B-52s, as promised, would attack that particular division. The leaflets promised a way out, as the commander of a Coalition psychological operations group recalled after the war:

> It wasn't just that we were going to bomb them but the alternative was to get away from their equipment, to desert, to come across the border. There was an alternative to death and that was an important message to get across. . . .

it reduced a great deal of the combat strength on the front, increased the feelings of isolation, and of being lied to [by Iraq].[24]

By the end of the first week of DESERT STORM Iraqi air defence capability had been reduced by 70 per cent and Iraq's ability to command by 80 per cent. Clearly, Iraq and its forces had effectively become both impotent and leaderless. During the following weeks successive air attacks using Precision Guided Munitions (PGMs) progressively destroyed the lines of supply to the deployed forces. Tactical leadership had never been strong in the Iraqi army and now there was an overpowering sense of isolation, of being cut off from both supplies and higher authority. Iraqi POW reports also suggest that this isolation gave rise to a conviction not only that there would be no relief but also that they were left to their fate – as cannon fodder. Such sentiments seemed all the more believable when rumours circulated that caught deserters were being shot by death squads, and that possession of Allied leaflets was a capital offence. The soldiers thus faced an impossible dilemma: to stay and be bombed (or destroyed in the inevitable ground assault that must follow), or to desert and face the death squads.

Fear of the Allies grew progressively and eventually outweighed the fear of death squads; at least 160,000 soldiers disappeared. As G-Day (the first day of the ground assault) approached, Allied Psyops, sensitive to the soldiers' dilemma, provided the answer – 'Surrender to your Arab brothers, surrender to Allah, walk in the direction of Mecca.' The latter appeal worked particularly well:

> One great psychological success was when we told them to defect and to go to Mecca; because they all knew what direction Mecca was, even though many of them didn't know where they were. . . . (We would have had more desertions except they didn't know how). First they had been told that they were going to be executed by the Westerners, and second they had their own guys shooting them, and some of the junior ranking Iraqi officers were sickened by this.[25]

Until G-Day few prisoners were taken, largely because of the Iraqi obstacles and minefields, but once these had been breached the trickle became a flood: 87,000 gave up, most without a fight. A number of common themes emerged in the POW reports:

- Psyop leaflets produced the highest threat to morale, second only to Allied bombing.[26]
- Psyop leaflets speaking of plentiful food and water caused soldiers to

desert to the South.[27]
* Rumours of deserters being shot caused soldiers to desert South rather than North.[28]
* Officers and leaders felt resistance was futile as they were 'against the world'.[29]
* Most desertions were caused by radio reports of B-52 bombings.[30]
* The Psyop campaign told soldiers to leave their vehicles to avoid injury; it proved what President Bush said about not fighting the Iraqi people.[31]

Phases III and IV of the air campaign had focused on destroying items of high military value, tanks and APCs in particular. (Phase II had been the suppression of enemy air defences in the Kuwait theatre of operations so that Phases III and IV could be pursued more easily.) The message to get away from your equipment was repeated frequently and widely believed. As one commander said, 'in the Iran/Iraq war the tank was my friend; in the Gulf war it was my enemy'.[32] Once the campaign against the ground forces began, Iraqi troops quickly learned to minimise the time spent in their vehicles, and slept well away from them at night. Thus the personal risk from Allied aircraft using 'smart' bombs or missiles, engaged in what was euphemistically called 'tank-plinking', was relatively low.

It is, however, surprising – and worth noting – that the Iraqis seemed unafraid of high technology weapons. The most likely explanation is that while 'smart' weapons demonstrated Allied omnipotence (and thus undermined Iraqi hopes of eventual success), they created little anticipatory anxiety, and the personal threat from them was low. In contrast, B-52 bombs were concentrated, devastating and intense. They were indiscriminate and unpreventable, so the anticipatory anxiety, particularly when preceded by leaflets, was high. Similarly, the potential threat of the A-10 attack aircraft was inescapable. Employed primarily against front-line infantry positions, it used a mixture of weapons equally capable of destroying vehicles and exposed troops.

The effect of the combined air and psyops campaign was catastrophic. For every Iraqi killed in the air and ground campaign, over 20 capitulated, most without a fight. This level of demoralisation is unprecedented in modern warfare and far surpasses similar ratios for Korea or Vietnam where the figures were as shown in the table below:[33]

Enemy Death in Action, Deserters and Prisoners of War

Conflict	KIA	Deserters	POWs	Deserters/POWs vs. KIA
Korea	400,000	unknown	152,200	0.38 : 1
Vietnam	850,000	121,200	36,700	0.19 : 1
Gulf War	10,000	160,000	86,743	24.67 : 1

Such figures prompt a number of questions. What 'demotivated' the Iraqi soldiery? Was the Gulf War a product of a set of circumstances that were unique to the Gulf, or could such a psychological victory be repeated in a future campaign? Was it the air campaign or the ground war that persuaded the soldiers to capitulate? If it was the air campaign, what factors contributed to its great success in demotivating the enemy? Was it the B-52 bombing, was it the Stealth and other high technology, or was it the psyop campaign of leaflets, radio and loudspeakers? Was the Iraqi army unconvinced of the justice of its cause and looking for an excuse to leave?

Information from Iraqi troops is understandably difficult to obtain but we at least have the testimony of those Iraqis treated by Allied hospitals. According to one specialised clinic:

> The Iraqis had been exposed to conditions specifically designed to lead to the development of Combat Stress Reaction (CSR). The incredibly intense and successful allied air campaign subjected many Iraqis to extraordinary stressors, including the constant fear of imminent death, frequent witnessing of the deaths and injuries of comrades, sleep deprivation, lack of food and water and disruption of command and control channels. Any of these circumstances separately would be expected to predispose a soldier to the development of CSR while their combination would multiply the risk. . . . All the EPWs [POWs] reported . . . anxiety, depressed mood, sleep disturbance and fear. Other CSR symptoms reported by most of the EPWs included intense memories and dreams, exhaustion, irritability, guilt. . . noise sensitivity, disciplinary problems, psychomotic disturbances, dissociative states, poor concentration and constricted affect. *Homicidal ideas were expressed by half of the EPWs . . . to kill their own officers.* There was little motivation . . . thoughts of surrender were commonly voiced as a way of coping with the stress of the air war. Thoughts of desertion were also frequently noted. Several soldiers did desert, only to be returned to their duties after being threatened with execution of themselves or members of their families.[34] [Emphasis added]

Unfortunately, it was not possible to quantify the level of trauma, nor to correlate it against particular attacks. Nevertheless, it was clear that all had been exposed to frequent bombings; several POWs indicated that bombings had occurred almost continuously. The *least* frequent was every two to three days. Living conditions were miserable, with little food or water, and starvation was common. Soldiers lived in small groups, they often witnessed death or injury and medical care was largely non-existent; there was a marked schism between officers and enlisted soldiers. Soldiers were asked to rate their combat effectiveness at the start of the ground war; all replied they were at nought per cent. Many methods of coping were employed: 'By far the most common response involved religious practices and prayer. Another common sustaining thought was of family members. POWs often expressed fear for their family members, indicating that they would have deserted except for anticipated reprisals against loved ones.'[35] The strength drawn from their small 'buddy' groups was important to sustain them but they openly discussed surrender and a third actively considered suicide.

It is noteworthy that the Iraqi leadership never gave up. In part, this may have reflected a realisation of the limited UN war aims, that Iraqi sovereignty was never threatened. Nevertheless, the costs in terms of lost manpower and infrastructure never precipitated an early surrender by Saddam Hussein or the Ba'ath Party. This reinforces the view that for tyrants the options are stark: cling to power or die; almost any level of loss is acceptable to the tyrant if it allows him to retain power. Just as Hitler tightened his grip as the bombing intensified, so the Iraqi secret police tightened theirs. Colonel John A Warden III's air campaign theory suggested that leadership should be the prime focus of an air campaign, which would be ideal if the leadership could be made to be vulnerable. In this case it was not, and psychologically it was the men of the armed forces who were both most vulnerable, and most critical to the outcome of the war. Compared with previous air wars, the Gulf air war achieved success in almost every psychological dimension. Iraqi expectancy, and the soldiers' hopes of victory, were progressively undermined. The intensity and severity of bombing sensitised the victims to repeat attacks. Overwhelming air supremacy created a feeling of impotence amongst its victims. Isolation, primitive living conditions and the inability to fight back, coupled with the pervasiveness of lethal allied aircraft, engendered not only fear but a sense of futility and hopelessness. Psychologically, the campaign gave the Iraqi soldier an impossible choice: die in the bombing, or die from the death squads. Only in escape – including escape into captivity – was there hope of life.

THE PSYCHOLOGY OF THE ATTACKED

The evidence suggests that the psychological responses of a civilian population to bombing mirror almost exactly the reactions of soldiers to enemy fire. Though there is therefore a shared universality of fear, a body of opinion posits that each culture should be treated from a different psychological standpoint,[36] and there certainly are large cultural differences which need to be borne in mind when constructing a psychological campaign. The responses of soldiers and civilians in differing cultures to bombardment have, however, a remarkable similarity. A number of writers, for example, J M Marcum and D W Cline, have suggested that the 'cross-cultural validity of symptoms appear to have more to do with response to overwhelming stress than with cultural or intrapsychic factors'.[37] This section will first analyse combat stress and combat psychology, before examining how the experiences are represented in later theories.

As reported in an Israeli journal of psychiatry, 'Most people are sustained in their daily lives by a deeply ingrained illusion of safety. Though aware of tragedy and suffering, we tend to view these as the plight of others. The illusion of safety is essential. In its absence there is little we would do without paralysing terror.'[38] If we accept that the soldier of today is little different from that of the fourth Century BC, it is his desire to survive that is his dominant characteristic, not his display of heroism. It is thus difficult to persuade a man to give his life in combat; it will require a considerable amount of altruism on his part, or a degree of coercion from another. For some, the promise of a place in the afterlife is a sufficient motive, but such religious fervour may require bolstering. Almost all soldiers, at one time or another, believe that they are prepared to give their lives for others, but their perception of death may be too idealised. In his mind's eye the soldier conceives of giving his life selflessly in a just, noble and victorious cause, perhaps in defence of his homeland. He will die heroically, respected by his peers, and loved by those at home. He will meet a clean, neat death and receive an honourable funeral; he will be revered and honoured by future generations and his family will be held in high esteem. In such circumstances a soldier is prepared to sacrifice his life. But the reality is very different. Indeed, in the mud of a Passchendaele or in the jungles of a Vietnam, few if any of these rosy ideals are likely to be met.

Battles of the eighteenth and even the nineteenth Century generally lasted a day: pitched battles were infrequent, fatigue was less important, little surprise was possible, troops had time to prepare mentally for battle, their responses were generally reactive, not cognitive, and they had the clear, visible support of their comrades. Moreover, there is at least some suggestion that soldiers in past battles were frequently fortified by alcohol, if not inebriated. Popular myth portrays war as a glorious undertaking, just as much now as previously. Soldiers entering a modern battle initially enjoy feelings of immortality and exhilaration, but are rapidly disillusioned when they realise for the first time that it is a fight to the death; they lose the illusion of immortality and, if wounded, are rendered all the more vulnerable to possible mental collapse.[39]

So much for the initial perceptions, what of the gradual changes as the fear of battle inexorably stresses a soldier? To consider this in detail requires an examination of combat stress, the various stressors, and what is now called Combat Stress Reaction (CSR). There is no common agreement over exactly what causes a rise in combat stress, but the following stressors enjoy a consensus:

Claustrophobia. Claustrophobia is the loss of personal movement through either regulation or enemy fire; the fear of being shut in, of being confined to a dug-out, or of being pinned down.

Impersonality. The realisation that 'we are expendable', and therefore no longer valuable persons, is demoralising.

Noise. People find difficulty in thinking when subjected to irregular and high levels of noise. The close proximity of many exploding shells emphasises the victim's vulnerability far more than the occasional very loud explosion. Alternatively, the battlefield sometimes becomes quiet: '. . . great quiet which seems more ominous than the occasional tempests of fire'.[40]

Isolation. 'A vital sustaining factor in combat is the presence, or presumed presence, of comrades.'[41] But modern formations are loose and spread out, with the result that the battlefield is a lonely place. The soldier finds himself alone in his greatest moment of danger and his mind can conjecture all forms of possibilities. 'Be a man even so accustomed to fire, experiencing it when he is alone and unobserved produces shock that is indescribable.'[42]

Risk. In anticipation of a battle each soldier undoubtedly assesses the degree of risk that he is to face. He creates a mental model of what he expects, but he knows that the model is a guess and the uncertainty gnaws at his resolve.

The Enemy and his Weapons. The enemy is frequently assumed at first to be 'ten feet tall'. A new or particularly effective weapon may become endowed with vastly overrated qualities, and thus act as a demoraliser. An example of the latter was the Junkers Ju 87 *Stuka* dive-bomber of the early Second World War.

Fatigue. Combat is not conducive to sleep. Extremes of climate, lack of shelter, the presence of the enemy, noise and the need to patrol reduce the opportunities for sleep to a minimum. In Exercise EARLY CALL three platoons of the British Army were subjected to varying levels of sleep deprivation. The platoon receiving three hours sleep per night remained effective for the full nine days of the exercise. The platoon receiving just one and a half hours per night experienced 50 per cent losses by day five; and the platoon prevented from sleeping at all became entirely ineffective after 72 hours.[43]

Climate and Terrain. Extremes of climate and adverse terrain are highly demoralising. Troops become highly demotivated if they believe that the enemy is better adapted or acclimatised for the theatre, for example during the early days of the South-East Asian campaign in the Second World War.

Personal Factors. Physical discomfort, a lack of privacy, poor personal hygiene and minor wounds undermine soldiers' self-esteem. Many soldiers reported a fear, not of death, but of being a coward, and thus of losing self-esteem.

Idleness. An idle soldier has time to ruminate and speculate about the risks that face him. Churchill noted of the French morale in 1939–40:

> Very many factors go to the building up of sound morale in an army, but one of the greatest is that the men be fully employed at useful and interesting work. Idleness is a dangerous breeding ground . . . visitors to the Maginot Line in 1940 were often struck by the prevailing atmosphere of calm aloofness, by the seemingly poor quality of the work in hand, by the lack of visible activity of any kind.[44]

Helplessness. Fear of being unable to fight back, fear of having one's options closed and fear of being trapped are major precipitators of panic. In addition, helplessness can also result where there is a belief that the enemy has superior weapons, tactics and ability. For example, French forces at Sedan in 1940 had no means of defence against the *Stukas* that assailed them at will.

Ignorance. 'Ignorance is bliss' could hardly be further from the truth in combat. Ignorance persuades men to dwell upon the worst possible outcomes. 'Besides encouraging rumours, lack of knowledge or of information, can also nurture fears and erroneous beliefs.'[45] Knowledge of the true capability of the enemy and his equipment leads to a realistic assessment and an accurate expectation. Ignorance is also closely associated with a lack of purpose where the soldier is unaware of the aims and objectives of the war. Soldiers need to be given a number of short-term tactical objectives which merge to accomplish the overall purpose of the campaign.

Casualties. The sight of casualties, of wounded and dying men, particularly for the first time, has been found to be highly demotivating. This reflects almost precisely the experience of the victims of bombing campaigns. In particular, weapons that burn, tear and rend are more demotivating than simple bullet wounds. Loss of comrades undermines a soldier's sense of security.

Defeats. Troops defeated in combat tend to exaggerate the enemy's powers, and frequently criticise their leadership and denigrate those perceived to be responsible. For example, following Dunkirk the evacuees heavily criticised the RAF for failing to keep the Luftwaffe away when, in reality, large-scale air battles had occurred out of sight, minimising the ability of the Luftwaffe to intervene against the evacuation fleet, to the benefit of the evacuees.

Under the pressure of the above stressors, the combat soldier experiences a profound reduction in his own confidence and abilities. Fear is endemic and erodes personal confidence and unit cohesion. The soldier's behaviour becomes increasingly passive or may become dangerously extreme, further threatening both his own safety and that of his comrades.[46] One US Marine Corps study has noted that research during the Second World War 'found that 68% of the men interviewed admitted that not only had they experienced fear and anxiety at some time in combat, but also that they had experienced it at a level that prevented them from completing their duties'.[47] From a personal point of view the first, and most important, factor is that in the end everyone will 'break'. As Lord Moran characterised it, a soldier has a quantity of courage as his capital; every time he enters combat he uses up some of that capital until, in the end, none is left. Such is true even of 'élite' military formations; all inevitably break at some point.[48]

Understanding of CSR has improved markedly since the Second World War. Amongst the leaders in the field, Israeli psychologists have carried out extensive research into the effects of combat stress, and their categorisation of combat stress reactions (and examples) are paraphrased below:[49]

Disturbance in the State of Awareness. Including confusion, disorientation and partial or complete loss of consciousness. (After a nearby tank was hit, the gunner went into a stupor in which he responded to external stimuli, but was not able to carry out orders or do the simplest things.)

*Depression.*Including sleep disturbance, loss of appetite, guilt feelings and suicidal ideation. (Many of the crew of an armoured personnel carrier were wounded; the driver was taken to the rear where he became depressive, would burst into tears, could not sleep and said he would commit suicide if he had to return to the front.)

Anxiety. Anxiety states include rapid heart beat, intense sweating or trembling. (A driver on his way home for leave was awakened by the sound of his bus being attacked. He subsequently began to suffer from palpitations, tension and anxiety.)

Dissociation. Typified by the most widespread dissociative state, amnesia. (An infantry officer was lightly wounded in the hand, but totally forgot the period preceding his injury.)

Somatic Complaints. These include cases where the principal manifestations are physical, for which no organic cause can be found.

Change in Motor Activity. This includes either an increase or decrease in motor activity. (An infantryman, under shelling, began to run from place to place for no purpose. He resisted the efforts of his buddies to restrain him. In the First World War many symptoms after shelling were similarly hysterical, and it has been hypothesised that this represented release by activity, as a substitute for the unfulfilled desire to escape.[50])

Psychosis. Psychosis is probably a latent state brought out by the stress and experience of war. (A tank driver began to have illusions that his commander was persecuting him and trying to kill him. He also suffered from hallucinations.)

The progression from confidence and equanimity to CSR exemplified by the above behaviour patterns and reactions may be sudden and pronounced, or more protracted with fewer symptoms. It is not yet possible to predict at what stage an individual will develop sufficient CSR to render him ineffective. Dr John Neill has described a typical progression from the First World War:

> The first evidences of incipient failure are irritability and disturbance of sleep, with a hypersensitiveness to minimal external stimuli, i.e. a beginning startle reaction. At a stage of partial disorganization, there is a general psychomotor slowing, seclusiveness, a tendency to discard even needed belongings, loss of interest, increased apprehensiveness and a dependence on others, confusion and tremor, vomiting, hysteria.[51]

The descent into CSR is not, however, irreversible and almost all combat stress reactions can be ameliorated or cured, at least in the short term. Using local simple treatment up to 90 per cent of stress casualties can be returned to active duty after approximately 72 hours' treatment.[52] Whether subjects are subsequently more susceptible to stress remains an open question.

It is important to understand how CSR affects the behaviour of groups and is manifested by them. A group provides for the social needs of the individual, including his need for security. The 'discovery' was made during the Second World War of the 'primary group'.[53] A soldier's participation in a group was found to actually enhance his ability to withstand physical pain.[54]

Commanders attempt to create and maintain loyalty to a large group through such things as *esprit de corps*. However, cohesion within the larger group can disintegrate under a variety of stressors. Its symptoms are frequently found in a large attendance at sick parades, absenteeism, desertion and 'fragging'.[55] Such symptoms reflect a lack of confidence in the larger group, and an individual's desire to place his own survival first. Moreover, where a larger group has had few successes and a number of failures, individuals inevitably lose confidence in the group and the individual's loyalty is re-directed to his friends. Some have argued that the American soldier was not as effective in Vietnam as in the Second World War and Korea because the decision was made to rotate individuals rather than units. As a consequence group cohesion suffered greatly. Where an army is unsuccessful, it is more likely to fragment. Under more severe stress, commentators have noted a survival reaction;[56] loyalty to higher authorities is withdrawn and the individual turns to his buddy group for comfort, support and survival. The soldier identifies more readily with a smaller, more cohesive body than a larger one; with, for example, the squad of his comrades rather than the larger and more impersonal company.[57] Such a reaction is similar to the survival response of the victims of bombing, where party, local and other loyalties were all relegated in importance, while the survivor looked to the needs of his immediate family only.[58] He became angry towards authority for it having let him down, or at still higher levels of stress, just apathetic.

Many writers have attempted to explain the *Wehrmacht*'s dogged determination in its long retreat of 1944–45 in terms of group cohesion, but Bartov[59], in his analysis of casualties, and hence replacement rates, stated that it would have been impossible to foster group loyalties before members of the group were killed or scattered. In his theory, German soldiers were primarily motivated by loyalty to the Reich and a personal loyalty to Hitler in particular. This is difficult to contradict but, equally, other evidence suggests that groups did form and continue quite successfully; those that were killed were generally the newer arrivals who were still flushed with the enthusiasm of youth. Veteran Guy Sajer – a survivor of the élite *Waffen* SS and thus an individual who might have been expected to have a larger sense of loyalty to Hitler, the Nazi party and the Reich – largely contradicts Bartov, recollecting that life on the Eastern Front was primarily concerned with survival: 'We fought from simple fear, which was our motivating power. . . .We fought for ourselves, so that we wouldn't die in holes filled with mud and snow; we fought like rats.'[60]

EXPLAINING THE PSYCHOLOGY OF VICTIMHOOD

Examination of the stressors and reactions listed above has prompted a number of researchers to hypothesise about the underlying mechanisms. I have identified six; the first three have been studied in detail by others and the latter three are developed here.

Sensitisation. Almost all young soldiers begin combat with exhilaration and a strange sense of invulnerability: if something unpleasant happens, 'it will happen to the other man'.[61] The most controversial topic is whether a victim then becomes sensitised – that is, rendered susceptible to degraded combat performance – or habituated – that is, accustomed and accepting – to the stress of battle. Little work has been done on relating stress levels to habituation. The most likely explanation is that a series of low-threat situations, or successes, are likely to reduce stress and allow habituation, while highly threatening situations or failures are likely to sensitise the victim. Indeed, studies now agree (see above) that every man has his breaking point, that high stresses will accumulate and that 'there is no such thing as getting used to combat'.[62] Commentators have attempted to deduce how long it takes to induce a CSR. More logical would be to relate it to duration of combat, level of success, degree of deprivation and intensity of battles. Sensitisation may take different forms; after the Battle of the Somme one British private noted the emergence of a minimalist attitude: 'From now on, the veterans, myself included, decided to do no more than was really necessary, following orders, but if possible keeping out of harm's way.'[63] Some find the level of stress so high that they are unable to cope even if offered prolonged rest.[64] For these, subsequent similar exposures would be cumulative in their effect, leading rapidly to flight or a stress reaction. Such an analysis mirrors the experience of frequently bombed civilians, where 36 per cent became habituated whilst at least 52 per cent never became adapted.[65]

Panic. Understanding flight and its extreme form, panic, has been a goal for many analysts. Useful as a precursor for deeper understanding are two analyses. The first is what 'the zoologist Hediger called the critical reaction . . . beyond a certain distance. . . – which varies from species to species – the animal would retreat; within it he would attack'.[66] This point of changeover is known as the critical distance. Others have thus hypothesised that at ranges larger than the critical distance man's natural temptation, when faced by a threat, will be to flee,[67] while when cornered he will turn at bay. Even when a soldier does not run, his repressed reaction degrades aggression; he may seek release in withdrawal symptoms (e.g. sleep) or his firing may become haphazard. Finally, he may simply hide or feign death. The second analysis, concerning the causes of panic, was advanced by Lieutenant A Argent in 1952. In his view (which I paraphrase) panic seems to split logically into two phases: 1) Gradual build up of stress or tension, followed by 2) a sudden surprise or shock, real or perceived, which initiates the panic. The first phase is characterised by: excessive nervousness and heightened imagination; pessimism; growth in wild rumours; and loss of faith in leadership.[68] L'Etang clearly agreed with Argent: he 'thought that a series of sudden changes and shocks in men who had had insufficient time to adjust to the rigours of war lowered their threshold of panic and alarm'.[69] Ikle found exact parallels in his study of the social impact of bombing; he also noted that flight changes to panic if the fleeing masses fear that they may be entrapped or that escape routes may become blocked.[70]

Expectancy. The expectancy theory advanced by Professor G H Quester[71] is supported in the writings of other analysts of combat motivation. The nub of the theory is that the brain is deluged with information and in order to process the data more rapidly it creates a model of what is expected, then compares input data with the model so that differences are immediately obvious. Where the expectancy is value laden (e.g. winning a bet) then achievement produces a feeling of well-being, while failure that of dejection. In war expectancy can have an effect out of all proportion to the event. As Kellett has noted, 'battle is potentially demoralising if, when it occurs, it differs substantially from the soldiers' mental image';[72] conversely, 'when people achieve more than they previously believed possible, morale soars'.[73]

Expectancy helps explain the British reaction to the Blitz on London. While, as noted above, those who were bombed were highly demotivated, for the un-bombed vast majority the raids were far less damaging than they had feared. Contrast for example the expectation created by evacuations, the shelters, the gas masks and Churchill's 'nothing to offer but blood, toil, tears and sweat' with the actual experience. The raids built up slowly, were inaccurate, delivered a small bomb load and did not cover the city in the poison gas predicted by pundits. During the summer of 1940 the public increasingly believed the RAF was winning the air war and they were excited that Bomber Command was paying Germany back. Göring's campaign failed to live up to Hitler's bombast, and the British public was thus pleasantly surprised and morale raised. On the other hand, Hitler had promised that not a bomb would fall on Berlin and when they did his propaganda created an expectation of German reprisal that was progressively undermined as the intensity of the Allied raids grew. Since the Allies made few hollow threats, German civilian expectation was based on hard experience and word-of-mouth reports. Thus, unlike the British experience where a dire expectation did not materialise, for the Germans, propaganda's predictions were discredited and the country became progressively apathetic and demoralised.

Expectations were shattered on at least two other occasions during the war, one German and one Allied. For the Germans, great faith in 1944 had been placed both in the V-weapons and in the ability of the *Wehrmacht* to defeat the Allies in France. In the event, neither succeeded, and by January 1945, 92 per cent regarded the war as lost[74]. On the other side of the coin, for the British the V-weapons had a disproportionately demoralising effect. Following the elation of D-Day the British public had become convinced that victory was in sight. Although vague warnings of new weapons had been given, German bomber attacks were minimal and the population looked forward to surviving the war. The V-1 attacks throughout the summer of 1944 shattered this illusion. 'The nightmare of the Blitz came flooding back. . . .They packed their bags and left. . . and the numbers [of evacuees] grew daily until they had reached 1,450,000.'[75] The outcry persuaded Churchill to make a stirring speech in the Commons with the defiant (if defensive) line 'London will never be conquered';[76] and – despite his assurance that no effort would be diverted from support of the troops in Normandy – fighters and guns were hastily redeployed to meet the menace, bombers and fighters were retasked against the launch sites, and by the end of August, British and Canadian armies were directed to take the area of the launch sites near the Pas de Calais.

Thus, expectancy is a highly important factor; if the outcome is better than expected morale will rise, but if worse, morale will fall. However, lest this should seem to be a recipe for always predicting disaster (in the hope that the outcome will be better), as Churchill probably did, then it would be important not to lessen the prospects of winning to the extent that one appeared impotent, or the position hopeless.

Impotence. Impotence and hopelessness are closely allied, but hopelessness springs in part from a realisation of one's impotence. A classic example is that referred to by Rommel earlier, of natives against the colonial armies of the last century. Although natives might attack with gusto, the realisation that a spear was almost useless against a rifle rapidly demotivated them and normally led to a rout, restrained only by the level of coercion exerted by tribal or other leaders. A further example, quoted above, is that of the German soldiers fighting fighter-bombers with pocket knives. A sense of impotence is exacerbated by other factors. For example, despite the knowledge that night bombing was less accurate, German soldiers and civilians were far more demotivated by night attacks than those by day. Unable to see the bomber coming, they believed (surprisingly) that the aircraft was all-seeing, and they felt powerless to take any countermeasures. *Wehrmacht* units frequently redeployed if overflown at night.

Thus a sense of impotence is, to a large part, a reaction to the enemy's perceived omnipotence and omniscience. To capitalise on this effect an attacker needs to demonstrate that he is not only all-powerful, and his weapons unbeatable, but that he knows where and how to apply this lethal force. For example, while the V-2 demonstrated British impotence, its inaccuracy mitigated against any belief in its omnipotence. From an air perspective, air supremacy is a clear demonstration of a soldier's impotence. Examples are from the Dunkirk experience mentioned above, and from Rommel's own sense that nothing could be done: 'Our own operations are rendered extraordinarily difficult and in part impossible to carry out [owing to] . . .superiority of the enemy air force. The enemy has complete command of the air over the battle zone and up to 100 km behind the front.'[77] It would be wrong to think that impotence inevitably terminates fighting, but troops are highly unlikely to look forward to a battle with no real hope of success.

Hopelessness. A sense of foreboding is likely to make morale fragile and impose severe strains on a soldier's ability to cope. Nevertheless, individuals or groups will often fight on even if their own position is one of impotence, provided either that there is the prospect of relief (reinforcements), or they believe that victory will ultimately be theirs. Britain's position in 1940 appeared hopeless, but the success of the RAF in the Battle of Britain reduced feelings of impotence, and the real prospect of aid from the United States, particularly after Roosevelt's re-election, held out hope for the future. An individual might feel the position hopeless if he were both impotent against the enemy's forces and had no prospect of turning the tables. In such circumstances he is likely to believe that there is little point in continuing such a senseless struggle for no gain. However, as at Stalingrad, such hopelessness does not mean immediate surrender. Troops continue to fight if there is sufficient coercion, if they are fighting in a noble cause (defence of hearth and home) or if continued fighting is less dangerous than surrender. An extreme form of hopelessness is sometimes manifested in martyrdom. In some cultures coercion, usually in the form of religious inducements, persuades soldiers to make the supreme sacrifice. But in desperate circumstances, a reasoning man may also recognize his position as hopeless and decide to 'take some of them with me': 'Since all was lost and there was nothing to return to, he should fight the hated enemy to the death, in revenge or despair.'[78]

Pervasiveness. The knowledge that the skies are owned by the enemy and that all aircraft seen are threatening is highly demotivating. Pervasiveness is closely associated with omnipotence. An occasional fighter-bomber across Normandy might be omnipotent, but if only one aircraft per day were seen then enemy ground troops would be hardly likely to rate the risk very highly. Aircraft may be pervasive but not omnipotent, in which case troops' freedom of action may be restricted, but any success in shooting an aircraft down would be likely to raise morale. Should enemy aircraft be both ever-present and omnipotent, then a sense of hopelessness is likely. While Allied aircraft at the end of the Second World War had become pervasive, and thus highly demoralising when they were seen, operations largely ceased at night and in bad weather, thus affording both physical relief from the threat, and a guaranteed period of psychological rest. In contrast, in the Gulf, operations took place around the clock, and there was no relief. Only the weather could stop the Allies from attacking.

The advent of military air power in the 20th Century added profoundly to the psychological burden of soldiers in combat. A review of the experience of air power and the psychological dimension of warfare indicates that, in conclusion, air power when used properly can be a devastatingly effective psychological weapon. To the air campaign planner seeking to capitalise on the psychological effects of air attack, the evidence from the Second World War and the Gulf suggests that air power should aim to increase the levels of combat stress by: pinning the enemy down; isolating him and creating a sense of expendability; maximising his discomfort and fatigue; and persuading him of the effectiveness of the air weapons by inflicting a large number of casualties upon him and by preventing him from retaliating. Furthermore, the bombardment should be intensive and frequent, thus preventing him from habituating. It should be more severe than his expectations; aircraft should be pervasive and create a feeling of impotence, hopelessness and panic. It should not, however, be so demoralising as to drive him to the point of martyrdom, and an individual must thus always be given a way out.

NOTES

[1] Smuts Memorandum August 1917.

[2] G Douhet, *The Command of the Air*, (Washington, DC: Office of Air Force History, 1983), p. 55.

[3] *London Gazette* 31 December 1918 – Postwar despatch of the RAF, quoted in R J Overy, *The Air War*, p. 13

[4] I L Janis, *Air War and Emotional Stress*, (The Rand Corporation), p. 128.

[5] Air Vice-Marshal N Baldwin (ACDS Overseas), in a briefing given at The Ministry of Defence, 24 May 1994.

[6] R J Overy, *The Air War* , p. 122.

[7] USSBS, *The Effects of Strategic Bombing on German Morale*, Vol. I. pp. 1 & 7.

8   W S Churchill, *The Second World War*, p. 360.

9   USSBS, *Consolidated Report of the Medical Services Branch*, available at Maxwell AFB.

10   Ronald Lewin, *Rommel as Military Commander*, (Batsford 1968), p. 162 in *ibid.*, p. 383.

11   Field Marshal E Rommel *Letter to his wife*, in R P Hallion, *Strike from the Sky*, p. 205.

12   Field Marshal von Kluge (Rommel's successor) in letter to Hitler, quoted in J Keegan, *Six Armies in Normandy*, (Penguin), p. 219.

13   R P Hallion, *Strike from the Sky*, p. 213.

14   USSBS, *The Effects of Strategic Bombing on German Morale, Vol. II*, pp. 39 and 41.

15   J Terraine, *The Right of the Line*, p. 675.

16   R P Hallion, *Storm over Iraq*, p. 147.

17   General H N Schwarzkopf, *It Doesn't Take a Hero*, (Bantam Press), p. 317 and 350.

18   *A Post-Operational Analysis: Psychological Operations During Desert Shield/Storm* (US Special Operations Command), pp. 4–10.

19   *Ibid.*, pp. 4–14

20   R A Blair and F L Goldstein, 'The Iraqi Propaganda Network', in *Psychological Operations: Principles and Case Studies* (US DoD), p. 161.

21   R P Hallion, *Storm over Iraq*, p. 169.

22   General C A Horner in an interview dated 2 May 1994.

23   *Ibid.*

24   Colonel Jones, Cdr. 4th Psyop Group, in an interview dated 20 April 1994.

25   General C A Horner in an interview dated 2 May 1994.

26   Brigadier General Ibrahim Adwan Abdul Hussein , Cdr. Iraqi 27th Infantry Division, *POW Debrief.*

27   Brigadier General Abdul Hamid Suleiman, Cdr. Iraqi 31st Infantry Division, *POW Debrief.*

28   *Ibid.*

29 Brigadier General Talal Shafiq Mohamed, COS, Iraqi 30th Infantry Division, *POW Debrief.*

30 Brigadier General Saheb Mohammed Alaw, Cdr 48th Infantry Division, *POW Debrief.*

31 Theme of several Senior Officer POWs.

32 Reported in *ibid.*

33 Dr Stephen T Hosmer, The Rand Corporation, drawn from a 1994 Rand Study on the psychological effect of air power in the Gulf War.

34 J M Marcum and D W Cline, 'Combat Stress Reaction in Iraqi Prisoners of War', *Bulletin of the Menninger Clinic* Vol. 57, No. 4 , Fall 1993, pp. 479–473.

35 *Ibid.*, p. 484.

36 Briefing with Heads of Regional Departments, 4th Psy Op Gp, Ft Bragg, 21 April 1994.

37 J M Marcum and D W Cline, *Combat Stress Reaction in Iraqi Prisoners of War,* (Bulletin of the Menninger Clinic Vol. 57, No. 4 , Fall 1993), p. 487.

38 Z Solomon, 'Twenty Years after the Yom Kippur War', in *Israeli Journal of Psychiatry and Related Science*, Vol. 30, No 3 (1993), pp. 128–129.

39 J Keegan, *The Face of Battle*, (Penguin), pp. 266–267, 326.

40 S L A Marshall, *Men Against Fire*, (New York, William Morrow & Co.), p. 44.

41 *Ibid.*

42 A Kellett, *Combat Motivation - the Behavior of Soldiers in Battle*, p. 98.

43 Major K Hartman RA, 'Battlefield Stress: Can we Continue to Ignore it?', *Defence Force Journal,* No 77 July–August 1989, p. 47.

44 W S Churchill *The Second World War*, p. 191.

45 A Kellett, *Combat Motivation – the Behavior of Soldiers in Battle*, p. 227.

46 Z Solomon *et al.* 'Post Traumatic Stress Disorder among Frontline Soldiers with Combat Stress Reaction', *American Journal of Psychiatry* 144.4, April 1987

47 'Fear and Motivation: An AWS Battle Study', in *Marine Corps Gazette*, August 1988. p. 65.

48   E J Hunter and Colonel H T Prince, 'Stress and the Combat Leader', in *Marine Corps Gazette*, August 1988, p. 58.

49   T Yitzhaki and Z Solomon, 'The Clinical Picture of Acute Combat Stress Reaction among Israeli Soldiers in the 1982 Lebanon War', in *Military Medicine*, Vol. 156, April 1991, p. 193.

50   John R Neill, 'How Psychiatric Symptoms varied in World War I and II', *Military Medicine*, 158, 3; 149, 1993.

51   *Ibid.*

52   A good description can be found in Lieutenant Commander P K True, 'Treatment of Stress Reaction Prior to Combat using the BICEPS Model', in *Military Medicine*, 157, .7.380, 1992.

53   See A Kellett, *Combat Motivation - the Behavior of Soldiers in Battle*, p. 41.

54   *Ibid.*, p. 45.

55   'Fragging', as used in the Vietnam War, was the grenading of unpopular officers by their own men.

56   R Pape in an interview at Maxwell AFB, dated 27 April 1994.

57   A Kellett, *Combat Motivation – the Behavior of Soldiers in Battle*, p. 44.

58   USSBS, *The Effects of Strategic Bombing on German Morale, Vol. I*, pp. 22, 31 and 56.

59   O Bartov, 'Indoctrination and Motivation in the Wehrmacht', in *Journal of Strategic Studies*, March 1986, pp. 16–33.

60   G Sajer, *The Forgotten Soldier* (Ballantine, New York, 1972), pp. 382-3.

61   A Kellett, *Combat Motivation - the Behavior of Soldiers in Battle*, p. 286.

62   *Ibid.*, p. 276.

63   *Ibid.*, p. 314.

64   Winter, quoted in A Kellett, *Combat Motivation - the Behavior of Soldiers in Battle*, p. 284.

65   USSBS, *The Effects of Strategic Bombing on German Morale*, Vol. I., p. 20,

66   J Keegan, *The Face of Battle*, p. 165.

67   *Ibid.* pp. 305 & 329.

[68] Lieutenant A Argent in W E Daugherty and M Janowitz, *A Psychological Warfare Casebook* (John Hopkins Press), p. 669.

[69] A Kellett, *Combat Motivation – the Behavior of Soldiers in Battle*, p.105.

[70] F Ikle, *Social Impact of Bomb Destruction* (University of Oklahoma Press 1958.) pp. 14 & 101.

[71] G H Quester, 'The Psychological Effects of Bombing on Civilian Populations', in B Glad, *The Psychological Dimensions of War* (Sage Publications 1990), p. 208.

[72] A Kellett, *Combat Motivation – the Behavior of Soldiers in Battle*, p. 217.

[73] *Ibid.*, p. 258.

[74] USSBS, *The Effects of Strategic Bombing on German Morale*, Vol. I., p.16.

[75] R Oglevy, *Doodlebugs and Rockets*, (Froglet 1992), p. 61

[76] *Ibid.*, p. 177.

[77] Letter from Rommel to Keitel dated 12 June 1944, in J Terraine, *The Right of the Line*, p. 637

[78] USSBS, *The Effects of Strategic Bombing on German Morale*, Vol. II, p.41.

4

PRECISION AIR ATTACK
IN THE MODERN ERA

by
Richard P Hallion
THE AIR FORCE HISTORIAN,
HQ USAF, WASHINGTON, DC

U ndoubtedly, one of the most important developments in the history of
20th Century warfare has been the emergence of the precision weapon:
the weapon which can be aimed and directed against a single target,
relying on external guidance or its own guidance system.[1] Launched from
aircraft, ships, submarines, land vehicles or even by individual soldiers on the
ground, the precision weapon exemplifies the principle of the low-cost threat
that forces a high-cost and complicated defence. Actually, efforts to develop
practical precision-guided weapons date to the First World War, though at that
time the vision of advocates for such systems far exceeded the actual
technological and scientific capability needed to bring them to fruition.[2] But
such weapons did appear in the Second World War, in rudimentary though
significant form, and it was that experience, and the experience of successor
conflicts such as Korea and Vietnam, that gave to us the generation of weapons
that now are incorporated in the arsenals of many nations.

WHAT CONSTITUTES PRECISION:
THE HISTORICAL PERSPECTIVE

Precision has always been recognised as an important attribute of weapon
development. The noted military theorist, strategist and historian Major General
J F C Fuller, considered 'accuracy of aim' to be one of the five recognisable
attributes of weaponry, together with range of action, striking power, volume
of fire and portability. (Of all of these, he considered range to be the attribute
which 'dominated the fight'.) It is worth noting that the modern precision
weapon combines the attributes of accuracy, range, striking power and

portability, and it is that combination that makes it a powerful force multiplier in today's military scene.[3]

With regard to the air weapon, two quotes give some perspective on the development of precision attack in this century.[4] The first is from the former chief of the US Army Air Corps, Major General James E Fechet, writing in 1933:

> In the past, wars' slaughter has been largely confined to armed combatants. Soldier has slain soldier. Unfortunately, in the next, despite all peace time decrees and agreements, the principal effort will be directed at trade and manufacturing centers. Obviously the airman, riding so high above the earth that cities look like ant hills, cannot aim his deadly cargo at armed males. All below will be his impartial target.[5]

The second is from Colonel Phillip Meilinger, the commander of the US Air Force's School of Advanced Airpower Studies, writing over 60 years later:

> Precision air weapons have redefined the meaning of mass. . . . The result of the trend towards 'airshaft accuracy' in air war is a denigration in the importance of mass. PGMs provide density, mass per unit volume, which is a more efficient measurement of force. In short, targets are no longer massive, and neither are the aerial weapons used to neutralize them. One could argue that all targets are precision targets—even individual tanks, artillery pieces, or infantrymen. There is no logical reason why bullets or bombs should be wasted on empty air or dirt. Ideally, every shot fired should find its mark.[6]

These two quotes serve as boundary references to the development and use of precision weapons in this century. The former (and the earlier quote of Fuller) reflects an attitude that accepted (if unhappily and bitterly) a philosophy of military operations typified by the large-scale, imprecise bombing campaigns of the Second World War, while the latter reflects the historical lessons of air warfare since that time. Seen from another perspective, the former reflects the view that precision is attainable only through aim, while the latter reflects the experience of technological development, which has emphasised both precise aim with precision guidance and control of the weapon itself.

Seeking precision through accurate aim remains an important aspect of military power projection, but the historical record indicates that the best combination is, not surprisingly, the trained operator on a smart platform with smart sensors dispensing a smart weapon. Precision, it must be remembered, is a relative word: relative to the time period about which one is concerned. For example, in the summer of 1944, 47 B-29s raided the Yawata steel works from bases in China; only one plane actually hit the target area, and only with one of its bombs. This single 500 pound general purpose bomb (which hit a powerhouse located 3,700 feet from the far more important coke houses that constituted the raid's aiming point) represented one quarter of one per cent of the 376 bombs dropped over Yawata on that mission.[7] In the autumn of 1944, only seven per cent of all bombs dropped by the Eighth Air Force hit within 1,000 feet of their aim point; even a 'precision' weapon such as a fighter-bomber in a 40° dive releasing a bomb at 7,000 feet could have a circular error (CEP) of as much as 1,000 feet.[8] It took 108 B-17 bombers, crewed by 1,080 airmen and dropping 648 bombs to guarantee a 96 per cent chance of getting just two hits inside a 400 x 500 ft German power-generation plant; in contrast, in the Gulf War, a single strike aircraft with one or two crewmen dropping two laser-guided bombs, could achieve the same results with essentially a 100 per cent expectation of hitting the target, short of a material failure of the bombs themselves.[9]

To appreciate better the impact–no pun intended–of precision weaponry, it is only necessary to examine trends in bombing accuracy from increasingly accurate bombing platforms equipped with increasingly advanced sighting systems used to dispense 'dumb' bombs. The following chart looks at the case of trying to hit, with a hit probability of 90 per cent, a target measuring 60 x 100 ft using 2,000 pound unguided bombs dropped from medium altitude:[10]

War	Number of Bombs	Number of Aircraft	CEP (in feet)
WW-2	9,070	3,024	3,300
Korea	1,100	550	1,000
Vietnam	176	44	400

By the time of the Gulf War, the capabilities of 'smart' aeroplanes dropping 'dumb' bombs from low altitudes were sufficient to place an unguided munition within 30 feet of a target. However, Iraqi air defences in the Kuwait theatre of operations, characterised by large numbers of man-portable surface-to-air missiles and rapid-firing light anti-aircraft cannon, simply would not permit such routine use of the low altitude operating environment. Operations from medium altitudes (15,000 ft. and higher) at longer slant ranges severely complicated bombing accuracy, particularly against targets that required essentially a direct hit to be destroyed, such as hangars, bunkers, tanks, and artillery. As one analytical study concluded:

> Medium and high-altitude bombing with unguided munitions posed problems, even with digital 'smart platforms'. First, the visual bombing pipper was 2 milliradians wide. At a slant range of 20,000 feet, typical for high-angle

dive deliveries, the pipper blanked out an area on the ground 40 feet across, often hiding the target. To the resulting errors must be added bomb dispersion errors. For example, the Mk. 84 [General Purpose bomb] dispersion was 5 – 6 milliradians. The result of both of these kinds of errors was a worst-case 160-foot miss distance, even if the pilot did everything right and the system worked perfectly.... Using 'smart platforms' to deliver 'dumb' bombs against point targets smaller than the circular error probable (CEP) may well require redundant targeting.[11]

The development of the precision munition and its undoubted influence upon modern military affairs is one that has sparked great debate. What anticipated changes to military affairs may be expected from the precision revolution? Is it, in fact, a revolution? Is there a continuing need for the so-called 'dumb' munition and weapon? What is the likely future role of the precision weapon *vis-à-vis* traditional weapon systems such as aeroplanes, tanks and ships? All of these are important issues that need to be examined. The following, then, are just some of the ways in which one can regard the advent of precision weapon warfare.

PRECISION WEAPONS AND
NATIONAL SECURITY DECISION-MAKING

One of the greatest advantages of the precision weapon is the confidence that it can offer a decision-maker confronted with having to contemplate using force in circumstances where so-called "collateral damage" would either be unacceptable or call into question the viability of continued military action. Even in high-tempo, high-level-of-violence conflicts, attitudes towards both 'enemy' and 'friendly' (or 'neutral') casualties have undergone a remarkable transformation since the days of the Second World War when, for example, a single air raid could kill tens of thousands of individuals and not raise any significant moral outcry.[12] Increasingly, conflict scenarios involve the use of force in dense, population-heavy environments where the negative publicity of misplaced weaponry could have profound implications for public opinion and policy.[13]

Adding to this problem has been a generalised lack of appreciation of how warfare has changed since the Second World War. On the eve of the Gulf War, for example, critics of proposed military action posited scenarios where tens of thousands of Iraqis would be killed by largely indiscriminate air attacks that would 'carpet bomb' population centres, particularly Baghdad. To give viewers some idea of what a 'modern' air war might be like, commentators, ironically, ran footage of Berlin and other German cities after VE-Day. In fact, of course, Coalition leaders had no intention whatsoever of using such a level of force against Iraq, recognising that, given the moral climate of the present day, this use of power would simply not be tolerated by the world community, or even the population of a Coalition nation that engaged in such action.

But, after being briefed on the air campaign plan for the Gulf War, Coalition political and military leaders were very comfortable with the notion of using precision weapons in attacks deep in the midst of major cities, once they had been assured that the accuracies claimed for such weapons were realistic and not the stuff of an overenthusiastic trade-show sales briefing. On the 'opening night' of the Gulf War, for example, Baghdad was struck by two kinds of precision weapons: ship-launched cruise missiles and air-launched laser-guided bombs. More recently, the extensive use of precision weaponry in the NATO air campaign in Bosnia without (to the author's knowledge) any collateral losses, affirmed again that this kind of attack offers decision-makers an option to exert force in circumstances that, just two decades ago, they would not have considered possible. Because of precision, decision-makers have a freedom to use military force closer to non-combatant-inhabited areas in an enemy homeland (or in enemy-occupied territory) than at any previous time in military history. They need not risk the broad-area 'seeding' of bombs characteristic of earlier wars. In a strategic sense, this can act as a powerful deterrent to an aggressor who, in previous times, might well have felt that the misery of collateral losses engendered by conflict designed to overcome his aggression would itself offer him some shield or defence. In both a strategic and tactical sense, precision robs the enemy of the material wherewithal to make war.

Further, since a precision weapon has a higher probability of scoring a hit on a target than a non-precision one, there is less likelihood that a target will have to be revisited or repeatedly struck. While never as 'surgical' as proponents might claim, precision attack nevertheless offers clear advantages in reducing risk to attacking forces, another encouragement for its use in conflict situations. Additionally, for a nation unwilling to risk military personnel in delivering precision weapons to a target, the somewhat less precise but still highly accurate cruise missile is an acceptable alternative.

Even in cases where precision weapons are used, there is, of course, some risk of collateral damage and consequent public outcry. Despite targets being clearly justified, this outcry can generate negative policy impacts mitigating against subsequent use of force. In the best-known example from the Gulf War, well-publicised attacks against bridges in downtown Baghdad, coupled with a precision attack against the Al Firdos command and control bunker that killed several hundred individuals using it as a shelter, generated a political reaction that included shutting down the strategic air campaign against Baghdad for ten days. This occurred despite clear evidence that the Hussein regime was trying to reconstitute key leadership functions destroyed or degraded by previous attack.[14]

Given the nature of precision weapon warfare, the education of decision-makers as to their capabilities and limitations is critically important. The majority of political leaders are individuals who come from non-military backgrounds, with the possible exception of brief periods of national service as conscripts, junior enlisted, or junior officers. There is, additionally, another form of decision-participant whose education needs to be considered: the journalist who, increasingly, lacks any military background whatsoever. Today, politicians and reporters alike are far more likely to be generalists in background, with no particular understanding of military issues or military technology.[15] With the rapidly changing state of such technology, it is incumbent that military and defence organisations offer them opportunities to become acquainted with the broad capabilities of modern military systems. This is particularly true for precision weaponry, for such weaponry has already demonstrated that, in particular circumstances, cherished notions of how wars are to be fought and the enduring value of such military constructs as the linear battlefield are questionable at best or even archaic.

Decision-makers are particularly vulnerable to looking at military events through the prism of the most recent conflict. Prior to the Gulf War, for example, the prism for American leaders was Vietnam; accordingly, there was profound scepticism and pessimism that military action could be accomplished in such a fashion as to achieve the coalition's ends quickly and with minimal loss of life. Even military professionals had considerable doubt; the former chief of staff of the US Army, General Edward C Meyer, estimated between 10,000 and 30,000 American casualties.[16] Now, there is some danger of the opposite: believing that future wars can be won virtually automatically with casualties as low as or lower than those of the Gulf War. Wars are obviously situational, and the casualties that one might expect to sustain in, say, a renewed Korean war (where a major population centre–Seoul–lies within range of North Korean artillery) are far different from those one would expect in a peacekeeping operation, or even a renewed or different Persian Gulf war.

THE LEVERAGE OF PRECISION WEAPONS:
HISTORICAL EXPERIENCE THROUGH VIETNAM

The precision weapon, within generalised boundaries, will perform roughly equally well in all circumstances, provided a target can be identified. Timescales may change and levels of effort may change, but the end result – a victory for the force making the best use of precision – is unlikely to change unless other factors (such as loss of national will, changing international support, 'wild cards', etc.) enter play. The single most important factor is how well the decision-

116

maker, both military and political, appreciates what precision weapons can and cannot accomplish, what mechanism or process has been established to assess the appropriateness of their use, and the rules of engagement that govern their use.

Historical experience with precision-guided munitions dates back over 50 years; as might be expected, the most recent use with the most sophisticated contemporary systems offers the best expectation of what might be accomplished; nevertheless, there is a considerable body of historical experience that suggests how precision weapons have dramatically transformed military affairs. The precision weapon era may be said to date from 12 May 1943, when a Royal Air Force Liberator patrol bomber dropped a Mk. 24 acoustic homing torpedo that subsequently seriously damaged the U-456, driving it to the surface where it was subsequently sunk by convoy escort vessels. On 9 September 1943, a German Fritz-X radio-guided glide bomb dropped from a Dornier Do 217 bomber sank the modern Italian battleship *Roma* as she steamed towards Gibraltar. Two months later, an anti-ship missile launched from a Heinkel He 177 sank a British troop transport with the loss of 1,190 American soldiers, one of the greatest of all maritime disasters. By the end of the war, Germany and the United States had employed various proto-smart weapons in combat, including radio-, radar-, and television-guided bombs and missiles, against targets ranging from industrial sites to bridges and enemy shipping.

Although not often thought of as a precision weapon, the various *Kamikaze* attackers that first appeared in the autumn of 1944 functioned much like modern anti-ship missiles and thus can legitimately be considered a part of the precision weapon story. The *Kamikaze* was the deadliest aerial anti-ship weapon faced by Allied surface warfare forces in the war. Approximately 2,800 *Kamikaze* attackers sunk 34 Navy ships, damaged 368 others, killed 4,900 sailors and wounded over 4,800. Despite radar detection and cuing, airborne interception and attrition, and massive anti-aircraft barrages, a distressing 14 per cent of *Kamikazes* survived to score a hit on a ship; nearly 8.5 per cent of all ships hit by *Kamikazes* sank. As soon as they appeared, *Kamikazes* revealed their power to force significant changes in Allied naval planning and operations, despite their relatively small numbers. Clearly, like the anti-ship cruise missile of a later era, the *Kamikaze* had the potential to influence events all out of proportion to its actual strength.[17]

The need to destroy precision targets such as bridges had driven development of rudimentary guided bombs in the Second World War, and Korea accelerated this interest. In Korea, US Air Force B-29s dropped the Razon and the much larger and more powerful Tarzon guided bombs on North Korean bridges, destroying at least 19 of them.[18] Off the Korean coast, modified Grumman F6F-5K Hellcat drones flew from the carrier USS *Boxer* against

North Korean bridges; the Korean bridge-bombing experience stimulated the Navy to pursue development of the postwar Bullpup, the first mass-produced air-to-surface guided missile.[19]

Accompanying this interest in anti-surface warfare was an equivalent drive to develop precision air-to-surface and surface-to-surface weapons for the anti-ship role. In particular, the Soviet Union pursued development of such weapons as a means of countering the tremendous maritime supremacy of the Western alliance during the Cold War. One of the most significant events in the history of precision weaponry occurred on 25 October 1967, when the Israeli destroyer *Eilat*, patrolling 15 miles off Port Said, was sunk by four Soviet-made Styx anti-ship missiles fired from an Egyptian missile boat, killing or wounding 99 of its crew. The sinking of the *Eilat* had profound impact; one surface warfare officer remarked that 'it was reveille' to the surface navy, and a Center for Naval Analyses study concluded: 'The threat is so great to all combatant ships of the Navy that a revolution in naval tactics may be required.'[20] Subsequent rumours that the Soviets had supplied Styx missiles to North Vietnam seriously constrained naval operations off the Vietnamese coast, particularly shore bombardment missions, and one senior naval officer called the potential Styx threat his 'worst nightmare'.[21]

The Soviet Union's alarming investment in increasingly sophisticated precision weapons, together with rapid expansion of the Soviet fleet, stimulated a tremendous response. This threat directly influenced the purchase of the Grumman F-14A Tomcat, armed with six long-range Phoenix air-to-air missiles, as well as more advanced airborne and surface early warning radars and fire control systems. Chief among these was the remarkable Aegis electronically steered radar which, coupled with a new surface-to-air missile (the General Dynamics Standard) and a fast-response launcher, promised some relief from the missile threat. Complementing Aegis was the creation of new shipboard gun and missile defences (notably the Phalanx and Sea Sparrow), the accelerated development of new anti-submarine warfare weapons and techniques and the likewise accelerated development of the McDonnell Douglas Harpoon, an American anti-ship missile. But despite such corrective measures, the problems posed by newer generations of weapons such as France's sea-hugging Exocet (which demonstrated its lethality in both the Falklands and Persian Gulf fighting) and the Chinese-manufactured Silkworm, continue to confront naval planners in the present day. Indeed, it can be argued that, at best, defensive measures have kept up with the threat, not surpassed it.[22]

As the anti-ship missile transformed war at sea, the advent of the laser-guided bomb (LGB), a result of United States Air Force-sponsored-research in the mid-1960s, revolutionised precision land attack, for even in its initial rudimentary form, it could function with an average circular error of less than

20 feet from the aim point. With this kind of accuracy, the need to operate mass flights of aircraft against a single aim point at last disappeared; it was as revolutionary a development in military air power terms as, say, the jet engine or aerial refuelling.[23] Even more significantly, an aircraft dropping an LGB could drop it from outside the majority of an enemy's air defences, thus further reducing the likelihood of incurring losses to enemy defences. First field tested in 1968, the laser-guided bomb was a powerful force-multiplier for the United States during the bitter fighting of 1972 when North Vietnamese mechanised forces invaded South Vietnam. In fact, the modern precision weapon era may be said to have begun on 13 May 1972, when four flights of LGB-armed McDonnell F-4 Phantoms perfunctorily took down the Thanh Hoa bridge in North Vietnam, a notorious graveyard for dozens of strike aircraft and airmen over the previous seven years.[24]

PRECISION ATTACK IN THE GULF WAR

The Gulf War showed how radically precision attack had transformed the traditional notion of running a military campaign and, especially, an air campaign. On the opening night of the war, attacks by strike aircraft and cruise missiles against air defence and command and control facilities essentially opened up Iraq for subsequent conventional attackers. Precision attacks against the Iraqi Air Force destroyed much of it in its hangars and precipitated an attempted mass exodus of surviving aircraft to Iran. Key precision weapon attacks against bridges served to 'channelise' the movement of Iraqi forces and create fatal bottlenecks, and many Iraqis, in frustration, simply abandoned their vehicles and walked away.[25] Overall, postwar analysis indicated that Iraq's ability to move supplies from Baghdad to the Kuwaiti theatre of operations (KTO) had dropped from a total potential capacity of 216,000 metric tons per day over a total of six main routes (including a rail line) to only 20,000 metric tons per day over only two routes, a nearly 91 per cent reduction in capacity; all others (including the railroad) had essentially been destroyed. What shipments did occur were haphazard and slow, and carried in single vehicles that were themselves so often destroyed that many Iraqi drivers simply refused to drive to the KTO.[26] This destruction had taken place in an astonishingly short time; whereas, in previous non-precision interdiction campaigns, it often took hundreds of sorties to destroy a bridge, in the Gulf War precision weapons destroyed 41 of 54 key Iraqi bridges, as well as 31 pontoon bridges hastily constructed by the Iraqis in response to the anti-bridge strikes, in approximately four weeks.[27]

In the Gulf War, only nine per cent of the tonnage expended on Iraqi forces by American airmen were precision munitions. Not quite half of this percentage – 4.3 per cent – consisted of laser-guided bombs, credited with causing approximately 75 per cent of the serious damage inflicted upon Iraqi strategic and operational targets.[28] The remaining precision munitions consisted of specialised air-to-surface missiles such as the Maverick and the Hellfire, as well as cruise missiles, anti-radiation missiles and assorted small numbers of special weapons. It was, overall, the laser-guided bomb that dominated both the battlefield, the counter-air campaign against Iraqi airfields, strikes against command and control and leadership targets, and the anti-bridge and -rail campaign. As the Gulf War Air Power Survey concluded,

> Against point targets, laser-guided bombs offered distinct advantages over 'dumb' bombs. The most obvious was that the guided bombs could correct for ballistic and release errors in flight. Explosive loads could also be more accurately tailored for the target, since the planner could assume most bombs would strike in the place and manner expected. Unlike 'dumb' bombs, LGBs released from medium to high altitude were highly accurate. . . . DESERT STORM reconfirmed that LGBs possessed a near single-bomb target-destruction capability, an unprecedented if not revolutionary development in aerial warfare. [29]

In particular, the advent of routine around-the-clock laser bombing of fielded enemy forces in the Gulf War constituted a new phase in the history of air warfare. These attacks were not classic close air support or battlefield air interdiction but instead, given the level of accomplishment over time, went far beyond the levels of effectiveness traditionally implied by such terms. Indeed, the vast majority were made in the 39 days prior to the ground operation when the coalition's land forces were, for the most part, waiting for their war to begin. Yet the Iraqi Army was, in effect, mortally wounded in this time. These attacks, against Iraq's mechanised formations and artillery, can best be described as a form of strategic attack directed against unengaged but fielded enemy forces, what might be termed 'DEA': 'Degrade Enemy Army'.[30] The combination of laser-guided bombs from F-111Fs and F-15Es, together with Maverick missiles using imaging infra-red thermal sensors fired by A-10s and F-16s were devastating, as were laser-guided bombs from British Tornados and Buccaneers, and AS-30L laser-guided missiles fired from French Air Force Jaguars. Particularly deadly were F-111F night 'tank plinking' strikes using 500 pound GBU-12 laser-guided bombs. On 9 February, for example, in one night of concentrated air attacks, 40 F-111F's destroyed over 100 armoured vehicles. Overall, the small (strong) 66-plane F-111F force was credited with 1,500 kills of Iraqi tanks and other mechanised vehicles. Air attacks by F-15Es and Marine A-6Es in the easternmost section of the theatre averaged over 30 artillery pieces or armoured vehicles destroyed per night.[31]

Once attack helicopters attached to surface forces entered battle, they demonstrated that such results were not limited to fixed-wing attackers. At sea, Royal Navy and US Navy helicopters destroyed numerous Iraqi small boats and military craft; 14 of 15 British Aerospace Sea Skua anti-ship missiles launched from Westland Lynx helicopters hit their targets, a hit rate of over 93 per cent. French, British and American gunships destroyed numerous Iraqi mechanised vehicles. McDonnell AH-64A Apache crews of one US Army aviation brigade destroyed approximately 50 Iraqi tanks in a single encounter. Another Apache unit scored 102 hits for the expenditure of 107 Hellfire missiles, a hit rate of better than 95 per cent.[32]

The reaction of Iraqi forces to direct precision air attacks indicated that the traditional powerful psychological impact of air attack had, at last, been matched by the equally powerful impact of actual destruction. One quote serves to highlight this, from an Iraqi battalion commander interrogated by a US Marine Corps intelligence specialist a month after the war ended:

Interrogator: How many of your soldiers were killed by the air war?
Iraqi Officer: To be honest, for the amount of ordnance that was dropped, not very many. Only one soldier was killed and two were wounded. The soldier that was killed did not die as a result of a direct hit, but because the vibrations of the bomb caused a bunker to cave in on top of him.
Interrogator: So, then you feel the aerial bombardment was ineffective?
Iraqi Officer: Oh no! Just the opposite! It was extremely effective! The planes hit only vehicles and equipment. Even my personal vehicle, a 'Waz' was hit. They hit *everything!* [33] [Emphasis in original text.]

This exchange illustrates another aspect of precision air war, particularly as it applies to the direct attack of enemy forces: what can be identified can be targeted so precisely that unnecessary casualties are not inflicted upon an opponent. In short, war, the great waster of human life, is now significantly more humane. Increasingly, war is more about destroying or incapacitating *things* as opposed to *people*. It is now about pursuing an *effects-based* strategy, rather than an *annihilation-based* strategy, a strategy with which one can *control* an opponent without having to *destroy* him.[34]

DELIBERATE FORCE:
REAFFIRMATION OF THE GULF EXPERIENCE
Nor was the Gulf War an isolated example. From 30 August to 14 September 1995, for the first time in its history, NATO forces engaged in combat operations, against Bosnian Serb forces in the former Yugoslavia. A total of 293 aircraft based at 15 European locations and operating from three aircraft carriers flew

3,515 sorties in Operation DELIBERATE FORCE, to deter Serbian aggression. Somewhat less than 700 of these sorties targeted command and control, supporting lines of communication, direct and essential targets, fielded forces, and integrated air defences. A total of 67 per cent of all such targets engaged were destroyed; 14 per cent experienced moderate to severe damage, 16 per cent light damage, and only three per cent were judged to have experienced no damage.[35]

In contrast to the Gulf War, the vast majority of NATO munitions employed in the Bosnian conflict were precision ones: in fact, over 98 per cent of those used by American forces. American forces employed a total of 622 precision munitions, consisting of 567 laser-guided bombs (303 GBU-10, 115 GBU-12, 143 GBU-16 and six GBU-24), 42 electro-optical or infra-red-guided weapons (10 SLAM, 9 GBU-15 and 23 Maverick), and 13 Tomahawk land attack cruise missiles (TLAM). American airmen dropped only 12 'dumb' bombs, consisting of 10 Mk. 83s and 2 CBU-87s. Precision weaponry accounted for 28 per cent of NATO munitions dropped by non-US attackers. Sorties by Spanish, French and British strike aircraft dropped 86 laser-guided bombs, and French, Italian, Dutch and British attackers dropped 306 'dumb' bombs. Overall, combining both the American and non-American experience in Bosnia, there were 708 precision weapons employed by NATO forces and 318 non-precision ones; thus precision weaponry accounted for 69 per cent of the total employed in the NATO air campaign. Combined statistics of American and NATO experience indicate that the average number of precision weapons per designated mean point of impact (DMPI) destroyed was 2.8. In contrast, the average number of 'dumb' general purpose bombs per DMPI destroyed was 6.6. The average number of attack sorties per DMPI destroyed was 1.5.[36] As a result of studying the Bosnian air campaign, the Institute of Defense Analyses subsequently concluded 'Precision guided munitions provide an essential capability for the effective prosecution of military operations other than war.'[37]

As a result of NATO's first sustained air strike operations, all military and political objectives were attained: safe areas were no longer under attack or threatened, heavy weapons had been removed from designated areas, and Sarajevo's airport could once again open, as could road access to the city. More importantly, the path to a peace agreement had been secured. In sum, for an overall expenditure of approximately 64 weapons per day – 69 per cent (44) of which were precision weapons – NATO forces achieved their military and political objectives. The leverage that this weaponry gave over Balkan aggressors and the recognition of what precision air attack means to decision-makers in the modern world was enunciated by former Assistant Secretary of State Richard Holbrooke after the conclusion of the campaign and the settlement of the Dayton Peace Accords:

One of the great things that people should have learned from this is that
there are times when air power – *not* backed up by ground troops – can make
a difference. That's something that our European allies didn't all agree with,
Americans were in doubt on it, but it made a difference. [38]

Holbrooke's statement hints at one of the major effects of precision, namely
that the traditional notion of massing a large ground force to confront an
opponent, particularly on a 'field of battle', is now rendered archaic. To a degree,
throughout military history, the span of influence of ground forces was always
spreading out the battle area at the expense of 'mass'. As the zone of lethality
an individual soldier could command increased, the spacing between soldiers
expanded as well. Such spacing meant that artillery fire, however well-targeted,
nevertheless could not achieve the kind of density on a day-to-day basis required
to control or eliminate opposition. For example, despite a truly gargantuan
leavening of artillery rounds per square yard of the Western Front during the
First World War, the Germans and Allied forces only rarely achieved decisive
effect, resulting in a war of attrition that generated millions of casualties. But
the precision attacker overcomes the expansion of the linear battlefield by
exercising the ability to undertake individual targeting at ranges far in excess
of even the most powerful artillery. Thus aeroplanes, 'smart' ballistic missiles
or cruise missiles, launched hundreds of miles away from a front-line, can then
pass beyond that front-line for a distance of hundreds of miles more before
targeting some key enemy facility or capability that directly influences the
success of enemy operations at the front itself. This is true flexibility, again of
a sort unknown to previous military eras.

PRECISION ATTACK VERSUS LIGHT INFANTRY

As hinted by the Balkan experience, the advantages of precision attack are not
limited to what might be termed 'traditional' encounters between massive
deployed forces possessing large and vulnerable weapons such as ships, tanks
and vehicles. Indeed, recent examinations of air power applications against
light infantry in typical Third World crisis conditions indicate that precision
offers very high leverage whether one is dealing with a mechanised force, a
guerrilla-type army in a wooded or jungle environment or, even, an individual
urban sniper *à la* Sarajevo.[39] The combination of new and enhanced sensor
technology, coupled with information exchange between targeting systems and
strike aircraft, helicopters or smart missiles, can defeat threats that, in previous
times, were considered too difficult to thwart without greatly widening the war
effort.

Even light infantry forces generate by their operations and equipment a
variety of detectable signatures–visual, chemical, infra-red, electromagnetic,

radar and acoustic – that render them vulnerable to a range of active radar sensor systems (such as synthetic aperture, moving target indicator and foliage penetrating radars) and passive air (and air-deployed ground-based) sensors (such as low light level TV, thermal imagers, multispectral analysers, engine electrical ignition and magnetic field detectors). These signatures betray the location and, indeed, strength of enemy forces, enabling targeting systems to then direct air attacks against them. A scenario by the RAND corporation details one possible mission against guerrillas moving heavy weapons by vehicle where many of these detection technologies might synergistically come into play:

> The JSTARS crew are directed to look for vehicle traffic along several roads. During its mission, the JSTARS' Moving Target Indicator radar detects suspicious vehicle traffic in the area of concern. This information is used to cue a UAV [Unmanned Air Vehicle] equipped with a FolPen [foliage-penetrating] radar and EO/IR [electro-optical/infrared] sensors. The UAV – using its thermal imager – detects and follows several trucks that appear to be carrying weapons. The trucks disappear into a wooded area. The UAV then uses its FolPen radar to follow the vehicles down the hidden road to an assembly area. Ground sensors are then dropped. Using acoustic and thermal imagers, remote operators are able to identify the personnel and vehicles as hostile. Tactical air (TACAIR) is called in to destroy the site.[40]

The capabilities of new detection systems are remarkable by the standards of previous conflict. One counter-sniper ballistic analyser, the Lifeguard sniper location system developed by the Lawrence Livermore National Laboratories, detects a sniper's bullet after the round has been fired, analyses its flight path and then establishes the bullet track back to its point of origin, all virtually instantaneously, and with an accuracy of within two feet of where the sniper is actually located. If multiple analysers are present, this track can be refined to within *one inch*. With this capability, even a sniper operating in the midst of a crowded urban environment is not immune to reprisal – for example, a helicopter gunship firing its cannon on precise co-ordinates, or a strike aircraft releasing a laser-guided soft and lightweight sticky foam bomb that could burst in a room and kill or disable a sniper without damaging or endangering the surrounding structure or building inhabitants.[41]

FUTURE DIRECTIONS IN PRECISION
WEAPON DEVELOPMENT AND USE

It is not unreasonable to expect that, in the future, a core ability of an advanced air force will be the ability to provide precision strike, with accuracies of less than two metres from an aim point, to any point on the globe within, at most, several hours.[42] In many ways, the 'calculus' of modern warfare has already changed. One study, by the RAND Corporation, concluded that:

> The results of our analysis do indicate that the calculus has changed and airpower's ability to contribute to the joint battle has increased. Not only can modern airpower arrive quickly where needed, it has become far more lethal in conventional operations. Equipped with advanced munitions either in service or about to become operational and directed by modern C3I systems, airpower has the potential to destroy enemy ground forces either on the move or in defensive positions at a high rate while concurrently destroying vital elements of the enemy's war fighting infrastructure. In short, the mobility, lethality, and survivability of airpower makes it well suited to the needs of rapidly developing regional conflicts. [43]

As technology changes, the nature of the precision weapon will change as well. Increasing stand-off engagement ranges is vitally important as a means of evading ever-changing ground defences and air threats; the current Joint Stand-Off Weapon is but a first step to even more advanced systems that are likely to emerge. Already, a long-range forecasting study by the United States Air Force has identified categories of 'smaller, lighter, agile, more lethal, and more affordable' air-deployed precision weapon concepts achievable over the next 10 to 30 years that could 'significantly enhance' the capabilities of the service.[44] These include advanced cruise missiles to conduct electronic countermeasure attacks, autonomous miniature munitions to stop invading armies, hard-target munitions and robotic micro-munitions to attack deeply buried hard targets, hypersonic missiles (of the order of 5 km/sec.) to strike rapidly and at long range, and precision thermoflux weapons generating very high temperatures of long duration to destroy chemical and biological weapons of mass destruction.[45] To further degrade the effectiveness of air defences, precision weapons themselves will develop the trappings of their launch systems, for example, stealth. The dividing line between what is now considered a precision-guided munition and an unmanned vehicle will increasingly blur. Aircraft dispensing such weapons will increasingly become multi-purpose 'battle' aircraft, capable of being applied to multiple long-range power projection tasks. The equivalent to the 'battle plane' likely will be not the questionably survivable (if even affordable) 'arsenal ship' but, rather, the 'arsenal submarine'.[46]

Intelligence, sensor development and targeting have always been key issues in aerial warfare, but are now of even greater importance than at any previous time.[47] Precision weapon employment requires intelligence of a sufficiently high order to enable a desired mean point of impact to be established on an individual target. In an era where, increasingly, military planners speak of conducting 'information warfare' against an opponent, the connection between intelligence, sensor suitability, targeting and combat operations is obvious. No less significant is the importance of bomb damage assessment. This was, together with intelligence collection and analysis, one of the most controversial aspects of the Gulf War. Bomb damage assessment relates directly to campaign assessment and to issues such as scheduling revisits to targets not considered sufficiently damaged. Failures in the intelligence and BDA process almost derailed the Gulf War air and land campaigns, and caused serious concerns in the minds of policy-makers as to whether their goals were being met.[48]

The story of Iraq's robust nuclear weapons programme offers a case in point. Prior to the war, failures in intelligence gathering meant that the Hussein regime had applied an astounding level of effort to developing weapons of mass destruction that was utterly unknown to the international community. Immediately prior to the war, only two nuclear targets had been identified in Iraq, one a uranium mine and the other the massive Al Tuwaitha nuclear complex. During the war, targeters identified seven other sites subsequently attacked. But after the war, inspectors learned that Iraq had, in fact, no less than ten major nuclear research facilities; eight uranium mining, production, processing and storage sites; 24 uranium enrichment sites; nine weaponisation sites; and 17 other sites devoted to supporting Iraq's nuclear weapons programme. In sum, what had been known had been targeted and much had been destroyed, but there was simply much more that was unknown and, thus, escaped attack.[49]

The profusion of advanced sensor and intelligence gathering and exploiting platforms – space-based assets, UAVs, manned airborne systems, for example – offer the hope that many of these problems will be overcome. But it is a continuing challenge, lest failures of understanding prevent the fullest possible exploitation of the precision-weapon capability now available to military forces, as well as that which will become available in the near future. Sensor development has been key to the evolution of practical precision weapons, and interest in sensors, particularly those that can penetrate foliage and adverse weather, and, literally, see through the fog, haze and smoke over a target area, is high. Sensors fall into three broad physical categories: electromagnetic (for example, electro-optical, radio frequency and low frequency); mechanical (acoustic, seismic and inertial) and chemical/biological. Fusing passive and active sensors into working architecture involving space-based systems, stand-off airborne systems (such as JSTARS), unmanned air vehicles, unattended ground sensors, ground and airborne command and control systems, and aircraft carrying precision weapons is a key requirement now and will obviously grow in importance in the future.[50]

Targeting offers its own particular challenges for appropriate precision weapon use. Traditionally, targeters have emphasised the systematic destruction of a target list; in the precision weapon era, there is far greater opportunity to target key nodes of a system for destruction, thus obviating a need for greater military effort, multiple strikes into high-risk areas, etc. Obviously, to accomplish this requires, again, the closest possible connections between the targeting and intelligence communities. Targeting also has to examine the appropriateness of precision-guided munition use against a particular target. Some targets, especially those covering large areas such as warehousing, truck parks, large industrial plants and army formations in the open, where issues of collateral damage are not a concern, may well be more suitable for attacks by aircraft carrying large numbers of dumb bombs, area denial munitions, cluster munitions, fuel-air explosives, and so on. This is particularly true of troop formations, where the shock, noise, and dislocation of air attack has essentially a paralysing and demoralising effect upon troops all out of proportion, on occasion, to the actual physical destruction achieved. In the Gulf War, for example, the attacker most feared by Iraqi forces was the B-52, a large capacity dumb-bomb-dropper capable of dispensing up to 38,250 pounds of ordnance.[51]

Though there is a continuing role for the dumb munition, as the above indicates, the reshaping of military affairs that has been wrought by the precision munition will increasingly dominate logistical and strategic planning issues. Small numbers of airlifters can bring precision weapons into a crisis region, generating levels of force projection that cannot be matched by older (and slower) forms of logistical resupply (such as so-called 'fast' sealift) bringing weapons more suitable to the conflicts of old, such as tanks and other armoured fighting vehicles, or large masses of infantry. The ability to field precision systems into a conflict region rapidly and to good effect – for example, the deployment of the largely experimental GBU-28 deep-earth penetrator in the Gulf War, or the US Army's ATACMS battlefield missile system, or the RAF's deployment of TIALD in the latter stages of the war to give the Tornado force an integral laser designating ability – has already emerged as a key characteristic and signal of whether or not a nation is, in fact, a modern military power.

Though precision weapons deployed from aircraft, helicopters, battlefield missile systems and ships and submarines off-shore undoubtedly offer a degree of leverage in warfare previously unknown, their cost is a serious concern, and one that must be addressed. Cost trends in precision weaponry are likely to force an evolutionary 'survival of the most capable for the least cost', particularly for those military services with scarce acquisition funding. (Such considerations in the United States killed the Aquila battlefield UAV in the 1980s, and, more recently, the Tacit Rainbow and Tri-Service Stand-off Attack Missile [TSSAM] efforts.) For example, by the year 2010, the US Army's Army Tactical Missile

System (ATACMS) will constitute but one-half of one per cent of the total American munitions inventory, but will account for *28 per cent* of the total cost of that inventory.[52] Whether such a system is thus, in fact, a suitable system for mass production is a serious question, given cheaper and more effective long-range power projection options. Looking at the air warfare case, the overall reliability and costs associated with piloted systems have traditionally been less than the costs associated with operating purely unmanned weapon systems. A case in point is that of the cruise missile, which carries a small and non-penetrating warhead and which is, once launched, incapable of being retargeted. The cruise missile does not endanger a human operator, and thus may be perfectly suitable for operations where a nation is unwilling to accept the risk of having personnel caught and interned. However, it lacks the survivability and flexibility of an aircraft carrying far more precise, larger and penetrating laser-guided bombs, which can attack multiple aim points on a single pass. Additionally, there are the tremendous cost penalties associated with using such missiles, which can range from 16 to over 60 times more expensive than precision-guided bombs.[53] In the Gulf War, for example, the total cost of the approximately 2,000 tons of laser-guided bombs dropped by the F-117A force was roughly $146 million; that same tonnage in Tomahawk Land Attack (TLAM) cruise missiles would have been $4.8 *billion*. Accepting for the purposes of argument that a ton of explosives delivered by a cruise missile is equivalent in military effect and significance to a ton of explosives delivered by other forms of precision weaponry, to replace all of the smart weapon tonnage delivered by the United States in the Gulf War (approximately 7,400 tons) would have required nearly $*18 billion* in TLAM missiles.[54]

Perhaps more intriguingly, precision weapons become themselves a justification and means to acquire more cost-effective precision-weapon platforms that can radically transform the capabilities of a nation to project power and influence, even when compared to other forms of precision attack. For example, a single sortie by a Northrop B-2A Spirit stealth bomber carrying 16 2,000-pound penetrating Global Positioning System-Aided Munitions (GAMs) delivers the same tonnage to a target as two non-stealthy Boeing B-52H Stratofortress sorties carrying 32 air-launched cruise missiles (ALCM) with 1,000-pound non-penetrating warheads. The cost differential of the weapons alone is $288,000 for the GAMs ($18,000 per weapon) against $32 million for the ALCMs ($1 million per weapon); the price of ship - or-submarine-launched TLAMs fired from well off-shore would be an even higher $38.4 million. Each B-2A / GAM sortie thus saves well above $31 million over using cruise missiles, thus enabling each Spirit bomber to essentially pay for itself after only 20 sorties.[55] Such cost savings, whether accumulated by substituting precision weapons for other, less cost-effective, precision weapons that may demand larger infrastructure investment or sortie generation, or by substituting precision weapons for large numbers of dumb weapons demanding even larger infrastructure, sortie and even force-structure investment, can thus constitute a powerful and significant argument for development of sophisticated multimission attackers, particularly stealthy ones.

Other cost trades are less obvious; for example, it is undoubtedly cheaper to have a smart aeroplane drop a dumb weapon, or a dumb aeroplane drop a dumb weapon, but the risk of revisiting targets and the previously discussed difficulties of ensuring that the target is actually hit will almost certainly mitigate against such 'cheap' – and misleading – solutions. The case of the dumb platform operating an autonomous or near-autonomous smart munition is, of course, more complex and worthy of analysis. Even so – as the experience of 'buddy' laser designation against strike aircraft having an integral laser designating ability has shown – results favour the sophisticated attacker. (In the case of buddy designation, the complexity and teamwork required between designator and dropper, as well as the risk from enemy defences, favours the self-contained striker such as an F-117A, an F-111F with Pave Tack or a Tornado with TIALD.)

The ongoing revolutions in aerospace and electro-optical technology will undoubtedly continue to shape the future evolution of the precision-guided munition, nowhere more so than in efforts to overcome current limitations on precision weapon use imposed by weather conditions. Two notable development efforts designed to produce acceptable accuracy in bad-weather conditions are the Joint Direct Attack Munition (JDAM) and the Joint Stand-Off Weapon (JSOW), both of which employ Global Positioning System satellite navigation terminal guidance as their primary means of achieving precision. Both JDAM and JSOW will generate their own families of precision munitions, with widely varying warhead and mission options (ranging from penetrating hard targets to dispensing submunitions in anti-armour attacks), and JSOW even offers a powered variant that renders it, in effect, a small cruise missile.[56]

The revolution in warfare that has been brought about by the precision-guided munition is one that has been a long time in coming; back to the Second World War, back, even, to the experimenters of the First World War who attempted, however crudely, to develop 'smart' weapons to launch from airships and other craft. Used almost experimentally until the latter stages of the Vietnam conflict, the precision weapon since that time has increasingly come first to influence, then to dominate, and now perhaps to render superfluous, the traditional notion of the linear battlefield. Given the experience of Iraq, the linkage of advanced sensors, advanced precision weapons, long-range combat aircraft, stealth, information technologies and the ability to strike multiple aimpoints virtually simultaneously, offers the best hope for militarily confronting the extraordinary dangers of the development of weapons of mass destruction by rogue nations. It is imperative that the implications of these developments and possibilities be assessed and studied lest the unwary discover themselves targets, not shooters, in some subsequent conflict.

NOTES

[1]   A version of this paper was presented at the H Silver and Associates (UK) Ltd. Precision Guided Munitions Conference, held in London, England, on 10–11 June 1996 and subsequently published in *Air Power History.*

[2]   The early history of guided weapon development is one well worth exploration. Good references include Heinz J Nowarra, *German Guided Missiles* (Atglen, PA: Schiffer Military/Aviation History, 1993); JR Smith and Antony L Kay, *German Aircraft of the Second World War* (Baltimore, MD: Nautical & Aviation Publishing Company, 1989 ed.), pp. 696–699; Rowland F Pocock, *German Guided Missiles of the Second World War* (New York: Arco Publishing Co., Inc., 1967); Kenneth P Werrell, *The Evolution of the Cruise Missile* (Maxwell AFB, AL: Air University Press, 1985); and William F Trimble, *Wings for the Navy: A History of the Naval Aircraft Factory, 1917-1956* (Annapolis: Naval Institute Press, 1990).

[3]   Major General J F C Fuller, *Armament and History: A Study of the Influence of Armament on History: From the Dawn of Classical Warfare to the Second World War* (New York: Charles Scribner's Sons, 1945), p. 7.

[4]   The subject of precision attack has been a generally neglected one. For this reason, Stephen L McFarland's *America's Pursuit of Precision Bombing, 1910-1945* (Washington, DC: Smithsonian Institution Press, 1995), is a most welcome addition to military aviation historiography, and recently won the Stuart Symington Book Award sponsored by the Air Force History and Museums Program.

[5]   Major General James E Fechet, ret., *Flying*, a volume in the *A Century of Progress* series (Baltimore: The Williams & Wilkins Co., in cooperation with The Century of Progress Exposition, 1933), p. 135.

[6]   Colonel Phillip S Meilinger, *10 Propositions Regarding Air Power*, (Washington, DC: Air Force History and Museums Program, 1995), pp. 41 and 45.

[7]   For further details on this raid, see Richard P Hallion, 'Prelude to Armageddon: The Troubled Beginning of the Air Offensive Against Japan', *Air Power History*, v. 42, n. 3 (Fall 1995), p. 46.

8   B-17 statistic from US Army Air Forces, *AAF Bombing Accuracy Report #2* (8th Air Force: Operational Research Section, 1945), Chart 2, 'Distribution of Effort and Results'. I wish to thank Tami Davis Biddle and W Hays Parks for making this information available to me. The fighter bomber statistic is from an AAF chart reprinted in the previously cited McFarland, p. 194.

9   This example is built using the experience of powerplant attacks in the European theatre of operations vs. powerplant attacks in the Gulf War. The Second World War data is computed on the basis of information from Major General Heywood W Hansell, Jr., *The Strategic Air War Against Germany and Japan: A Memoir* (Washington, DC: Office of Air Force History, 1986), pp. 280–281.

10   HQ USAF/XOX, 'Air Power Lethality and Precision: Then and Now', (Fall 1990). I wish to thank Colonel John A Warden III and then-Lieutenant Colonel David A Deptula for making this chart available to me. The number of aircraft calculations, based on the bomb requirements, are my own.

11   *Gulf War Air Power Survey*, v. IV, *Weapons, Tactics, and Training, and Space Operations* (Washington, DC: GWAPS, 1993), p. 86.

12   For example, research undertaken by Professor Harvey M Sapolsky and his associates at the Defense and Arms Control Studies program, Massachusetts Institute of Technology, has shown that American citizens are not only intolerant of friendly deaths in combat, but increasingly intolerant of enemy ones as well, all at the same time that they show a remarkable tolerance for high levels of domestic violence within American cities. For implications of this thought in military affairs, see Harvey M Sapolsky, 'War Without Killing', in Sam C Sarkesian and John Mead Flanagin, eds. *U.S. Domestic and National Security Agendas* (Westport, CN: Greenwood Press, 1994), pp. 27–40; and Harvey M Sapolsky and Jeremy Shapiro, 'Casualties, Technology, and America's Future Wars', *Parameters*, XXVI, n. 2 (Summer 1996), pp. 119–127.

13   Some of these issues are discussed cogently in Alan Vick, David T Orletsky, John Bordeaux, and David A Shlapak, *Enhancing Air Power's Contribution Against Light Infantry Targets* (Santa Monica, CA: RAND, 1996).

14   Richard G Davis, *Strategic Air Power in Desert Storm* (Washington, DC: Air Force History and Museums Program, 1995), p. 36.

15   This was highlighted in the United States on a talkshow discussion following the shootdown of Korean Airlines Flight KAL 007 by a Soviet fighter. When, in the run-up to the 1984 Presidential election, a reporter

asked one potential candidate what orders he would give to American fighters intercepting an unknown aircraft approaching the United States, the candidate replied that he would ask them to 'look inside the windows' and 'see if anyone was wearing a uniform'.

[16]   John J Fialka and Andy Paztor, 'Grim Calculus: If Mideast War Erupts, Air Power Will Hold Key to U.S. Casualties', *New York Times*, 15 Nov, 1990.

[17]   Rikihei Inoguchi, Tadashi Nakajima, and Roger Pineau's *The Divine Wind: Japan's Kamikaze Force in World War II* (Annapolis, Naval Institute Press, 1958) is still the best single history of the *Kamikaze* story.

[18]   Futrell, *USAF in Korea*, p. 320. Razon, for range and azimuth, was far more accurate than the earlier Azon. Tarzon, a 12,000-pound bomb, had the same guidance package as Razon, but with greater mass and a much more powerful explosive charge. All of these, however, were more 'OT & E' (Operational Test and Evaluation) weapons rather than standard 'in-the-inventory-ready-to-go' military options.

[19]   Richard P Hallion, *The Naval Air War in Korea* (Baltimore: Nautical and Aviation Publishing Co., 1986), pp. 193–196. The results were one hit, one miss, and four aborts.

[20]   Quoted in Malcolm Muir, Jr., *Black Shoes and Blue Water: Surface Warfare in the United States Navy, 1945–1975* (Washington, DC: Naval Historical Center, 1996), pp. 168, 174.

[21]   *Ibid.*, p. 169. The officer in question was the then-commander of Cruiser-Destroyer Flotilla 7, Rear Admiral Elmo Zumwalt, (later the Chief of Naval Operations in the Carter administration).

[22]   *Ibid.*, pp. 170–194.

[23]   For the early history of laser-guided bomb development, see David R Mets, *Quest for a Surgical Strike: The United States Air Force and Laser Guided Bombs* (Eglin AFB, FL: Air Force Systems Command Armament Division History Office, 1987).

[24]   Eduard Mark, *Aerial Interdiction in Three Wars* (Washington, DC: Center for Air Force History, 1994), p. 387.

[25]   In one notable video clip from an Army helicopter shown after the war, a column of abandoned Iraqi vehicles, some destroyed by subsequent attack, wends its way across Kuwait. After about two minute's worth of film—which, given the apparent ground speed of the helicopter, equates to

approximately three miles of congestion–the cause of the jam is apparent: a bridge destroyed by a laser-guided bomb. As an aside, it is worth noting that even in the Second World War, an era of far-less-precise and effective air attack, troops typically abandoned their transport when exposed to it and preferred to take their chances on foot. A good example of this is the wholesale abandonment of motor vehicles by the German *Wehrmacht* during the Nazi retreat from France in 1944, or, earlier in the war, the abandonment of vehicles by the French Army in the face of Nazi assault in 1940.

[26]   Thomas A Keaney and Eliot A. Cohen, *Gulf War Air Power Survey: Summary Report* (Washington, DC: GPO, 1993), pp. 95–97. Suitably impressed by interdiction strikes, Jordanian drivers routinely charged $18,000 for risking a one-way trip to Baghdad; see Milton Viorst, 'Report from Baghdad', *New Yorker*, v. 67, n. 18 (24 June 1991), pp. 55–73.

[27]   DoD, *Conduct of the Persian Gulf War: Final Report*, p. 158. Further, not all of the 54 had been targeted, for a variety of reasons including political and humanitarian ones. For a provocative analysis of what the precision revolution means to interdiction warfare (and the interplay of air and land forces) see Lieutenant Colonel Price T Bingham, USAF (ret.), 'U.S. Air Interdiction Capability Challenges Ground War Doctrine', *Armed Forces Journal International*, (Oct. 1992), pp. 62–63.

[28]   GWAPS, IV, p. 85 states that 'laser-guided munitions constituted only *6.7* per cent of bombs dropped from tactical aircraft during Desert Storm', but this statistic requires reconsideration and clarification. It does not include the 77,299 dumb bombs from B-52s. Further, this is only an American statistic, and does not include Coalition bombs dropped by Coalition attackers. Additionally, the '9,494' *laser*-guided bombs listed in this study actually include 152 missile rounds–SLAM, Skipper, and Walleye, the latter an *electro-optically* guided glide bomb. The 4.3 percent reflects dividing 9,342 by the *total* of 219,498 bombs dropped by USAF, USN, and USMC attackers.

[29]   *Ibid.*, p. 87.

[30]   This term represents an effort by the author and Dr Diane Putney of the Air Force History Support Office to characterise the kinds of new attacks that took place in the Gulf War. The term DEA is that of Dr Putney, but seems to the author to perfectly summarise what, in fact, took place, and what, in fact, can be expected of air attacks of a similar nature in future wars.

[31] Lieutenant Colonel Richard B. H. Lewis, *Desert Storm—JFACC Problems Associated with Battlefield Preparation*, a paper in the *U.S. Army War College Military Studies Program Paper* series (Carlisle Barracks, PA: AWC, 1993), p. 19. (Hereafter cited as Lewis Army War College paper). See also Richard P Hallion, *Storm Over Iraq: Air Power and the Gulf War* (Washington, DC: Smithsonian Institution Press, 1992), p. 203; Keaney and Cohen, p. 155; and Reuters Transcript Report, Address of General Charles Horner to the Business Executives for National Security Education Fund, 8 May, 1991, Washington, DC, pp. B-7 and B-8. I also wish to acknowledge with appreciation information from Brigadier General Thomas J Lennon, USAF, who commanded the F-111Fs in the Gulf.

[32] Department of the Army, 'Army Weapons System Performance in Southwest Asia', (Washington, DC: Department of the Army, 13 March 1991), pp. 3–4; John G Roos, 'Sergeant Pilot Recalls First Hit Delivered by France's "Iron Fist"', *Armed Forces Journal International* (August 1991), p. 35. Statistic on Hellfire usage from Terry Gordy of the Rockwell Corporation.

[33] John G Heidenrich, 'The Gulf War: How Many Iraqis Died?' *Foreign Policy*, n. 90 (Spring 1993), p. 116. A 'Waz' (Vaz) is a small Jeep-like command vehicle, an indication that literally no vehicle, no matter how small, was safe from Coalition attacks.

[34] I wish to acknowledge contributions to my thinking on this issue by Colonel David A Deptula, USAF. For a more complete description of this, see his essay 'Parallel Warfare: What is It? Where Did It Come From? Why is It Important?', in William Head and Earl H. Tilford, Jr., eds., *The Eagle in the Desert: Looking Back on U.S. Involvement in the Persian Gulf War* (Westport, CN: Praeger, 1996), especially pp. 138–141, and his more extensive *Firing for Effect: Change in the Nature of Warfare* (Arlington, VA: Aerospace Education Foundation, Aug. 1995).

[35] Lieutenant General Ralph E Eberhart, 'Airpower: An Airman's Perspective', a briefing paper prepared by AF/XO, April 1996, Slide 129. Copy in the files of the Air Force Historical Support Office, Bolling AFB, DC.

[36] Statistics on NATO weapon usage is from a briefing by Lieutenant General Michael Ryan, USAF, the commander of Allied Air Force Southern Europe, presented to the February 1996 Corona South meeting, Orlando, Florida. Copy in the files of the Air Force Historical Support Office, Bolling AFB, DC.

37   Quote from L D Simmons, et. al., *Lessons and Implications from the U.S. Operations in the Former Yugoslavia, 1992–1995 (U)*, v. III (Arlington, VA: Institute for Defense Analyses, 1996), p. X-49. This is a classified study at the SECRET level, but the quote is from an unclassified portion of the text.

38   Transcript of statement by Richard Holbrooke to Elizabeth Farnsworth, *Newshour with Jim Lehrer*, PBS television, 21 February 1996. The Holbrooke view is echoed by a veteran NATO peacekeeper, Colonel Edward E. Doyle, Irish Army (ret.). See his talk 'Peacemaking in a Divided Society', a lecture given at Trinity College, Dublin, on 27 August, 1996. Copy in the files of the Air Force History Support Office, Bolling AFB, DC.

39   See the previously cited Vick, Orletsky, Bordeaux and Shlapak, *Enhancing Air Power's Contribution Against Light Infantry Targets*, *passim*.

40   *Ibid.*, pp. 9–27, quote from p. 28.

41   *Ibid.*, pp. 54–57.

42   I wish to acknowledge with appreciation discussions with Lieutenant General George Muellner, USAF, SAF/AQ that have influenced my thinking on some of the following issues.

43   Christopher Bowie, Fred Frostic, Kevin Lewis, John Lund, David Ochmanek, and Philip Propper, *The New Calculus: Analyzing Airpower's Changing Role in Joint Theater Campaigns* (Santa Monica, CA: RAND, 1993), pp. 83–84.

44   The quotes are from the Scientific Advisory Board, *Munitions*, a volume in the *New World Vistas: Air and Space Power for the 21st Century* series (Washington, DC: HQ USAF/SAB, 1996), p. v.

45   *Ibid.*, pp.

46   See, for example, John Mintz, 'New Ship Could be Next Wave in Warfare', *The Washington Post*, 23 June 1996. The record of ships surviving three-dimensional attackers is not a good one; previous 'arsenal ships' such as the *Bismarck*, *Tirpitz*, *Prince of Wales*, *Mushashi*, *Shinano* and *Yamato* succumbed to air and submarine attack, as did many lesser known ones even when protected by escorting vessels. The notion of a stand-off battle aircraft and an arsenal submarine are, in the author's view, altogether more useful, survivable, and practicable than the chimera of an 'arsenal ship'.

47 For some relevant case studies, see John F Kreis, ed., *Piercing the Fog: Intelligence and Army Air Forces Operations in World War II* (Washington, DC: Air Force History and Museums Program, 1996).

48 One recent suggestion to overcome the BDA problem is to deploy small 'parasite' winged BDA sensors from a precision munition during the terminal engagement stage of its flight; during its own terminal flight, this 'BDA glider' could then observe the resulting impact and relay via satellite whether the strike was, in fact, successful. See the previously cited SAB, *Munitions*, p. 37.

49 For a discussion of the Iraqi programme and its implications for defence decision-making, see Robert W Chandler with Ronald J Trees, *Tomorrow's War, Today's Decisions* (McLean, VA: AMCODA Press, 1996), especially chapters 2–7.

50 For a discussion of sensor development trends, see Scientific Advisory Board, *Sensors*, a volume in the *New World Vistas: Air and Space Power for the 21st Century* series (Washington, DC: HQ USAF/SAB, 1996).

51 The best overall study of morale and air warfare is Group Captain A P N Lambert's *The Psychology of Air Power*, a volume in the Royal United Services Institute Whitehall Paper series (London: Royal United Services Institute for Defence Studies, 1994). For the Gulf experience in particular, see J M Marcum and D W Cline, 'Combat Stress Reaction in Iraqi Prisoners of War', *Bulletin of the Menninger Clinic*, v. 57, n. 4 (Fall 1993). See also GWAPS, IV, pp. 256–266.

52 Data from an Institute for Defense Analysis weapons inventory study presented in Colonel David A Deptula, 'Deep Attack/Precision Conventional Strike', a draft manuscript for the Commission on Roles and Missions, 3 March 1995, p. 18. Copies of this manuscript are in the files of the Air Force History Support Office, Bolling AFB, DC, and the Air Force Historical Research Agency, Maxwell AFB, AL.

53 The comparison is between a $1.2 million TLAM vs. a $73,000 GBU-27 laser-guided bomb (16 : 1), a $40,000 GPS-guided Joint Direct Attack Munition (30 : 1) and a $18,000 GPS-Aided Munition (GAM) (67 : 1).

54 Details on how these statistics were derived are as follows: a Gulf War-era TLAM costs approximately $1.2 million, and delivers a 1,000-pound warhead. Thus, to match a ton of high explosive delivered by a strike airplane means using two TLAMs at a total cost of $2.4 million. F-117As dropped approximately 2,000 tons of smart bombs (approximately $73,000 per bomb). Therefore:

(2,000) x ($73,000)   = $146,000,000

(2,000) x ($2,400,000)   = $4,800,000,000.

Total precision tonnage dropped by American forces was approximately 7,400 tons. Therefore:

(7,400) x (2 x $1,200,000) = $17,760,000,000.

[55]   This analysis is from 'B-2 1996: The Revolution is Here', (Pico Rivera, CA: Northrop Corporation, 1996), pp. 32–33. I wish to thank Dr Christopher J Bowie for making this available to me. Even with the more expensive JDAM ($640,000 per load of 16 weapons, versus $288,000 per load of 16 GAMs), the B-2 still saves $31,360,000 over B-52s deploying ALCMs, or $37,760,000 over ships and submarines firing TLAMs.

[56]   I have drawn on information from two briefings, Lieutenant Colonel James McClendon, USAF's 'The Joint Direct Attack Munition', and Mr. Robert Pergler's 'The Joint Stand Off Weapon', presented at the previously mentioned H Silver and Associates (UK) Ltd.'s Precision Guided Munitions Conference. Information on receiving copies of these briefings may be obtained by writing to HSA (UK) Ltd., Africa House, 64–78 Kingsway, London, WC2B 6BD.

5

JOINT AIR WARFARE: HALFWAY THERE

by

Rear Admiral James A Winnefeld, USN (ret.)

FORMER CONSULTANT, RAND, WASHINGTON, DC

Jointness is fighting together at the seams. . . . The seams are
where the enemy can hurt us and where we kill ourselves.[1]

In the past 55 years of joint air operations, the air forces of the US armed services have fought 'joint' exactly one and a half times.[2] The real joint air campaign was fought in the Solomons 1942–44, an example that carried over through most of the following campaigns of the Pacific War. In those campaigns, there were in most cases true joint commands with a joint staff, joint planning and joint operations involving multi-service packages of aircraft. The environment that shaped true 'jointness' on those occasions involved a fight to the death against a proficient, brave and resourceful enemy. To be sure, there were turf arguments and parochial sideshows among the services, but the enemy forced a focus and sacrifice of service concerns that was to be missing for most of the ensuing 50 years.

In reviewing these joint campaigns, one could conclude that there is a direct correlation between the degree of jointness achieved and the incentives in place. Unfortunately, the history of such matters suggests that negative incentives (e.g. the prospect of defeat on the battlefield or the loss of service prerogatives) have been more important than the more abstract benefits of efficiency and effectiveness.

The 'half-joint' air campaign was fought in DESERT STORM where there was a single joint forces air component commander (JFACC) whose largely single service staff did the planning and provided the operational direction for a collection of air forces. But we should be a bit sceptical about assertions that Operation DESERT STORM was a full-up demonstration of jointness. Gulf War air operations appeared to be a major improvement because:

- The two previous major conflicts – Korea and Vietnam – were only superficially and episodically joint insofar as air operations were concerned;

- The plentiful air resources available to Lieutenant General Charles Horner, USAF (the Central Command JFACC) during the Gulf War, permitted his letting each air component do mostly what it wanted to do in its own way; and, finally,

- The Gulf War (unlike Korea and Vietnam) was a success in the narrow sense of decisively defeating the enemy's forces – and success tends to blur the visibility of organisational and doctrinal problems.

Nevertheless, Operation DESERT STORM demonstrated progress and appeared to bear out some of the more optimistic claims that a new era in jointness had arrived. Basking in the glow of victory, many were quick to identify the sources of the new era in joint air operations. For example, some pundits and editorial writers placed the credit on the Defence Reform Act of 1986 (more popularly known as the Goldwater-Nichols Act) by claiming that legislation was the source of greater jointness. But, service advocates were more sceptical, stating that the trend was well underway before the Gulf War and that solid progress continues regardless (or in spite) of various pronouncements from Washington.

Some airmen claimed that increased jointness is a natural byproduct of the increased role that air power plays in modern warfare and, furthermore, that airmen have always believed in unity of command. They assert that the argument has been over who is to exercise such command and under what circumstances. Meanwhile defence reformers continue to state that we can no longer afford 'four air forces', but that if we insist on keeping them, a single joint command structure is a necessity.

There are other voices. For example, some defence analysts state that the critical dimensions are good and rapid intelligence, targeting and delivery systems regardless of service origin. They observe that the environment and the systems have changed so dramatically that the old almost-joint paradigms don't work anymore. Or, at a minimum, they don't work well or are not affordable. Yet many of these analysts also recognise the dangers represented by system enthusiasts and service advocates who favour single point solutions that sub-optimise around an attractive new (or traditional) concept.

This essay examines these and other views on recent experiences in joint air operations, points out their strengths and shortcomings, and attempts to gauge what the future direction of jointness is as it pertains to airmen. To these ends a short prologue is offered, a diagnosis of current progress and problems is conducted, and a prognosis of what the future may hold is advanced.

THE GOOD NEWS

The good news is that joint air operations are now more joint than they have been at any time since 1945. This slow but steady progress is the more remarkable because it has been achieved without the pressure exerted by a clear, immediate and very dangerous threat. The JFACC concept, dormant since 1945, has been rediscovered, dusted off, 'legitimised' and accepted by all services.[3] The argument is now about the extent of the JFACC's command, control or co-ordination authority and to what degree he should be kept on a leash by various targeting boards, need to consult, geographic constraints, etc.

At the squadron level, the threshold dividing largely single service from truly joint tactical air operations has been crossed. We have started the painful process of jointly manning some specialised service aircraft.[4] The 'one service can do it all' concept probably received its death blow during the Gulf War, but there are still a few who believe in the heat of Washington budget and system acquisition battles that one service or one force application concept is the war winner. There are others whose beliefs imply that their service's force application and command and control concepts should be protected from the intrusion of joint concerns. Fairly or not, the Air Force has been associated with the former view and the Marine Corps with the latter view.[5]

While some early progress towards jointness was in evidence during the Korean and Vietnam conflicts, it was the exception rather than the rule. The ruling air power application paradigm in those earlier wars was the 'route package' concept wherein each service conducted its own air war within pre-defined geographical boundaries (or even within assigned time periods).[6] As recently as 1986, during the Operation EL DORADO CANYON strikes against Libya, the operations of the Air Force and Navy/Marine units were separated geographically – though there was some limited joint support. However, by the time of Operation DESERT STORM, there had been numerous joint operations that went beyond the usual 'in support of' concepts and approached the degree of integration realised in the Solomons during the Second World War.

Perhaps the most remarkable, yet seemingly little noticed, development of the Gulf air war was the explicit recognition (in the form of mixed strikes set out in the air tasking order) that a single service no longer had all the air capabilities that were needed. Although some partisans hung on to the old beliefs centering on service self-sufficiency, it became clear that many important capabilities were unique (or near unique) to one service, yet were needed for the effective operation of the whole. The Air Force had the only stealth (the

Lockheed F-117A) and air target recognition systems. Moreover, it had the only up-and-running theatre-wide command and control system, whatever its faults were. The Navy had the only surface-launched cruise missiles and (with the Marines) the only air platform (the Grumman EA-6B Prowler) that combined both lethal and electronic defence suppression. The Army and Marines had lesser, but nonetheless near unique air capabilities that, if not essential to victory, were nevertheless important contributors. The upshot was that no service could go it alone in the prosecution of the war, or the air war itself for that matter.

Over the decade preceding Operation DESERT STORM, the Navy had gradually become dependent on USAF AWACS and tankers. Even as far back as the Korean War, the Navy was dependent on the Air Force to take on the MiG threat in the absence of adequately capable carrier-based fighters.[7] The Air Force came to accept a legitimate Navy role in early combat air operations including base defence, until the greater numbers and payload of USAF forces could be brought to bear and fully supported. Moreover, the Air Force learned that it must take on a major role in expeditionary warfare that had long been the niche role of the Navy and Marine Corps. The USAF's composite wing (established with expeditionary warfare in mind) was a concept that had long been in Navy and Marine Corps use and was adapted (with some pain) to existing USAF operational strengths.

This trend towards increased integration was both pulled by enlightened service leadership and pushed by a combination of astonishing technological development and the associated steeply rising costs. It became clear that no service could afford what it would have preferred to do: be a full-service air operations system. Increases in costs drove increases in dependence, which in turn drove the need for increased jointness. But it is that need for increased jointness that exposed the difficulties in putting aside the old ways. Therein lies a residue of bad news.

THE BAD NEWS

The bad news is that, while the services and the CINCs accept the need for a JFACC in joint air operations and there are largely agreed doctrinal publications outlining his duties and authority, in practice there is considerable room for disagreement. These differences are avoided or papered over in current joint doctrinal publications and by the instructions (the concept of operations, or 'conops') the CINCs have developed to cover joint air operations in conflict.[8] The result is that while there is some posturing about the success of jointness, the real decisions are not necessarily based on published doctrine but lie with the CINC and his joint force commanders – where they should lie in the opinion of the author. The CINC under Goldwater-Nichols is given wide latitude to organise his command as he sees fit. The result of this latitude is an ongoing striving among the services for the hearts and minds of CINCs and other joint force commanders present and future to shape the latter's views on how the air weapon should be organised and wielded.[9]

Unfortunately, this dialogue among proponents and outside experts has been conducted in a continuing atmosphere of suspicion and mistrust. Whatever its other merits, the Congressionally-mandated Commission on Roles and Missions gave air jointness a severe setback.[10] Zealous staff members of the Commission and the services turned a serious dialogue about roles and missions (more accurately, 'functions') issues into a fight about the merits of specific air weapons systems and the prowess of the various services in meeting the needs of the national strategy. Sharp words, charges and counter-charges were exchanged. Acerbic service-oriented briefings were given to the Commission. Slick brochures were printed. Narrowly drawn, self-serving arguments were advanced. The result, as one service chief confided to the author, was that all were 'glad when this debate is over so we can get on with real business'.

When one puts the procurement issues aside, and the arguments of who can get there first with the most, the pre-eminent joint air warfare issue centres on the role of the JFACC in practice, the form and extent of his co-ordination with service components, where his advice comes from, and how cherished service component prerogatives associated with their preferred style of warfighting can be preserved.

THE JFACC AS AN INSTITUTION

The JFACC's role is so crucially important that each service has attempted to either expand or limit his authority depending on expected gains and losses to their concerns. In most cases, this has pitted the Air Force against the other three services, though there have been different alignments on specific sub-issues. The Air Force has sought the widest possible scope of action and authority for the JFACC. The other services have in general attempted to tether that authority to need for advice from a Joint Target Co-ordination Board (JTCB) or from special embedded organisations within the Joint Force Commander's staff. Their objective is to insure a clear formalised method for ground (or other surface) commanders to influence targeting and apportionment recommendations to the JFC. Paralleling these interests is a continuing effort to carve out single service component authority for geographic areas of special interest to them in terms of high density traffic control zones (HDTCZS) or the set back of the fire support control lines (FSCLS) from friendly ground units.

The Marines have long seen the JFACC not as a *commander* but as a *co-ordinator*. His job in their view is doing strategic air planning and managing airspace deconfliction and support in the theatre. The Air Force sees Marine interests as an attempt to sub-optimise amphibious or other expeditionary operations at the cost of denying the CINC the full power of a single air weapon under unitary command. Officers whose principal interest is control of the earth's surface (with forces on the earth's surface) remain deeply sceptical of the promises of airmen. The latter repay the compliment by saying the former do not understand how technology has changed to give air forces a decisive role and, therefore, we can no longer afford to exert power the old-fashioned way with vulnerable troops and expensive (and redundant) surface systems.[11]

These are the cross currents that continue to swirl around the joint force commander as he decides (or has decided for him) how the functional air component is to be organised, directed and wielded in combat. It remains for the JFACC to employ the compromise that inevitably results. The JFACC sees himself as a commander, but he knows only too well that he must be a diplomat ('co-ordinator') as well. He needs command and control authorities, but he is wise if he takes and uses only what he needs to win and no more. This blend of firm direction, skilful diplomacy and restraint is what characterised General Charles Horner's direction of the Gulf air war. Very few air command and control arguments arrived on General Schwarzkopf's desk for resolution thanks to Horner's larger conception of his role and his putting aside service operational preferences to use what would work in the circumstances.

This need for diplomacy in the integration of fielded forces bothers some who see in simple terms the command and subordination issues involved. But I would caution that trust and confidence among commanders from different backgrounds (regardless of subordination) are the glue that hold any military system together. Today's Air Force JFACC may, in different circumstances, become tomorrow's Marine JFACC as mixes of capabilities (needed and available) shift. Services other than that from which the JFACC is drawn need to have confidence that their concerns will receive full consideration in the decision and execution processes and that single service agendas will not be pursued.[12]

Since DESERT STORM there have been two prominent applications of the JFACC concept: continuing SOUTHERN WATCH and DENY FLIGHT operations in the Gulf and the air operations over Bosnia.[13] These applications have profited greatly from the Gulf experience. The JFACC has been assisted by a deputy from another service and the staffs have been joint (and combined) nearly from the start. The air task order concept has been retained and improved with the help of better standardisation of procedures and more modern software and equipment. But to face the question squarely, these latter operations have been relatively (compared to DESERT STORM) small scale and with a lower tempo. Problems can be solved with hand-tooling and the price of failure, while possibly high in diplomatic terms, has been relatively low in military terms, e.g., excessive casualties or even defeat on the battlefield.

Preparing for the establishment of future JFACCs has been helped immensely by the increasing use of contingency Joint Task Forces (JTFs) by the regional CINCs. The JTFs have in due course been exercised and JFACC issues encountered and solved. There is a growing body of knowledge, gradually being codified in joint publications at the national and CINC levels, that is gaining service acceptance – or at least understanding.

The services, with the Air Force in the lead, have not been bashful about advancing their ideas on the duties and responsibilities of the JFACC. The Air Force is working on the third edition of its 'JFACC Primer'. This primer is an off-the-shelf set of rules, guidelines, and authorities that a CINC or joint force commander of like mind can go ahead and implement. At a less formal level the other services each has a set of primers for setting up and commissioning a JFACC.[14]

To sum up, the JFACC as an institution is an accepted general concept, but there remain arguments about what should be the limits placed on his authority and how targeting and apportionment advice for the JFC is developed. One way to look at the associated issues is to answer the following question:

ADVISING THE CINC OR JFC: WHO HAS HIS EAR AND WHAT IS HE TOLD?

The critical relationship in joint air war fighting is the relationship between the CINC (or subordinate Joint Force Commander) and his JFACC. Service component commanders tend to be jealous, suspicious or otherwise worried that their narrower (which appear broad and war winners/stoppers to them) concerns will be overridden in the CINC's (or JFC's) relationship with his JFACC. What are the underlying sources of this tension and anxiety? The simple answer lies in how one considers subordination, geographical demarcation, apportionment and targeting issues. The CINC/JFC makes important decisions on each as he plans and directs his campaign.

Subordination. The doctrine, whether in the joint publications or the CINC's conops, is clear: the JFC has the choice of establishing a JFACC, or not. Moreover, if he does establish a JFACC he must establish the geographic bounds of his authority both horizontally and vertically, the functional bounds on that authority (e.g., tactical control of joint sorties provided), and what associated tasks he is given (e.g., air defence commander, air space co-ordinator). While doctrine has something to say on each of these points, it is broad enough to provide an umbrella over the arena in which service component issues are joined. The current trend is to give the JFACC more rather than less authority. Route packages (recalling the air war over North Vietnam) appear dead as a concept, but it is conceivable that a future theatre of operations may be large enough to warrant separate sub-theatre JFACCs.

The Late 20th Century Version of the Route Package. The crude way of overcoming air service interoperability problems and operational preferences is to carve the theatre up into regions that each 'belong' to a single service. This practice was widely used in the Korean War and the Vietnam conflict. The Air Force detested it as a manifestation of putting air power into 'penny packets' and denying the commander the ability to wield a massive air instrument with unity of command. The other services saw it as a way to keep air responsive to engaged surface commanders, or to permit a service to exercise its weapon employment preferences, or to head off a perceived grab for its needed air resources. The advantages and disadvantages of the route package concept have been overdrawn by its advocates and critics.

Although an explicit route package system was not used during the Gulf War – and most Air Force officers deny it existed – there was evidence that the concept was alive if not well. For example, PROVEN FORCE units in Turkey were under General Horner's control and hit the classes of targets he wanted hit, but the PROVEN FORCE commander exercised more discretion in operations than did similar commanders based in the Gulf. The over-water part of the theatre was in effect a Navy route package. Certain air operating areas (with an altitude ceiling) and sorties were under marine control once ground operations began. Army commanders exercised a form of route package control by their tight control over the Fire Support Control Line (FSCL) – a control that was roundly criticised by airmen for allegedly denying Coalition forces the chance of an air kill against retreating Iraqi forces.

These examples notwithstanding, Air Force officers are correct that the old route package concept was not employed in Iraq. Rather, the JFACC exercised some flexibility in his command and co-ordination arrangements to gain the benefits of centralised control together with elements of decentralised execution. The essential elements of that command and co-ordination were the Air Tasking Order (ATO) and the JFACC's concurrent authorities as air space and air defence co-ordinators.

During the deliberations of the post-Gulf War Congressionally-mandated American Commission on Roles and Missions (CORM), there was considerable discussion of how control of airspace beyond friendly front lines should be exercised and by whom. Surface warfare proponents wanted control farther out, arguing that they had to have the opportunity to engage the enemy's operational reserves with their long-range weapons and to 'shape the battlefield'. Air proponents argued that air forces were the only forces capable of conducting massive and precise attacks on forces beyond the range of conventional artillery, and that air forces should not be constrained by the lower firepower rates of fast moving ground forces. The issue remains unresolved in specific terms and will be an item on any future JFC agenda.

Apportionment. Apportionment is defined as 'the determination and assignment of the total expected effort by percentage and/or priority that should be devoted to the various operations and/or geographic areas for a given time period'.[15] It is the JFC's duty to apportion, a duty that is not delegated. The issue is how component and staff advice is arrived at. The JFACC is the principal focal point for the development of this advice and he is required to co-ordinate with the service component commanders in its preparation. The extent, timeliness and influence of the products of co-ordination can become an issue.

During Operation DESERT STORM, there was a breakdown in communications between the JFC (the CINC in this case) and his service components in conveying the commander's intent (operational security and deception against battlefield preparation). A healthy, functioning co-ordination mechanism would have highlighted and led to resolution of these issues prior to the JFC's decision, and headed off the need for the subsequent tardy explanations and recriminations.

The scale and focused nature of joint air operations since the Gulf War have pushed apportionment issues into the background.[16] However, the lack of salience in the last five years should not lead one to believe that the doctrinal and systemic issues have been resolved.

Targeting. Joint doctrine provides for a Joint Target Co-ordination Board (JTCB). The establishment and functions of such a board are up to the JFC.[17] The naval CINCs, in their JFACC conops, put major emphasis on the JTCB role, where the non-naval CINCs do not. Most USAF officers I have interviewed oppose the concept, seeing it as an infringement on the JFACC's authority and effectiveness.[18] Officers of the other services see the JTCB as a check on airmen to see that ground component concerns are adequately addressed in targeting. I will discuss my views on the future of the JTCB later in this chapter. Suffice to say that some form of targeting board has been an important feature of every war the United States has fought since the Second World War.

With this view of the past and present of joint air operations, it is now time to look at what the future may hold.

LOOKING TO THE FUTURE

What is the shape and content of the future of joint air operations? To answer this question, we need to look at the trends which are already visible: more peace operations; more combined operations; more expeditions; the shifting of support functions to the rear; and increased service specialisation.

More Peace Operations. While peace operations can have a largely stand-alone air component, as was the case of air operations in Bosnia in 1995, more often the air contribution will be in support of peacekeepers, peacemakers and peace-enforcers on the ground. Completely apart from any joint issues that may arise, such support places very stringent demands on air forces.[19] Operating a major airlift to Bosnia (e.g. 50 heavy airlift sorties per day), while at the same time continuing Operation DENY FLIGHT and maintaining a round-the-clock close air support capability with both fighter-bombers and helicopters, involves a degree of diversification and control, co-ordination and intelligence integration rarely required in the past in peacetime. But the diverse air operations in Bosnia may be more the pattern for the future than a clone of Operation DESERT STORM.

Bosnia has been a laboratory for developing and improving co-ordination and force application techniques at both the joint and combined levels. Mass will not be as important as highly specialised, precise (the word 'surgical' has been misused), nuanced, rapidly applied and tightly controlled capabilities. These requirements argue for capabilities on-scene or in near proximity exercised by a commander, probably also on-scene, supported by a wide array of regional and global capabilities. Such needs argue for not sacrificing modernisation to maintain force levels. They also suggest that tomorrow's peace operations JFACC will require a level of jointness in outlook and experience in combined air operations not routinely found among officers nominated today for JFACC and associated staff duties.

More Combined Operations. This is a corollary of the trend towards more peace operations. But there remains the case of coalition operations outside the rubric of peace operations as that term is used today. Possible future operations in South-West and East Asia (not just on the Korean Peninsula) may require coalition warfare without the peace operations backdrop experienced in Somalia and Bosnia. It is clear that effective joint air operations are an essential building block for combined air operations. But there is already some blurring of the division between joint and coalition warfare as the United States leads the way in packaging and deploying expeditionary air forces.

In my view, the trend towards more coalition air warfare (including air logistic operations) plays to Air Force strengths in organisation, doctrine development and its close relationships with the air forces of likely coalition partners. The simple fact of the matter is that the air forces of those partners are more aligned with USAF concepts than they are with the more specialised air power concepts of US Army, Navy, and Marine Corps. At the risk of appearing to contradict a point made earlier, I think the point is fast approaching when the United States Air Force will need to shift its focus from smoothing out the speed bumps in the joint air arena to developing the complete tool kit for combined air operations and the experience to use it. Not only will our future coalition partners look to the USAF for such leadership, but the other US services will increasingly look there as well. In my book, every dime we spend on getting Air Force officers in representational and planning billets overseas is well spent.

Fewer Bases, More Expeditions. Another trend that has become clearer since 1990 is that we will have fewer US bases overseas. While we may operate as coalition partners, the timely availability and suitability of overseas bases will become a major concern. I believe it is somewhat glib to say that because we are likely to operate as coalition members in a future operation, overseas base access will be automatically provided by threatened security partners. There are two elements of this formulation that warrant caution:

• The timing of, and restrictions on, base availability and usage; and

• The suitability of the bases made available.

Typically, a country needing our assistance will worry about provoking the danger they fear, while at the same time hedging by providing some form of base access to US forces. We saw some evidence of this ambivalence in late July and early August 1990. Access was attained after several days, but with a different Saudi leadership the result could have been much more adverse.[20] There are several corresponding scenarios in East Asia that should be troubling.

Even if bases are made available in a timely fashion we may find that they are not entirely suitable – or adequately supported – for basing our first line aircraft. These considerations argue for the importance of pre-positioning and infrastructure development during the pre-crisis period. The development of such capabilities is an important, but low key, form of overseas presence. While CONUS-based bombers can make a rapid initial contribution, it is likely that a combination of bombers, carrier aircraft, submarine or ship-launched cruise missiles (SLCMs) and fast arriving land-based expeditionary tactical air power forces will be needed. Orchestrating the development of a 'seamless web' of air power application is a major challenge to jointness.[21] Rapid shifts in the location and operational responsibilities of the JFACC – across service lines on occasion – may be necessary as part of this process.

In my view, these considerations pose a particular challenge to the Air Force. If CONUS-based bombers can indeed do most of it, well and good. But the more likely case will involve a smooth blending of disparate forces from all services and the special operations forces (SOF) community.

More Support Functions Moving to the Rear. While the trend has been obvious for decades, I believe we can expect most maintenance to move to the rear, including CONUS. There will be some blend of organisational and intermediate maintenance accomplished in theatre, but more intermediate maintenance will join depot maintenance in the rear areas – a point well demonstrated during the Persian Gulf War.

This may not seem to effect jointness, but differences in maintenance and support concepts across services will result in different capabilities (particularly in sustainability) and force future JFACCs to consider more than tactical questions in force commitment and employment.[22] I see the seeds here for giving the JFACC more operational control (OPCON) authority than the tactical control (TACON) authority reflected in the contemporary Air Tasking Order system. This is not necessarily an adverse development, but it will not be implemented without some heartburn across the services.

Increased Service Specialisation. Earlier in this essay the trend towards increased specialisation was mentioned. This trend is most obvious in the joint EA-6B enemy air defence suppression programme and the heavy reliance of all services on USAF tankers, AWACS and JSTARS. The Army is clearly the lead service on attack helicopters and is likely to remain so. The Lockheed-Martin F-22 stealth air superiority fighter programme promises to make the USAF the principal air-to-air player if a future opponent has a sophisticated fighter. It is likely that the Navy's Tomahawk will be the principal theatre missile weapon. The service orientation of future missile defences is less clear, but the Army and Navy seem to have the lead entries at the moment.

This varied stable of capabilities – few of which are useful in the standalone mode – crossing service and time of arrival lines poses a major challenge to future JFACCs in both planning and execution. Tools for putting it all together, beyond such generalised concepts as Joint Mission Essential Task Lists (JMETLs) and Joint Force Packages, are needed. While each service has its own ideas as to the optimal mix and method of employment, it will be up to the CINCs to see that integration occurs. For me, the trend in all this is away from service doctrine and preferences, and towards joint doctrine and employment concepts developed in the field.

There are other trends that could be explored in detail (e.g. more capable C4-IW [Command, Control, Communications, Computers – Information Warfare]). But what are some of the implications for joint air warfare? That question is the focus of the conclusion of this essay.

TOWARDS JOINT AIR WARFARE IN THE 21ST CENTURY

I believe the JFACC concept will become stronger and become firmly embedded in the American way of fighting war. The trend will be for Joint Force Commanders to give him or her more authority. I also predict the JFACC concept will decline as a focus of intra-service controversy. This will happen because JFACC staffs will become more truly joint in their composition and there will be ample scope *within the staff* to insure component views are heard and legitimate concerns accommodated.

I also believe that a parallel development will be decreased use of Joint Target Co-ordination Boards as trust is developed across components. These positive developments are contingent on Congressional restraint in not provoking future unnecessary roles and missions battles. If a JTCB is needed, it will be an entity within the JFC's staff.

I believe there will be more standing JFACC organisations and fewer skeleton or cadre units. A JFACC and his staff will be tools the CINC or JFC can pull off the shelf, just as he does a fighter wing or a carrier battle group. The standing JFACC organisations will be the engines that drive joint and cross-service air training. This will cause some problems for commanders concerned with cherished service functions in organising and training forces. But I believe they slowly but surely will lose ground. Jointness is moving upstream in the force packaging 'food chain', whether the services like it or not.

Moving away from JFACC staff and organisational issues, I believe we are slowly moving towards a joint wing structure. This will not happen quickly and there will be zigs and zags along the way. But I see a future scenario (perhaps by 2010?) when a composite wing ashore may be comprised of units from several services. As more intermediate level maintenance migrates to the rear, some of the current problems with the joint wing concept will move with it.

Moving closer to the battle line, I see the FSCL moving closer to the Forward Edge of Battle (FEBA). Air concepts for shaping the battlefield will achieve equality with (or superiority to) ground force concepts that now dominate. The JFC will have a menu of options for setting the line depending on the situation. But as field commanders are better served by their C4I systems and more trust and confidence in the JFACC occurs, the FSCL distance will shrink. But this will not happen automatically: airmen will first have to gain the confidence of their earthbound comrades-in-arms.

Phrases such as 'air campaign plan', 'ground scheme of manoeuvre', and 'missile strikes at operational depth' will need to be transformed to meet the demands of truly joint operations.

Perhaps no military operation is more vexing to the achievement of true air jointness than close air support (CAS). Classic close air support grew up in an environment where there was a fairly clear territorial demarcation (the FEBA) between the opposing forces. In its traditional form, CAS was intended to replace or supplement artillery. Increasingly CAS has been orientated to the support of relatively small friendly formations engaged in mobile warfare. As the range of ground force weapons has increased, the application of CAS has moved out farther from the FEBA except in truly desperate situations or where friendly forces are inserted by air or from the sea.

The distinction between CAS and 'battle area support' or interdiction has become blurred. In some situations, as in Operation DESERT STORM, it all but disappeared. I believe that classic CAS on the Second World War and Korean model is a relic. Though it is a capability that needs to be retained – as are bayonets, pistols and 'dumb' bombs – the need for it is very, very situation-specific and increasingly rare.[23] Forces composed of Marines or airborne units will still need it to support forced entry, but they are special cases. Though CAS is not dead, then, it will have a much lesser role in the future than it has had historically. This is not to argue with the Marines or others that it is not still needed on occasion; but to assert that it is not a proper central rationale for air power.

All in all, the diagnosis and prognosis that I have suggested should be comforting to Air Force officers. But since the focus of this essay is on doctrine, I should close with a few cautionary words. The major role of air power in future conflict is assured. Air power has come of age and is an equal partner with the other forms of military power. In some cases it will be the pre-eminent, and in others the supporting, partner. Airmen must ensure that their own doctrinal tent is large enough to support their comrades-in-arms and that their proper striving for unity of command in air operations does not work to deny others full partnership in advising how the air weapon can best be used. Combined arms need not be the enemy of unity of command.

NOTES

[1]   William G Welch, 'We're Still Not Joint', *Naval Institute Proceedings*, February 1996, p. 61.

[2]   The author is a retired naval aviator and a consultant with the RAND

office in Washington, DC. He has authored or co-authored books, articles, and book reviews on joint air operations. The views expressed in this article are his own and do not necessarily reflect those of RAND or its research sponsors. By 'joint' he refers to the interfaces among the nation's four air forces and their service components. This essay does not deal with separate and important interfaces between air and land components.

3   Welch (p. 59) suggests the limits of this acceptance.

4   Steven Watkins, '4 Fliers Help Start New Era: Air Force, Navy Team Up in Joint EA-6B Squadron', *Air Force Times*, 13 November 1995, p. 3. Similar integration is occurring in various air training squadrons, integration that goes beyond the long-standing and well-publicised 'exchange pilot' system. The NATO AWACS programme contains elements of both combined and joint integration.

5   See Eliot A Cohen, 'Air Power, the Next War, and the Marine Corps', in *Marine Corps Gazette*, November 1995.

6   Moreover, there was considerable direct involvement of the Joint Force Commander (and/or CINC) in the targeting process. In many ways, the air campaigns were directed by commanders above the component command level.

7   During the Vietnam War, the MiG suppression role was performed by both services.

8   The latter observation is not meant to be derogatory. The CINC and Joint Force Commander must be left latitude to organise and manage affairs as the combat situation and other circumstances require. The most relevant joint publication on joint air operations (Joint Pub. 3-56.1) reflects the ambivalence in concepts that on the one hand suggests that doctrine is merely guidance or distilled experience and on the other hand that it is authoritative, prescriptive, or to be violated only in exceptional circumstances (see 'purpose' and application paragraphs in the preface of Joint Pub. 3-56.1). General purpose escape clauses recognize the JFC's prerogatives to organise and fight the way he wants to regardless of the often lawyerly wording in joint publications.

9   'Only the Joint Force Commander has the authority to reassign, re-direct, or reallocate a component's direct support air capabilities/forces .... The authority and command relationships of the JFACC are established by the JFC.' Joint Pub. 3-56.1, pp. v-vi.

10   Some will argue with this finding, maintaining that the Commission merely provided a forum that brought out into the open disagreements that had long simmered in the back rooms of all the services. However, the acrimony that developed during the course of the dialogue had an intensity and 'my service first' aura that had not been approached since the corrosive arguments advanced during the bomber-carrier controversies of 1946–50. I believe that period did great damage to inter-service trust and confidence that carried over into sub-optimal joint performance in the Korean and Vietnam wars.

11   This implication is clear in David A Fulghum's 'Glosson: U.S. Gulf War Shortfalls Linger', *Aviation Week and Space Technology*, 29 January, 1996, pp. 58–60.

12   Single service agendas take several forms. Some appear under the rubric of combat necessity, putting bombs on target regardless of which service provides the aircraft, and working as a team, putting aside the fact that there usually are a number of good ways to perform a given task. Others emphasise the pre-eminent importance of the air-ground interface, disregarding or downplaying the possibility that under some circumstances a primarily air or ground operation may be the most effective and/or efficient.

13   'JTF-SWA does not have a separate JFACC since the operations size and nature allow the JFC to accomplish the functions. . . '. See 'Lessons Learned', *Joint Forces Quarterly*, Autumn 1995, p. 122. We are examining JFACC functions, recognising that in some cases those functions will be performed by the JFC. In a combined operations context, the JFACC might be referred to as the operational director of a Combined Air Operation Center (as in the Bosnia case).

14   Service views are skillfully blended and differences muted in joint publications such as Joint Pub. 3-56.1 (*Command and Control for Joint Air Operations*). But they become more evident in the somewhat different approaches taken by the various CINCs to JFACC issues. For example, successive CINCs for US Pacific Command and US Atlantic Command (officers from the Department of the Navy), in their JFACC 'conops', put much more emphasis on the role of Joint Target Coordination Boards (JTCBS) and potential conflicts and disagreements in air operations planning than do USCINCEUR and USCENTCOM (the Deputy CINC in US European Command is a USAF officer and the JFACC in Central Command has with few exceptions been a USAF officer).

15 Joint Pub. 3-56.1, p. IV-6. The timing dimension of apportionment is frequently overlooked in discussion of apportionment issues.

16 Some feel it is an unnecessary function given the JFC's authority and the variations among the capabilities of the diverse types of aircraft 'apportioned' .Welch, *op. cit.* 1 p. 60.

17 'Typically, the JTCB reviews targeting information, develops targeting guidance and priorities, and may prepare and define joint target lists.' Joint Pub. 3-56.1, p. IV-1.

18 Indeed, in the 2nd edition (Feb 1994 edition of the USAF's *JFACC Primer*), the JTCB is scarcely addressed except as an issue between airmen and others.

19 See Craig Covault, 'NATO Air Power to Enforce Peace', *Aviation Week and Space Technology*, 4 December, 1995, pp. 20–23.

20 Even Italy, a staunch security partner, refused a request for basing some specialised US aircraft in that country as major NATO intervention in Bosnia became a reality.

21 It does not centre on the question of which service's assets get there first and in strength. The central challenge is to orchestrate their arrival and employment for prompt, maximum and sustained effect.

22 For example, how much support is needed for alternative force packages, how vulnerable is it?

23 I agree with Cohen, *op. cit.*, on this point.

6

OPERATIONS IN SEARCH OF A TITLE: AIR POWER IN OPERATIONS OTHER THAN WAR

by

Air Vice-Marshal Tony Mason CB CBE MA RAF (ret.)

PROFESSOR OF AEROSPACE POLICY, UNIVERSITY OF BIRMINGHAM

'Operations other than war' (OOTW) is an awkward expression, used to describe the use of air power in peace support, humanitarian and constabulary activities. Such operations may involve combat aircraft discharging weapons as well as transport aircraft delivering succour to populations stricken by natural disaster. The latter is, undoubtedly, a peaceful mission; the former, on the other hand, may involve procedures similar to those of traditional combat and, in the eyes of the recipient at least, differences may be difficult to identify.

This essay will assume that OOTW take place in an environment where air power is not being used against a hostile state, nor in support of either a constituted government or its opposition in an insurgency or revolution. When air power is bringing force to bear, it will be to induce belligerents in a civil war to prefer a negotiated settlement rather than depend on their own military strength to impose a favourable solution. Humanitarian operations may be flown in benign circumstances when an undisputed sovereign authority needs assistance in the aftermath of a natural disaster, or in the more complex and hazardous environment of a war zone. Constabulary activities are those flown in support of a civil power, for example against smuggling and piracy.

The differences between the use of air power in OOTW and in traditional conflict are relatively easy to identify. Arguably, they have in recent years tended to obscure principles and procedures essential to both.

PEACE SUPPORT OPERATIONS

In the aftermath of the Gulf War, air power enthusiasts were exultant, and with good reason. Air power had denied Saddam Hussein the opportunity to impose a strategy of ground force attrition on the Coalition; it had isolated his occupation forces in Kuwait and shattered their morale and war fighting cohesion to such an extent that they could be swept aside by Coalition land forces in 100 hours with but a handful of friendly casualties. Air power's capacity had finally caught up with the promise of so many years.

However, in a little more than 12 months, exultation began to turn to frustration, as a very different operational environment began to evolve in the territory of the fractured state of Yugoslavia. In the Gulf, the 'enemy' had been clearly identified, the political objective was unambiguous and agreed among Coalition members; military objectives were defined and executed in a unified military command structure; the Coalition enjoyed considerable numerical and technological superiority in the air; the enemy ground forces were largely static and highly visible on terrain favourable to air attack; and the weather, despite unseasonable lapses, was generally favourable to air operations.

It is difficult to envisage more contrasting circumstances than those of Bosnia. For over three years there was constant disagreement among nominal Coalition partners about political objectives and strategy. While the Serbs were frequently identified as aggressors, only in 1995 was Coalition combat air power heavily and systematically applied against them. There were few formal ground force deployments, no recognisable 'front lines' and frequently little separation between belligerent formations and the surrounding civil population. Terrain was mountainous, inhibiting surveillance and reconnaissance, while the local topography provided cover for small mobile units.

It is impossible to forecast whether the unusual combination of circumstances which favoured air power in the Gulf will ever be repeated. In passing, it may be noted that the same circumspection is not always demonstrated by those who confidently forecast that the Bosnian experience is likely to be the model for 21st century conflict. It is equally possible that interstate conflict may arise in less favourable surroundings for air operations and fail to stimulate unanimous international response, while civil war may erupt in a region conducive to air power application towards objectives strongly supported by the international community.

Some circumstances, however, affecting the application of air power in peace support operations, are likely to remain constant. They have their roots in the strongly contrasting political considerations of the participants.

Political Considerations

There may be several reasons why a state or a supra-national organisation may wish to intervene in a civil war, but the objective is likely to differ considerably from intervention in a conflict between a government, however frail, and insurgents. In Afghanistan, Western support of the Mujahidin was intended to discomfit the USSR. In Vietnam, the situation had been the reverse. In OOTW, the objective of intervention is to stop the conflict and to bring the belligerents to the conference table. Intervening states may be concerned about the impact of the war on essential natural resources in the region or access to them. Without the escalatory constraint of superpower confrontation, there may be a risk of the civil war spreading across frontiers and stimulating regional conflict. Alternatively, instability may tempt intervention from a potentially hostile power which should be forestalled. A smaller state may wish to build up international credit by participating in a coalition. In the absence of any of these *raisons d'etat* there may be the pressure to 'do something' prompted by international media transmission of scenes of atrocities.

One factor is common to all these dispositions to intervene: the core security interests of the putative intervener are not at stake. Since the ending of superpower confrontation, the states from whom the intervening power would most likely be drawn have two levels of option: first, whether to intervene or not; and second, if so, then how far and for how long. From this basic assumption a number of sensitive political and military considerations flow which are likely to re-occur whenever peace support intervention is being considered. Some states may view international peacekeeping as a means to fund their armed services, but most western governments are seeking to reduce defence expenditure and intervention will inevitably interrupt that process. Consequently, the cheapest method will be attractive. Finite, preferably short duration, small-scale commitments will be preferred.

In democratic states, the absence of threat to core security interests leaves room for political opportunism. A government may be condemned for becoming involved, or for not becoming involved. It will be vulnerable to partisan politics if 'success' appears illusory, or if military mistakes are made, or if 'needless' casualties are incurred.

The media is likely to be influential, highlighting the horrors which stimulated the demand for intervention and then publicising any collateral damage or suffering inflicted by peace-supporting forces. Public opinion will itself be volatile, fluctuating between outrage at scenes of horror and concern at casualties among friendly forces incurred in trying to stop them.

Susceptibility to public opinion may induce governments to adopt ambivalent positions and to be disproportionately influenced by relatively small numbers of casualties, as in Somalia in 1993 after the mutilated bodies of 15 American servicemen in Mogadishu were shown on international television. From 1992 to 1995 the vulnerability of British troops in Bosnia to reprisals stimulated consistent British opposition to the use of offensive air power against recalcitrant Bosnian Serbs.

Every country will evaluate likely benefits and costs of intervention. In a coalition, consensus will be determined by the compounded caution of the entire group. There may be a common interest in inducing the belligerents to reach a peaceful settlement, but there may not be agreement on the extent of the commitment to be made or the price to be paid. As a result, the hesitation and disagreement between the US and European governments over the use of force in Bosnia may be repeated elsewhere.[1]

Conversely, the political considerations of the factions in a civil war are likely to stimulate very deep commitment to clearly defined objectives. Recent events suggest that the belligerents will be fighting over the remains of a fragmented or decaying political entity as in Rwanda, Somalia, Moldova or Bosnia. The conflict may have tribal, ethnic, ideological or cultural roots and it may have erupted spontaneously or it may have been stimulated by more cynical political opportunism. While their motivation may be deep and intangible however, the faction's objectives are likely to be territorial and political control. Their motivation and historical perspectives will stimulate hatred, fear and suspicion, leaving little room for compromise or conciliation. They are likely to equate security with territorial and political domination. The imminence or actual outbreak of civil war will signal their determination to achieve that security or aggrandisement by armed force. Throughout history, civil war has been characterised by brutality, destruction and intimidation frequently applied by formations lacking traditional military discipline, organisation or command and control structure. There is no reason to assume that such characteristics will disappear from future peace-support environments.

The belligerents do, however, share one major military weakness. They will have inherited the military resources of the original state, but without agreement and thereby with the shortcomings of arbitrary division. Military supplies, formations, command, control and logistic organisation will have been split. Air defence co-ordination is particularly likely to have been weakened by fragmentation. Arms factories might have been inherited; if so, their location will be well known. Both sides will have finite supplies of war stocks and spares, especially of heavy weapons, aircraft and armoured vehicles. Their locations, too, are likely to be well known.

As a result, both sides are likely to be dependent on external assistance to sustain any protracted military engagements. Both are likely to be particularly vulnerable to losses of stocks or interdiction of resources. Therefore, while the chosen instrument of factions is coercion, their ability to sustain it on a large scale, over a protracted period, may be in doubt. This vulnerability can be exploited by the intervening powers.

The Role of Force

While the factions are relying on force to achieve their political objectives in classical Clausewitzian mode, the use of force by the interventionists has a very different purpose, varying in application in different phases of peace support but sharing an underlying objective.

The application of intervening force is unlikely to elicit reconciliation between the belligerents or to impose a political settlement. It will be used concurrently with other inducements and diplomatic pressure to persuade the belligerents that they are likely to achieve a better outcome by negotiation than by force and that, once having reached a negotiated settlement, it is in their own interests to adhere to it.

Four categories of peace-support activities have been defined by the United Nations (UN).[2] They are:

1. *Preventative Diplomacy.* Action to prevent disputes from arising between parties, to prevent existing disputes from escalating into conflicts and to limit the spread of the latter when they occur.

2. *Peace Making.* Diplomatic action to bring hostile parties to negotiated agreement, essentially through peaceful means as those foreseen in Chapter VI of the Charter of the United Nations.

3. *Peace Keeping.* The development of UN presence in the field, hitherto with the consent of all the parties concerned, to implement or monitor arrangements relating to the control of conflicts and/or to protect humanitarian relief.

4. *Peace Enforcing.* May be needed when peaceful means fail. It consists of action under Chapter VII of the UN Charter, including the use of armed force, to maintain or restore international peace and security in situations where the Security Council has determined the existence of a threat to the peace, breach of the peace or act of aggression.

In all four activities, or phases, a distinctive feature is the fact that all the pressures and inducements are applied by a third party and, therefore, subject not only to the perceptions of the belligerent who is particularly being 'targeted' but also to those of his adversary. Yet this is an environment of deep-rooted mistrust, suspicion, subjective perceptions, reluctance to make concessions, unpredictable responses and local intransigence, even when the belligerent leadership has acquiesced in the peace process.

If force is to be included among the inducements, it is essential that it be applied impartially and with legitimate authority. Consent, however grudging and resentful, may be induced by force as well as by cajolery and promises of economic assistance. Impartiality does not imply equality of force against both belligerents when one is intransigent and the other is not.

The Potential of Air Power

Air power can contribute to all four phases of peace inducement. It is, in many respects, particularly suited to the complex political sensitivities of intervening powers and the vulnerabilities of belligerents.

Aircraft do not need to be deployed to disputed or turbulent territory to influence events within it. Operating from secure bases in the region, aircraft do not require extensive and vulnerable logistic links within the territory itself. Such deployment may be deterrent in nature, especially in the preventive diplomacy and peace making phases, or it may be to contribute to peace inducing coercive operations. If no airfields are available in the region, or if neighbouring states are hostile to the intervening powers, the ability to sustain any intervention, not just the application of air power, must be highly debatable.

Air power may be swiftly deployed and equally swiftly removed from a theatre, without the military and political penalties of the highly visible withdrawal of ground forces. Its operations may be concentrated in space and time, or intermittent: activated and suspended in cadence with diplomatic and other pressures in the peace building process. It may be held at various levels of readiness over long periods without the problems associated with sustaining ground forces during a cease-fire among a resentful population.

Most of the traditional roles of air power are relevant to peace inducement. Throughout the process, surveillance and reconnaissance will be essential: to disclose belligerents' intentions and capabilities to locate weapon, ammunition, fuel and other stocks; to identify supply routes or breaking of embargoes; to locate fortifications, command posts, road blocks and heavy weapons; to monitor treaty compliance and contravention; and to investigate, swiftly, claims or even rumours of atrocities.

All these tasks will be required whether ground forces are deployed or not. When friendly ground forces or other agencies are deployed, their effectiveness can be enhanced by the provision of tactical air mobility and reinforcement when roads are blocked or otherwise impassable. Belligerent forces can themselves be outflanked and enveloped from the air.

Just as there is a requirement for armed soldiers in all phases of peace inducement, so there will be a need for combat air power. Any residual belligerent air and surface-to-air assets will need to be neutralised, not so much because of their likely impact on the outcome of the civil war, but because of the disproportionate political effect on the intervening powers of even moderate aircraft losses, or of small hit-and-run indiscriminate bombing raids on friendly forces or opposing belligerents.

Reconnaissance and surveillance facilitate many forms of diplomacy and coercion; air mobility enhances the coercive capacity of ground forces; and air superiority enables a range of other activities to proceed without interference:

all contribute to the reduction of belligerents' ability to pursue their own objectives by force.

Air-to-surface attack, on the other hand, can directly reduce the military advantage held by a belligerent to a point where, not only is he incapable of imposing his will on a competitor, but he may actually be in danger of conceding the coercive advantage to him. Under such circumstances air power becomes a force equaliser.

Offensive air power can deny a belligerent the ability to concentrate his own ground forces or to move them confidently into excluded territory. Thereby, air power confers escalation dominance on the interveners.

Some targets will, however, be off-limits or unproductive. Snipers or light mortars operating from built-up areas, even if precisely located, are unlikely to be neutralised by air attack without civilian casualties and collateral damage. Attacks on social and economic infrastructure – power stations, oil refineries, industry etc. – will increase the discomfort of all concerned but will prolong and complicate economic reconstruction essential to cement the peace making process, without necessarily furthering it. They are just as likely to stiffen belligerent support as undermine it.

Similarly, while the character and intransigence of some belligerent leaders may tempt personal targeting, their violent removal is as likely to induce martyrdom as it is concessions. Discrediting them by military failure is likely to be more effective and permanent.

Overall, air power can, despite all the attendant environmental constraints, make a similar contribution to peace inducement as it did to DESERT STORM. It can reduce the number of ground troops required, thereby reducing the potential casualties, and it can deny the opposition, in this environment an intransigent belligerent, opportunity to pursue the ground force strategy of his choice. As in the Gulf, it capitalises on the technological advantages likely to be possessed by the intervening powers and on long-standing habits of operational co-operation and cultural affinity shared by many air forces.

Learning From Bosnia

Assertion of such potential for air power prompts a very obvious question: 'Why did it take so long to be effective in Bosnia?' In 1996, the Bosnian tragedy had not reached its last Act, but circumstances from 1992 to September 1995 already offered almost as many lessons about how not to apply armed force as did the earlier tragedy of Vietnam. The impact of air power for most of that period was largely a casualty to those circumstances. As usual, hindsight is a valuable attribute.

Croatia and Slovenia seceded from the former Yugoslavia in June 1991, followed in October by Bosnia Herzegovina. After an increasing spiral of ethnic brutality, bloodshed and destruction, the UN proposed, in December 1991, a peacekeeping force, mandated to oversee the demilitarisation of a number of protected areas and to separate warring Serb and Croat factions.[3]

By July 1992 14,000 foreign troops had been deployed, with Britain and France providing the largest contingents, but widely publicised atrocities and the interruption of humanitarian aid prompted increasing internal frustration and irritation. Twelve months after the outbreak of the crisis, the debate about the application of air power was begun by the American Secretary of Defense Richard Cheney, when he offered US fighters, close support aircraft and intelligence-gathering resources for the limited objectives of identifying and reacting to forces which were threatening or attacking the humanitarian relief effort.[4] Three weeks later a British opposition politician, Paddy Ashdown, moved closer to identifying a major role for air power when he called from Sarajevo for the airspace above the former Yugoslavia to be taken over by the UN with the mandate to bomb impartially any heavy weapons or tanks employed by either side. 'This would freeze the war at a lower level so that the people being attacked would have the chance to defend themselves with small arms. It should end the awful bombardments we are now seeing.'[5]

These straightforward proposals were quickly ensnared in the overall political and strategic confusion about the role of force in such an environment, with the further complications of misunderstanding, exaggeration and mistrust of air power.

Because there were insufficient United Nations Protection Force (UNPROFOR) ground troops to enforce their mandate to ensure the delivery of humanitarian relief, separate the warring factions and protect refugees, local UN commanders were heavily dependent on the consent of the belligerents to discharge their responsibilities. Worse, they became vulnerable to retaliation when air strikes were threatened or made. When the ground forces were originally dispatched, no thought appears to have been given to the consequences of failure, or to the possibility that their presence would ultimately inhibit execution of UN mandates rather than discharge them.

This fear of retaliation and the disruption of their humanitarian mission in the event of air strikes was to prove an enduring concern. In January 1993, British Defence Secretary Rifkind told a press conference that the role of British forces in Bosnia would continue to be 'the provision of humanitarian aid. . .'.[6] He subsequently asserted that 'our primary responsibility as the United Kingdom is obviously the safety of our own forces'.[7] In August that year, Foreign Secretary Hurd said that the 16 North Atlantic Treaty Organisation (NATO) countries had agreed to prepare plans for air strikes 'subject to arrangements for the UN to be involved so that our troops are not at risk. . .'[8] Lest there should have been any remaining doubt, Rifkind observed the following day from Bosnia, 'It remains essential to ensure that any new initiative by the UN is fully compatible with the physical safety of British and UN forces in Bosnia.'[9] Meanwhile, less senior Europeans were frequently and explicitly critical of US initiatives to launch air strikes when no US soldiers were deployed in the territory. 'The Americans need to do the sort of high-level visit to Bosnia Mr. Rifkind has just done,' said one British official, 'They might whistle a different tune.'[10]

Other concerns about retaliation may have been less well founded. Some argued that there were no 'appropriate targets' for punitive strikes, that collateral damage would be unavoidable and that minority communities would become the victims of retaliatory attacks.[11] Others were concerned that air attacks would not discriminate between the innocent and the guilty, while the aggressors would compound the difficulty by locating their heavy weapons 'in orphanages, hospitals, refugee centres and schools'.[12]

Both points of view were questionable. As events three years later were to illustrate, there were 'appropriate' targets, well away from risks of collateral damage. Attacks on heavy weapons would have been designed to neutralise their impact on specific areas; by compelling their withdrawal to civilian communities, the objective would have been achieved. Retaliation on minority communities could hardly have been worse than contemporary experiences and at least, as Ashdown argued, the communities had a better chance of defence if their opponents' strength was reduced.

At first, the doubts of the sceptics seemed well founded. The air exclusion zone established by UN Security Council Resolution 781 in October 1992 was given enforcement authority in March 1993. With the exception of one dramatic incident in February 1994 when four Bosnian Serb Super Galeb aircraft were shot down by US Air Force F-16s after attacking Bosnian targets, the air operations had little practical impact on events on the ground. Helicopter flying by all belligerents continued and as late as August 1995, Serbian aircraft attacked Croatian positions without loss.

After Serb aircraft attacked Bihac, a UN designated 'safe area,' in November 1994, 30 NATO aircraft attacked their base at Udbina. The single runway, SA-2 'Guideline' anti-aircraft missile and anti-aircraft gun emplacements were hit. At the request of UN officials to reduce the risk of casualties, no aircraft on the ground, their hardened shelters or their maintenance hangars were attacked. Mr. Akashi, UN special envoy in the former Yugoslavia, stated: 'This was a limited action, a proportionate and judicious reaction to a number of unacceptable offensive actions. But now is the time for all sides to show utmost restraint.'[13] NATO commander Admiral Leighton Smith also noted the limited nature of the attack – 80 guided and unguided bombs on runways and taxiways – and commented, 'It's fairly easy to fill up a hole in an airfield so I don't expect this one to be out of commission for an awfully long time.'[14]

The Serbs were unimpressed and undeterred by an attack which caused only minor inconvenience and had no impact on their campaign to overrun the 'safe enclave' of Bihac. Instead, they took 150 UN peacekeepers hostage and increased their humiliation and harassment of UNPROFOR units. Despairing comments echoed round the NATO alliance and UN hierarchy. NATO Secretary General Willy Claes said that the UN peacekeeping force was 'in an impossible position, unable to keep the peace and unable to enforce it'.[15] US Secretary of Defense William Perry observed:

> The Serbs are in control of Bihac. NATO air strikes can punish the Serbs but they cannot determine the outcome of ground combat. It would take 100,000 troops with heavy weapons even to enforce the peace. To affect the outcome of the war, to win the war, would take several hundred thousand troops with heavy weapons, undoubtedly involving significant casualties.[16]

The thinking of such clear-sighted men was in a rut: the situation was impossible; but apparently only overwhelming ground forces could resolve it; yet such a commitment was too expensive, too risky and, by implication, politically out of the question. Nor was the object 'to win the war'.

Within days the situation had deteriorated still further. 'Top level negotiations between the UN and the Serbs, that once focused on peace settlements or aid to civilians, now centre on getting food and fuel past Serb check points to increasingly desperate peacekeepers.'[17] Specific pressure on the UN Bangladeshi battalion in Bihac was described by a UN spokesman as 'a deliberately designed, carefully calculated insult against the United Nations which can only be allowed to pass at great cost'.[18]

Yet there was little prospect of relief by NATO air strikes. The tortuous 'dual key' command and control structure with responsibilities for authorisation and despatch divided between UN and NATO commanders was being unscrambled only with great difficulty.[19] Inevitably, responses to calls for offensive air support from beleaguered UNPROFOR units was seldom productive. The difficulty was compounded, even after UN authority for such attacks had been given, by stringent roles of engagement laid down in early 1994 by General Sir Michael Rose, commander of the UN forces in Bosnia:

> In each case [offensive air action] can be carried out only against a unit deemed responsible for the initial aggression; the NATO response must be proportionate to the original force, and reports from the ground must be verified from the air or vice versa before an attack could be launched.[20]

166

On one occasion, in March 1994, when French troops requested air attack on Serbian artillery, several hours delay ensued, with the result that the guns had withdrawn when the aircraft arrived.[21] On another, rapid response placed NATO aircraft overhead Serbian tanks, but because it was not possible to verify that they were the specific ones responsible for an attack, they were allowed to withdraw unscathed. In August, four US OA-10 Thunderbolt IIs, six Dutch F-16 Fighting Falcons, four French Mirage F1-CTs, four UK Jaguar GR-1As, one US EA-6B Prowler, one US EC-130F Hercules, two E-3 Sentry airborne warning and control aircraft (AWACS), one unidentified ELINT aircraft and several tankers were involved in action against Bosnian Serb positions. Two OA-10s destroyed one self-propelled gun; no other targets were engaged because of bad visibility and the strict rules of engagement.[22]

The chain of command was, indeed, unwieldy, involving UN civilians, UN ground force commanders and UN operational staff. The rules of engagement were tight. But they were all determined by the political circumstances of the environment and, as long as they pertained, offensive close air support would continue to be ineffective. Air power's primary attributes of speedy response and technological advantage could not be exploited to inhibit Serbian fire power.

Some NATO commanders had favoured a 'more robust response' to Serbian violations rather than 'hitting one tank in the middle of a field', as expressed by one commander in chief.[23] The successes of DESERT STORM were still recent and the temptation to translate procedures and strategies to the Balkans was strong. The vulnerability of the Serb electrical network to non-lethal weapons was noted, with the subsequent impact on oil and gas pumping stations, food preservation and processing, transportation, water and sewage.[24] Others argued for the direct targeting of the Bosnian Serb leadership.[25] But the UN principle of 'Proportionate Response' and the constant fear of retaliation still prevailed at the end of 1994.

Moreover, the UN Security Council consensus was threatened by Russian opposition to increased air strikes while Hungary, hitherto supporting the Operation DENY FLIGHT food resupply operation by providing base access to E-3 AWACS aircraft, had threatened to withdraw it should air attacks be made. Such withdrawal would have had little operational impact, but would have illustrated the sensitivities of the peace-supporting mission to legitimization by international consensus. Overall, military logic was at odds with the political environment. Notably, it was not just air power that was at odds, but all military force.

In early 1995, the harassment of UN forces continued, even prompting considerations in Europe about their withdrawal.[26] In March, during heavy Serbian pressure on the 'safe area' of Gorazde, British patrols were attacked twice and the local Serb commander told a UN liaison officer that he did not want UN peacekeepers in the area; his men were deliberately aiming at the patrol, and would not cease fire. NATO aircraft were overhead for much of the four-hour engagement, but were not summoned to attack the Serb positions. When asked why the NATO aircraft had not been tasked to destroy weapons which were violating the Coalition's exclusion zone around Gorazde and firing on UN troops, the UN military spokesman stated that 'the UN's policy was not to escalate such incidents'.[27]

Ceasefire agreements collapsed as Bosnians, Serbs and Croats increased their military activities in several areas of the disputed territory. A warning in March 1995, issued by the new British commander of UN forces in Bosnia, Lieutenant General Rupert Smith – 'Attacks which come from outside a safe area and which deliberately target civilians will meet a resolute response from us including the use of air power' – went unheeded; not surprisingly in view of the numberless previous unsubstantiated threats.[28]

In April and early May, fighting intensified,[29] culminating in Serbian shelling of Bihac and Sarajevo. When the Serbs failed to meet another UN deadline to withdraw heavy weapons, NATO aircraft, for the first time, were freed from the constraints of previous rules of engagement and, instead of striking the offending weaponry, hit Bosnian Serb ammunition bunkers near Pale. This attack was to be the turning point in the peace inducement process. For the first time, the air strike had not been 'proportionate'. It hit the weakest point in the Serbs' coercive strategy: their finite war stocks. The versatility, reach and precision of air power had finally been exploited without civilian casualties or collateral damage. The damaging potential of the attack was realised immediately by the Bosnian Serbs, who swiftly and indiscriminately retaliated by shelling Sarajevo, Bihac, Gorazde, Srebrenica and Tuzla, inflicting heavy civilian casualties and taking 300 UN troops hostage as human shields against further air attacks.

The international response was illuminating and probably relevant to future peace inducement operations. The air attack was widely seen as counter-productive, producing exactly the disastrous results forecast by many policy-makers and analysts. The reason for the violence of the Serbian response was scarcely remarked upon, nor were the longer-term implications for the Bosnian Serb leadership of breaking Geneva Conventions on the treatment of prisoners of war. They would have been well pleased with a 'Commentary' in the London *Times* under the heading 'Disaster Lurks in West's Folly of Macho Vengeance', which unreservedly blamed 'those who ordered air strikes . . . for the deaths of dozens of young people in Tuzla when the Serbs retaliated, and for the subsequent fate of the UN hostages'.[30] The international media broadcast pictures of UN soldiers apparently chained to weapon stores' gate posts and interviewed tearful wives, mothers and sweethearts. 'Pictures of the chained peacekeepers have evoked desperation and pity', wrote the same commentator, 'but what if the Bosnian Serbs televise executions? Nobody should doubt they would do this, or something similarly gruesome, if attacked again.'

Contemporary decisions by the British and French governments to increase their troop contributions to UNPROFOR, dire warnings to the Serbs of retribution should the hostages be harmed, proposals by the UN Secretary General 'to consolidate peacekeepers into more defensible positions',[31] and a NATO decision to establish a Rapid Reaction Force did not have the same media appeal. Consequently, the real significance of both the air attack and the beginnings of a revised UN posture were submerged amidst confused and dismayed public opinion.

Nor did subsequent events inspire much confidence in the creation of a more forceful and coherent UN – NATO strategy. The loss of a single USAF F-16 aircraft (fortunately its pilot was subsequently rescued) on 2 June to a SA-6 'Gainful' surface-to-air missile prompted a withdrawal of NATO combat air patrols out of SAM range and at the same time reopened European criticisms of US political over-sensitivity to even the most negligible casualties. Srebrenica and Zepa fell to Serbian forces, accompanied by refugee reports of large-scale massacres of the defending population. The Dutch battalion in Srebrenica called for, and was given, close air support against Serbian armour but a third air strike was cancelled at the request of the Dutch Defence Minister after '[The Serbs] threatened to shoot dead the 30 Dutch soldiers they are holding hostage and to raze the Dutch battalion's headquarters to the ground'.[32] Operation DETERMINED EFFORT, the NATO contingency plan to withdraw UNPROFOR, seemed close to implementation in early July.

In London on 21 July, however, NATO foreign ministers agreed to launch intensive air strikes against the Bosnian Serbs if they threatened to attack a further 'safe area' at Gorazde. In the following week the 'dual key' command chain was simplified by the removal of the civilian Mr Akashi from it, leaving authorisation in the hands of UN General Bernard Janvier, General Smith and their NATO counterparts. Reports from Brussels suggested that air strike targets would not be proportionate but would include munition stores, command and control units, roads and bridges.

Meanwhile the Croatian and Bosnian Muslim armies, reorganised and re-equipped despite official embargoes, began to exert pressure on the Serbs at several critical points in West and East Bosnia, forcing the Serbian forces to draw down more heavily on their military resources and become more dependent on reinforcement and re-supply. British and French ground forces used heavily reinforced fire power to counter Serbian pressure near Sarajevo. Other UN troops were withdrawing to secure positions reducing their vulnerability to

169

retaliation and hostage taking.

On 27 August, US Assistant Secretary of State Richard Holbrooke applied direct diplomatic pressure on the Bosnian Serbs to cease their obstruction to a peace settlement: 'If this peace process does not get dramatically moving in the next week or two, the consequences will be very adverse to the Serbian side. One way or the other NATO will be heavily involved and the Serbs do not want that.' Asked to clarify if NATO was prepared to launch bombing raids beyond anything seen before against Bosnian Serb positions, he replied, 'That is a fair inference to draw, but it is part of a larger package.'[33] Here for the first time was an explicit threat of air power not to retaliate or defend, but to coerce a belligerent to the negotiating table.

Following the NATO Council meeting on 25 July, a press statement amplifying the alliance's determination to apply 'timely and effective' air power to defend Gorazde had noted that, 'There is a strong feeling among allies that such operations, once they are started, will not lightly be discontinued.'[34] The following week, Bihac, Tuzla and Sarajevo were explicitly added to the list: 'As is the case already with Gorazde, our planning will ensure that military preparations which are judged to represent a direct threat to UN Safe Areas or direct attacks upon them will be met with the firm and rapid response of NATO's air power.'[35]

On 28 August a mortar shell, apparently fired from Bosnian Serb positions, exploded in a Sarajevo market place killing 37 civilians and injuring many more. The scenes of carnage were given international media cover. Two days later, NATO air power was finally unleashed in Operation DELIBERATE FORCE.

In less than 24 hours, 90 Bosnian Serb targets were struck, including command bunkers, radar and control centres, munitions and ammunition storage depots.[36] The purpose of the air strikes, and accompanying artillery attacks, was spelled out. In addition to demands for Serbian heavy weapons to be withdrawn from around Sarajevo, for no further attacks on safe areas and complete freedom of movement of UN personnel, NATO Secretary General Claes expressed the hope that this action 'will also demonstrate to the Bosnian Serbs the futility of further military action'.[37]

Attacks were suspended between 2–4 September to await a Bosnian Serb response, while diplomatic negotiations with the Serbian government continued. In the face of a defiant Bosnian Serb leadership, air attacks recommenced on 5 September. The targets included roads and bridges whose destruction impaired Bosnian Serb resistance to Croatian and Muslim pressure. Finally, after attack sorties by NATO strike aircraft and the launch of 13 Tomahawk cruise missiles, the Bosnian Serb leadership accepted the UN ultimatum. The air offensive was halted on 14 September and on 21 September was indefinitely suspended, but with a warning of resumption if any agreement should be breached. A total of slightly over 3,500 NATO sorties, approximately 20 per cent of them attack, had been flown between 30 August and 16 September.[38]

The 16 September edition of *The Economist* went to press before the bombing campaign was completed on the 14th. Its leading article began, 'NATO's aerial onslaught on the Bosnian Serbs does not seem to be working', and continued with very pessimistic speculation on possible outcomes.[39] Similar sentiments were shared by other European media. The expectations from air power in 14 days, after three years of ground force impotence, were interesting to say the least. Extracts from the following week's edition of that prestigious international journal must have made satisfying reading for air force commanders everywhere:

> The combination of western air power and Croat-Muslim ground forces has confounded the sceptics. . . [presumably including the previous week's *Economist* leader writer!] The NATO air strikes have also had an impact on the rout of the Bosnian Serbs in the northwest of the country. . . damaged the morale of an overstretched, war weary army. . . . General Mladic, the symbol of Bosnian Serb defiance, remained in a Belgrade hospital apparently with kidney problems while his troops retreated. . . . Remarkably, neither the NATO air strikes nor the Croat-Muslim ground offensive seems to have diminished the desire of all parties for peace. [40]

Spasmodic conflict continued until a formal ceasefire came into effect on 12 October. On 21 November the peace accords were agreed. Temporarily, at least, the belligerents had been induced to accept a negotiated settlement rather than pursue their objectives by force. Undoubtedly a major factor in the Bosnian Serb decision was the realisation that not only had NATO air power removed their military advantage, but that its impact was threatening to tip the military balance heavily in favour of their opponents.

Bosnian Lessons

Caution must always be applied when drawing lessons from one arena to project forward to others, but several may be confidently drawn from the Bosnian morass. The differences between the strategic environments of DESERT STORM and Bosnia were well understood. Conversely, the similarities between principles for the use of armed force in traditional conflict and in peace support operations were not.

Among the principles which were overlooked were: the need for a clearly defined objective; the need to provide adequate military force for the tasks allocated including escalation dominance; the need to decide what kind of force was likely to be needed; the need to ask, 'What if that doesn't work?', before any action was taken; the need to establish a single chain of command; the need for constant and timely reconnaissance and surveillance; and the need to retain the military initiative.

The impact of these omissions was compounded by three other principles believed to be intrinsic to peace support operations: proportionate force, impartiality and consent. The first denied the Alliance the opportunity to exploit superior force, the second failed to distinguish between different degrees of intransigence among belligerents and the third conferred an advantage to the side which exacted the highest price for consent.

In the end, a combination of pressures brought the Bosnian Serbs to the conference table: resurgent and threatening Croatian-Bosnian ground forces; heavy diplomatic pressure and sanctions; increased Allied artillery fire in the critical area of Mount Igman; and the 'disproportionate' impact of Allied air power.

However, one has only to speculate on the outcome if any one of those pressures had not been applied to see that air power was the catalyst which threatened to destroy Bosnian Serb ambitions so quickly that further procrastination was impossible. Concentration of force; versatility and depth in targeting; destruction of instruments of power; exploitation of technological superiority; weapon precision; minimal casualties and collateral damage; greatly reduced requirements for ground forces (4,000 troops of the UK Air Mobile Brigade, although now available, were not employed); and a sense of powerlessness among the Bosnian Serbs: the circumstances had been very different from those of the Gulf War, but the impact of air power was very similar.

There is, however, no point in chafing over 'lost time' before NATO air power was unleashed in 1995. Similar circumstances may again arise in which political considerations constrain the use of combat air power. As in Bosnia the circumstances must be changed, or the comparative ineffectiveness of air power should be acknowledged. It would, however, be a dereliction of political and military responsibility to allow circumstances to evolve again which then induced constraints. Air power's potential contribution to peace inducement intervention should be identified at the outset, before any other forces are committed.

HUMANITARIAN OPERATIONS

Air power has much to contribute to humanitarian operations in war-torn or benign environments. In the former it is virtually impossible to disassociate humanitarian relief from the perception that one side or the other is being strengthened. There is, indeed, no guarantee that such relief will reach its 'legitimate' destination of civilian sufferers.

UNPROFOR's task was severely complicated by conflicting humanitarian and coercive priorities. The only air force fatalities in Bosnia were an Italian transport crew lost on a humanitarian mission when their Fiat G222 was shot down by a missile. Subsequent humanitarian relief flights into Sarajevo were frequently threatened or attacked but the local UN commander was loath to invoke air-to-surface retaliation for fear of even greater disruption of the relief task. Unified command of all activities would have determined priorities but would not have removed the potential for misunderstanding or hostage vulnerability.

In a benign environment, a natural disaster may prove beyond the capacity of the responsible government. Earthquakes and flooding are sadly familiar, providing opportunities for swiftly responsive delivery of medical supplies, food, shelter and mobile communications. Such operations, frequently in circumstances which provide realistic training for aircraft crews, provide opportunities for political credit, international good will and public approbation which should be grasped willingly by air forces which may have fewer opportunities to demonstrate their value and professional competence. Indeed, military skills, combat awareness, the need for protection and unqualified willingness to enter threatening environments will remain prerequisites for the discharge of the full range of humanitarian tasks.

All applications of air power should be 'political' in the sense of supporting a political objective, and humanitarian operations should not be regarded as somehow inferior. Perhaps the most significant single contribution of air power to the Cold War was the Berlin Airlift of the late 1940s. Protected by fighters and backed by the deployment of nuclear-capable bombers, it changed the fate of Europe and the course of the Cold War without a shot being fired.

CONSTABULARY OPERATIONS

Throughout the world, air power is being used more and more for constabulary tasks against piracy, smuggling, illegal fishing and other criminal activities. Airborne surveillance and reconnaissance can facilitate the interception of aircraft and ships plying illegal trade. (For example, one US Navy Grumman E-2C Hawkeye airborne early warning squadron, VAW-122, was directly credited by American law enforcement authorities with interdicting 14 metric tons of cocaine and two tons of marijuana over the course of 1,247 sorties flown over the Caribbean and South America.)[41] Drug crops and processing plants can be identified and destroyed from the air. More controversially, palatial residences, boats and other highly visible material benefits from illegal profit, beyond the reach or inclination of local law enforcement, could become vulnerable to aerial destruction. In campaigns against piracy, surveillance and

173

identification of home ports could precede precise destruction of boats and harbour facilities when local authorities have proved ineffectual.

Such activities would not stop international crime but they would disrupt the market flow and depress the material benefits accruing from it. They would, in some circumstances, raise delicate questions of sovereignty but would introduce sanctions commensurate with the scale and brutality of the illegal activities themselves.

CONCLUSIONS

Peace inducing, humanitarian and constabulary actions are not cost free nor can they alone justify the existence of a national air force. That must be based on its contribution to core security and the protection of vital interests.

Air power does, however, possess two advantages over other forms of military power. First, much of the equipment required for high intensity 21st Century air operations are also appropriate for OOTW. Surveillance, reconnaissance, all-weather multi-mode target identification, precision munitions, air superiority, defence suppression, self-defence and airlift will be required in most operational environments.

Second, with the one major exception of training, procedures, command, control, and communications (C3), and infrastructure may be readily adapted to various scales of commitment. If the principle is generally adopted that air power may, under many different circumstances, shape a combat environment and reduce the risks of friendly ground force casualties, the inherent versatility of air power can be exploited still further.

The 'exception' contains a hidden cost. OOTW missions may be flown in addition to traditional peacetime training and exercises for major conflict, in which case aircraft fatigue life, engines and spares are consumed more rapidly. Either peacetime aircrew and ground crew manning levels must be increased, or workloads must be expanded, risking overstretch and dissatisfaction. If OOTW were to replace peacetime training, quantifiable costs may be contained, but combat air crew are unlikely to be prepared for the intensity and attrition of conflict between peers conducted in the dense fog of electronic warfare. There may also be a temptation to reduce priorities in the procurement of advanced platforms, weapons and systems.

There is an uncomfortable precedent of an air force preoccupied with low intensity operations in a period between major wars. In the 1920s and '30s the Royal Air Force made a very significant contribution to 'Imperial Policing', sustaining its independence in a period of international uncertainty and defence resource restraints. In doing so, it failed to prepare or equip for modern large-scale warfare until the eleventh hour, with tragic results in the early years of the Second World War.

Exploitation of Versatility

The contribution of air power in the widely different circumstances of the Gulf War of 1990–91 and the Bosnian tragedy of 1992–95 demonstrated its enormous versatility and potential for the international uncertainties of the 21st Century. OOTW may not be accorded the same political enthusiasm after the Bosnian experience as in the heady days of 'the new world order', but they are likely to re-occur in the spectrum of conflicts where coercion is required to protect interests or sustain diplomacy. Air power which is deemed only relevant when national security itself is threatened is unlikely to retain either public respect or fiscal support.

On the contrary, politicians, the general public and the other armed services must constantly be reminded of its attractions and utility as a primary, highly versatile instrument which can, in many circumstances, reduce the risks and costs of large-scale surface force commitment. 'In many circumstances'; not in all. It is up to air power advocates to persuade political masters of their instrument's versatility, not to seek to shape political circumstances to make it fit. Usually they will be able to make a very strong case.

NOTES

1   For a concise but comprehensive analysis of the difficulties faced by the United Nations Protection Force from 1992–96 see 'Post Mortem on UNPROFOR' by Richard Caplan, London Defence Studies Paper Number 33, Brassey's for the Centre for Defence Studies, 1996.

2   Report by the Secretary General, 'Improving the Capacity of the UN for Peace Keeping', dated 14 March 1994.

3   UN Doc S/23280, 11 December 1991 Annex III, cited in Caplan *op cit.* p. 3.

4   London *Daily Telegraph*, 10 July 1992

5   London *Daily Telegraph*, 4 August 1992

6   UK Secretary of State for Defence Rifkind, London, 14 January 1993. Press conference transcript.

7   *Ibid.*

8   BBC Radio interview, 3 August 1993, reported in London *Daily Telegraph*, 4 August 1993.

9   London *Daily Telegraph*, 5 August 1995.

[10]   *Ibid.*

[11]   e.g. Professor Lawrence Freedman, London *Independent*, 5 August 1992.

[12]   Unnamed 'British government official', London *Independent, ibid.*

[13]   London *Daily Telegraph*, 22 November 1994.

[14]   London *Times*, 22 November 1994.

[15]   London *Times*, 28 November 1994.

[16]   *Ibid.*

[17]   London *Times*, 6 December 1994.

[18]   *Ibid.*

[19]   For a detailed analysis of the command and control problems see the author's *Air Power: A Centennial Appraisal* (London: Brassey's, 1994) pp. 168–181.

[20]   UNPROFOR spokesman, London *Times*, 14 March 1994.

[21]   *Jane's Defence Weekly*, 26 March 1994.

[22]   *Jane's Defence Weekly*, 3 September 1994.

[23]   Admiral Leighton Smith, CINC Allied Forces Southern Europe, *Jane's Defence Weekly*, 15 October 1994.

[24]   Warren Piper, assessor of war damage in Iraq, *Aviation Week and Space Technology*, 17 August 1992.

[25]   US sources quoted in London *Daily Telegraph*, 5 August 1993.

[26]   James Gow, *The World Today,* RIIA London, July 1995 p. 127.

[27]   London *Times*, 17 March 1995.

[28]   London *Guardian*, 28 March 1995.

[29]   For a concise chronology of the accelerating events in the theatre during 1995, see *Strategic Survey* 1995/96 (London: IISS), pp. 241–246.

[30]   Misha Glenny, London *Times*, 30 May 1995.

[31]   London *Times*, 30 May 1995.

[32]   London *Times*, 12 July 1995.

[33]   NBC TV 'Meet the Press', 27 August 1995, as reported in the London *Times*, 28 August 1995.

34   Press statement on Gorazde by NATO Secretary General Willy Claes following North Atlantic Council Meeting on 25 July 1995 as reprinted in *NATO Review*, September 1995, p. 7.

35   Press statement on other safe areas by Secretary General following North Atlantic Council Meeting on 1 Aug 1995, *ibid.*

36   London *Daily Telegraph*, 1 September 1995.

37   London *Times*, 31 August 1995.

38   *Aviation Week and Space Technology*, 25 September 1995.

39   *Economist*, 16 September 1995, p. 47.

40   *Economist*, 23 September 1995, p. 47.

41   Commander Will Dossel, 'The History of VAW-122: Sunset for the Steeljaws', *The Hook*, XXIV, 2 (Summer 1996), p. 33.

7

'YOU'LL REMEMBER THE QUALITY LONG AFTER YOU'VE FORGOTTEN THE COST': STRUCTURING AIR POWER FOR THE SMALL AIR FORCE

by

Alan Stephens

HISTORIAN, ROYAL AUSTRALIAN
AIR FORCE AIR POWER STUDIES CENTRE

F or over half a century air power has been the decisive expression of military force for the liberal democracies, even though many analysts have been reluctant either to recognise or acknowledge that fact. Air operations in general and offensive action in particular have been *the* capability which has given allied military forces a war-winning advantage in major conflicts. When that advantage has been used forcefully and with resolute political support the desired result has invariably been achieved, the Second World War, the Six-Day and Yom Kippur Wars and the Gulf War being prime examples.[1] When those essential conditions have not been observed, failure or at best an uneasy stalemate has resulted, with Korea and Vietnam illustrating the point.

It will be a major challenge for air forces to maintain that decisive edge during the present period of extraordinarily rapid technological, geostrategic and managerial change. For example, the two countries which more than any other have underwritten air power's combat dominance, the United States and the United Kingdom, are both subjecting their defence forces to severe budgetary cuts. Similar large reductions are being applied to other leading air forces, such as those of France, Australia and Canada. And at the same time there is a broad consensus amongst senior officials that the greatest threat to nation states will not be major conflict with other states, as has generally been the case for the past 350 years, but rather terrorism and the proliferation of weapons of mass destruction.[2] It is debatable whether the 'traditional' model of air power will be best suited to meet those kinds of non-traditional threats.

More than ever before, therefore, there is an imperative for defence officials to structure their forces precisely; to spend their defence dollars on the air power capabilities their country needs rather than those their air force might like. Of all the arts of the defence bureaucracy, none is more arcane or more subject to personal bias than force structuring. It would be a strange admiral, general or air marshal who did not want capital ships, divisions or bombers respectively. But such preferences have never been a legitimate force structure determinant (although they have been immensely influential), and they are even less so now.

In attempting to provide clear guidance on the basic considerations for structuring a small air force, this essay starts by reviewing the politics of air power and the key doctrinal issues. Against that essential background it then examines two diametrically opposed force structure methodologies.

THE POLITICS OF AIR POWER

The French couturier Pierre Cardin reportedly dismissed criticisms that his fashions were too expensive with the response, 'You'll remember the quality long after you've forgotten the cost.' Cardin's attitude could equally serve as the guiding principle for those airmen responsible for force structuring. The aphorism that 'quantity has a quality all of its own' applies to armies, not air forces.

In a modern air force, 'mass' (in the context of force application), or 'striking power', or 'combat effectiveness', or whatever term one may wish to use to describe the desired outcome of an offensive action – namely, applying the right amount of force at the right place at the right time – is more a function of quality than of sheer numbers. The first conspicuous demonstration of this air power truism took place over the Western Front in November 1915. On the ground, where massive armies had become bogged down in a ghastly stalemate, tactically moribund generals sought to break out of the morass by pouring in more men and applying more firepower. They were almost invariably unsuccessful. By contrast, in the air, the emergence of one high-quality fighter, the Fokker Eindecker, suddenly and dramatically swung the advantage to the Germans. A highly manoeuvrable monoplane, the Eindecker had a singular ability to sustain long, almost vertical dives. Its great strength, though, was its status as the first warplane fitted with an effectively synchronised forward-firing gun. So superior was Germany's new fighter that, until the Royal Flying Corps was able to fit its own aircraft with similar guns, British and Commonwealth pilots were instructed to engage in combat only under highly favourable conditions.[3] It was the quality of the Eindecker, not the numbers involved, which was the decisive factor.

More recent demonstrations of the dominance of quality over quantity in the war in the air include the Six-Day War of June 1967, when the numerically inferior but qualitatively overwhelmingly superior Israeli Air Force effectively destroyed its Arab opponents in four hours; and the Gulf War of 1991 when, through the medium of superbly led, trained and equipped American forces, Coalition airmen swept aside large and ostensibly powerful Iraqi air defences in several days and with scarcely any losses.[4] Also worthy of mention is the IAF's astonishing victory over the Syrian Air Force in the Bekaa Valley in June 1982, when at least 80 Syrian aircraft were destroyed for the loss of one Israeli fighter.[5]

Sorry examples of the adverse consequences of trying to substitute quantity for quality are not confined to the Middle East. China's People's Liberation Army Air Force is a case in point. Immensely strong on paper with more than 4,000 fighters and bombers, the PLAAF nevertheless 'does not constitute a credible offensive threat against the United States or its Asian allies' and nor will it for at least ten years, despite a current modernisation programme.[6] Using the Six-Day and Gulf Wars as guidelines, the huge but poorly trained, badly led and largely obsolescent PLAAF would certainly suffer the same fate as the Egyptians, Syrians and Iraqis if China's leaders decided to pit their low quality air power against a smaller but first-class opponent.

After quality, 'size' is the second issue which warrants comment here, given that this is an essay about structuring 'small' air forces. Like everything else, the size of an air force is relative. In this instance the benchmark for relativity is the United States Air Force. The fact is, there are now two kinds of air force in the world: the USAF and everyone else. The material, technological and qualitative superiority of the USAF (and its Navy, Army and Marine adjuncts) is simply overwhelming. No other nation or combination of nations comes close to matching the quality of the USAF's platforms, weapons, people and training and technological base. Those fundamental elements of air power translate into a range and variety of capabilities – air supremacy, strike, airlift, reach, sustainment and so on – which in sum constitute a dominant force. Of all the world's air forces, only those of the United States could realistically plan to apply air power globally in all its forms.

The point here is that in relative terms the USAF is 'big' and every other air force is 'small'. Yet even the USAF is subject to troublesome constraints, as the debate during 1995–96 over the Service's ability – or lack thereof – to fight two major conflicts simultaneously demonstrated. In other words, to some extent the caveat 'small' applied to this essay is irrelevant. All air forces operate under constraints, and identifying, accommodating and working within those constraints is one of the main tasks of force structure planners, an issue which is addressed later in this chapter.

There are also significant external pressures which planners must accommodate. Like land and sea power, air power must remain responsive to a range of influences from the wider civil and military communities which will affect the translation of ideas into combat power.

National security policy is the most senior external influence. It may not always be a straightforward matter to identify a national policy, as in all probability it will be contained in a number of major speeches or statements made by different senior officials. Nevertheless, a hierarchy of policy guidance and direction to which force structure planning must respond does exist. As far as security policy is concerned, a nation's defence, foreign affairs and economic postures are the most important. There are clear force structure implications, for example, for the air service of a nation which has endorsed the Nuclear Non-Proliferation Treaty. A similar but more complex example for the future might involve national attitudes towards the Missile Technology Control Regime.

Economic constraints comprise the second external force. The Asia-Pacific region provides a useful case study. Despite generally increasing levels of expenditure, no air force in the region has the full range of air power capabilities. The Royal Australian Air Force, for example, has been one of the region's best equipped, best trained and most experienced air forces for decades, but remains to this day without such vital capabilities as operational air-to-air refuelling, airborne early warning and control platforms and advanced air-to-ground missiles. The absence of those capabilities has nothing to do with the RAAF's force structure preferences and everything to do with constrained budgets. Similar observations could be made about the region's numerically strongest air forces, those of India and China. It is manifestly clear that financial constraints determine the shape of air forces just as much as does any force structuring preference.

A third major external force which can bear on the order of battle is the pressure to support local industries.[7] This is usually a two-edged sword, as the RAAF experience again illustrates. Achieving and maintaining a qualitative edge is an imperative of Australian air power doctrine. In terms of hardware, that imperative has been expressed through such leading-edge platforms as the General Dynamics F-111 Aardvark, McDonnell-Douglas F/A-18 Hornet, Lockheed AP-3C Orion and Lockheed C-130J Hercules. Less satisfactory have been the attempts to support the local industry by designing and producing indigenous aircraft, ranging from the mediocre Boomerang fighter and ill-conceived Woomera strike/reconnaissance bomber of the Second World War, through to the disappointing Nomad light transport and failed Wamira trainer of more recent years. The fact is that, for over 60 years the RAAF has been disadvantaged by having to accept, under government pressure, locally produced equipment that has been either inferior to its foreign-built competitors or uncompetitively expensive. The imperative at work has not been the demands of a rational force structure, but rather the political reality of local jobs. Current examples of that imperative at work include India's Light Combat Aircraft, Japan's FS-2 fighter and Taiwan's Ching-Kuo Indigenous Defensive Fighter.

The consequences of having to support indigenous industries need not necessarily, however, be all negative. An invaluable spin-off from local production is the ability to modify combat systems in-country at short notice to meet prevailing circumstances. Few better examples can be found than that of the (British) Royal Air Force during the Falklands War of 1982 when, faced with enormous distances from the home base in the United Kingdom to the battlefield in the South Atlantic, aircraft like the Hercules transport and Nimrod maritime patrol aircraft were modified for air-to-air refuelling within weeks. Similarly, the existence of a sound local aerospace industrial base has enabled the RAAF to modify many of its strike/fighter aircraft to carry an exceptionally wide range of weapons, a valuable capability for a small airforce. Thus, when planning a force structure, it may be preferable to accept slightly inferior locally-produced support aircraft (for example, basic trainers and light transports) in order to develop and sustain the industrial capacity to modify front-line weapons systems.

The fourth and final significant external pressure which impacts on force structuring, and which is sometimes unspoken but is nevertheless very real, is inter-Service rivalry. Air power entered the combat arena explicitly subordinated to armies and navies. Notwithstanding clear evidence from the First World War of the importance of control of the air and the potential of strategic strike, that dependent relationship continued for decades. Despite stunning demonstrations of the impact of air power on the battlefield—consider, for example, Normandy in 1944, the USAF and the RAAF along the Pusan Perimeter in 1950, LINEBACKER II in December 1972, the Coalition in the Gulf in 1991 and NATO in Bosnia in August/September 1995—many surface commanders still seem unwilling to acknowledge the equal place in the military family of Douhet's 'Third Brother'.[8]

It is a considerable irony that, while insisting on the ultimate 'superiority' of surface forces in general and armies in particular, those same commanders are, according to one analyst, currently spending some 60 per cent of their budgets on air power-related systems such as fixed- and rotary-wing 'ground support' aircraft, unmanned aerial vehicles, cruise and ballistic missiles, and aerial surveillance and navigation platforms.[9] The issue is and will remain a difficult one for airmen. To illustrate the dimensions of the problem by reference to Australian doctrinal principles, RAAF airmen maintain that their nation's air power should be unified and commanded at the highest practicable level by a single, experienced commander with expertise in the application of air power.[10] In fact, the Australian Army and Navy both maintain substantial (and growing) air arms, with the Army likely to operate more aircraft than the RAAF inside the next decade. Nor is this situation limited to small air forces. Indeed, the United States Army already has more aircraft than the world's most powerful air force, the USAF.[11]

The challenge this poses for independent air forces is both real and escalating. Specifically, as defence forces increasingly focus on operations at the lower end of the combat spectrum (those resulting from internal disorder, terrorism, drug trafficking, resource disputes, organised crime, illegal immigration and so on), force structure decisions – that is, who gets what – are likely to favour helicopters and light attack aircraft over the 'traditional' air power systems of air superiority fighters and strategic bombers.

AIR POWER DOCTRINE, ROLES AND MISSIONS

Against the background of those general considerations (which in most cases will tend to inhibit rather than encourage an ideal force structure), and before turning to the central question of force structure methodologies, it is necessary to identify the kinds of tasks an air force might have to undertake. It will almost certainly be the case that most nations will neither need nor want the full range of air power capabilities. Individual priorities will be determined by individual circumstances. Nevertheless, unless a planned force structure is tested against a comprehensive doctrinal model, its designers may not fully appreciate the strengths and, just as importantly, the weaknesses of their product.

The combination of theory and practical experience which comprises doctrine suggests that there are five main roles for the application of air power. The first four are directly concerned with warfighting activities, while the fifth provides the essential support base upon which air power rests. Those roles are:

- Theatre Control;
- Strategic Strike;
- Force Application;
- Force Multiplication; and
- Force Support.

Each of those roles is implemented by conducting one or more of a number of air power missions.

Theatre Control

Since the First World War many air forces have listed the ability to 'control the air'–that is, to secure the freedom to conduct air operations while denying the enemy that capability – as the 'prime' air activity. But as the Coalition air forces demonstrated through their stunning dominance of the entire battlespace during the Gulf War, that definition has become too restrictive. Limiting the 'control' function of air forces to only one element of the combat environment – the air – is inconsistent with the capabilities of modern air power and is therefore doctrinally incomplete. Any description of an air force's 'control' role should encompass the full extent of what is possible, not merely part of what is possible. The fact is that, in the right circumstances, for more than half a century, air forces have been (and are) just as capable of controlling the land and the sea as they are of controlling the air. That vital capability perhaps tends to be overlooked because of the emphasis doctrine has placed on air control.

Consequently, a much broader description of that role than simply 'control of the air' is necessary. The term 'theatre control' most accurately describes an air force's 'control' capability over the modern battlefield. The use of 'theatre' instead of, say, 'battlespace' (a term which implies almost infinite size and which incorporates space) recognises the constraints of size: the USAF is the only air force which could realistically expect to establish 'battlespace' control. Theatre control is a wide-ranging role containing three subsets:

- Air Control;
- Surface Control (including sub-surface control); and
- Information Control.

Depending on circumstances and the overall campaign plan, the three subsets of theatre control could be prosecuted separately or in parallel, or they could be ignored. However, experience has shown that control of the surface is unlikely to be achieved without first gaining control of the air. The timing of information control missions is less certain at this early stage of the phenomenon of 'information warfare', but it may well prove to be the case in future that the need to establish some degree of information control will precede the other control roles.

Air Control: In most circumstances air control will remain an air force's prime task. One or a number of missions can be conducted to achieve air control: offensive counter air; defensive counter air; suppression of enemy air defences; and so on. It is probable that surface forces will contribute to the air control role through special force missions (to sabotage enemy air defences etc.), radar picket ships and the like. At the least, the involvement of surface forces will be essential for such enabling missions as air base defence and logistic support.

Surface Control: Instances where air forces have dominated the movement of surface and sub-surface forces abound: Bosnia in September 1995, the Gulf in 1991, the Falklands in 1982 and the Battle of the Atlantic after 1944 are only a few. At a time when joint operations are being increasingly recognised as the preferred method of prosecuting a campaign, it is incumbent upon airmen to remind their army and navy colleagues of the full range of possibilities their Service brings to the planning process.

Information Control: Acknowledging the importance of information to warfare is scarcely original. What is new, however, is the ability of many military forces rapidly to gather, process, analyse and exploit information, to the extent that 'information dominance' must now be regarded as a distinct and crucial military activity; as a potent weapon and a lucrative target. The driver for this phenomenon has been the extraordinary advances made in the last 20 years in the technical means of collecting, storing, transmitting and analysing information.

By itself, that technical revolution might be worthless; it is only when the capability is reflected in doctrine that it acquires military significance. Information warfare has three objectives: to attack, exploit and defend information. Currently the priority for technologically developed states must be on defence. The world's sole remaining military superpower, the United States, is vastly more vulnerable to assaults on its information systems than are Third World states, for whom information attacks may be of little consequence.

Strategic Strike

The single quality which above all others has distinguished air forces since the First World War has been air power's ability to strike directly against an enemy's instruments of power, be they leadership, oil, electricity or whatever: that is, to conduct strategic strikes. Notwithstanding the advent of surface- and sub-surface launched cruise and ballistic missiles, long-range aircraft equipped with precision missiles remain the pre-eminent expression of strategic strike.

Force Application

Force application deals with the application of combat air power for purposes other than the theatre control and strategic strike roles. Missions which force application might incorporate include battlefield interdiction, close air support, anti-shipping strikes, anti-submarine warfare and reconnaissance.

Force Multiplication

The RAF's first chief of staff, Sir Hugh Trenchard, may not have been familiar with the term 'force multiplication' but he understood its meaning: 'to expand the effectiveness of man and machine without increasing the numbers of either; in that way lies economy'.[12] Force multiplication can be achieved through the exploitation of such air power capabilities as air-to-air refuelling, superior command and control systems, multi-role aircraft, electronic support measures and better personnel practices.

Force Support

Force support is the essential base upon which all other air roles depend, and is concerned with activities like logistics, recruiting, training, research and development, and air base defence. No matter how good the aircrew, the aircraft and the weapons systems, it is unlikely that an air force without a high quality support organisation will succeed. As is the case with other air roles, there is no reason why land and sea forces should not be employed to conduct this action, an important consideration in an environment of constrained resources.

* * *

To return to the observation made previously by most air forces would not be able to satisfy this idealised doctrinal model. For example, there would be little sense in the air force of Guinea-Bissau, with its fleet of four 1950s-vintage MiG fighters, aspiring to the role of 'Theatre Control'. The Canadian Forces provide another good example, but one starting from a different logic. For many years Canadian airmen have been able to omit specific capabilities from their order of battle because of the certainty that any direct air threat to Canada would be viewed in Washington as a direct threat to the United States, thus drawing a response from the USAF. The point is, before a force structure is planned, its authors must clearly understand which roles are essential to their purposes, just as they must appreciate which roles they will be excluding.

STRUCTURING AN AIR FORCE

There are two basic and diametrically opposed methodologies for structuring any air force, small or large. The first involves shaping the force to meet a specific threat, while the second is intended to develop a force in a 'threat-free' or 'threat-ambiguous' environment. Each of those contrasting methodologies is examined in detail below.

However, before proceeding with that examination, brief mention should be made of two other possible approaches to force planning, one utilising weapons of mass destruction and the other the concept of a 'balanced' air force.

The intellectually least-demanding response to the considerable challenge of force structuring would be to invest in weapons of mass destruction; to

187

place all of one's security eggs in the deterrence basket. If a country's threat assessments strongly indicated that the greatest danger to national security came from other nation-states which could not accept the risk of massive counter-value strikes, then weapons of mass destruction might not be a bad option. The acquisition by a small nation of, say, 20 nuclear warheads would generate a powerful deterrent effect which no rational aggressor could ignore. Further, that small nation might then decide that, on the balance of risk probabilities, it could dispense with most of the components of a conventionally armed and traditionally structured air force, thus saving a great deal of money.

The problems, however, are significant. First, there is the difficulty of acquiring both warheads and delivery platforms (noting that the latter need not be aircraft). Second, no matter how awesome the weapons concerned, deterrence simply cannot guarantee security. The threat of retaliation may not be enough to deter terrorists or irrational groups, while it is not hard to envisage circumstances in which responding to aggression with the use of weapons of mass destruction would be unacceptable or inappropriate, or both.

The so-called 'balanced' approach to force structuring also brings with it considerable difficulties. For almost 50 years the concept provided the doctrinal foundations of the Royal Air Force and, by association, its Commonwealth protégés. The idea was, quite simply, that an air force should be structured to conduct the full range of air power roles; namely, theatre control, strategic strike, force application, force multiplication and force support.[13] In a sense the concept was threat-ambiguous, for if properly applied it meant the 'balanced' air force would be capable of confronting any kind of defence contingency immediately. The question, though, was how well?

At the time the methodology was developed conflicts were often drawn-out, as in the case of the Second World War, the Malayan Emergency and the Korean War. Thus, factories had time to gear up and increase production of the most-needed types of aircraft, just as the training system was able to increase the output of bomber pilots, fighter pilots, or whichever specialisation the nature of the conflict demanded. To some extent, therefore, the concept of a 'balanced' air force relied on aerospace technologies which were suited to quick production times and brief training courses. Consequently, the evolution of more complex technologies with their concomitant longer production and training times created problems. Additionally, by trying to do a little bit of everything instead of concentrating on one or two vital roles, an air force runs the risk of becoming a 'jack of all trades and master of none', of becoming an organisation that can prosecute many roles poorly instead of a few very well. In the modern era air wars tend to be fast and furious; that is, they are fought on a 'come as you are' basis, with no time for the mass industrial and personnel mobilisation of the past. The 'balanced' approach to force planning, with its inherent delay in reaching the optimum warfighting structure, thus represents a high risk approach.

Nor does the concept have general relevance. It is unlikely, for example, that the air force of a land-locked country like Switzerland would need too much in the way of an air/sea warfare capability. Similarly, few countries have ever possessed a strike force capable of delivering enormous firepower over long distances. In general, and especially during peacetime, air forces have been structured to meet their nation's most pressing security needs, within the political constraints outlined earlier in this chapter.[14]

FORCE-STRUCTURING METHODOLOGIES

The two most useful force-structuring methodologies are based on *threat-specific* and *threat-ambiguous* planning respectively. The former is a relatively straightforward process, the latter is complex. In both cases, however, the start point is the same, namely, a rigorous analysis of prevailing strategic circumstances, including geography, economy, population, infrastructure, internal political factors, alliances and, of course, threat assessments.

Threat-Specific Planning

There are few better examples of threat-specific force structure planning than the Israeli Air Force prior to the 1967 Six-Day War. The threat was crystal-clear: nothing less than the destruction of the Israeli nation by armed force. Also crystal-clear was the source of the threat: the surrounding Arab states, especially Egypt and Syria.

Geography and demography largely determined the way in which the IAF had to be structured to fight for national survival. Israel is a very small country, measuring only 370 kilometres from north to south and as little as 14 kilometres across. In 1967 Israel's population was 2.5 million, compared to the 52 million of its most immediate enemies. Land borders were shared with Egypt, Syria, Jordan and Lebanon, the first three of which were overtly hostile to Israel's existence. A jet bomber could fly from Cairo to Tel Aviv in 35 minutes, from Suez to Tel Aviv in 20 minutes, and from Damascus to Haifa in nine minutes. Invading armies similarly could reach key population and government centres in a matter of hours.

Egypt and Syria maintained ostensibly powerful land and air forces and, in the event of a war, could reasonably expect substantial reinforcements from Jordan and Iraq. In broad figures the Arab forces amounted to about 750 combat aircraft, 1,650 tanks and 300,000 troops, against which the Israelis could field 320 combat aircraft, 800 tanks and 264,000 troops.[15]

Lacking strategic depth and dangerously outnumbered, the Israelis made two key planning decisions. First, it was clear that they needed to fight over

189

enemy territory, not their own. Second, they had to take the initiative and seek a rapid victory to deny other Arab states the time to mobilise against them. Control of the air thus became a *sine qua non* of their campaign plan. Air power alone offered the speed of action, strategic reach and striking power which could both eliminate the possibility of Arab attacks on Israeli population centres and seize the initiative from the outset, leaving enemy forces vulnerable to strikes from the sky.

The Israeli Air Force was structured precisely to achieve that objective. It consisted predominantly of jet fighter/ground attack and light bomber aircraft which could be used either for pre-emptive raids to win the air war on the ground by destroying the Arabs' aircraft on the ramps; or, failing that, for a classic 'dogfight' campaign to gain control of the air. Flexibility was an important consideration as most aircraft had to be able to change quickly from one role to another: for example, from air defence to ground attack, depending on the state of the battle. In contrast to its large number of strike/fighter aircraft, the IAF contained relatively few airlifters as, given the short distances to Israel's borders and the open, flat terrain, land forces could move to trouble spots almost as quickly by truck and armoured personnel carrier as they could by air. For similar geostrategic reasons, the IAF had placed few resources into other air 'support' capabilities such as maritime patrol and rotary-wing transport.

That rational assessment of operational priorities was complemented by an emphasis on quality. The IAF was an élite organisation, well-trained, aggressive and confident. Its strike/fighter aircraft, mostly French, represented leading-edge technology.[16] The contrast with their well-equipped (with Soviet aircraft) but operationally and doctrinally inept enemies was stark.

It is a matter of record that, when the theory behind the IAF's force structure had to be transformed into action, the Israeli airmen all but destroyed their prime threat, the Egyptian Air Force, on the ground in some three hours. Subsequently they gave the same treatment to the Syrian and Jordanian Air Forces in less than half an hour. Having achieved the first objective of the classic air campaign, the IAF was then free to pursue the other two: interdiction of the enemy army's resupply system, followed by close support for ground forces. The IAF's prosecution of those two objectives was no less devastating than that of the first.

While many factors contributed to what was probably the most stunning air campaign in history to that time, it is clear that the IAF was ideally structured to confront the specific threat to the Israeli nation.

Thirty years later the IAF continues to apply the same sensible methodology to its force structuring deliberations. Notwithstanding changes to some territorial boundaries since 1967, the nature of Israel's security problem remains the same. Thus, the three critical imperatives of achieving control of the air, of fighting over the enemy's territory and of being able to mount powerful strike operations, preferably pre-emptively, continue to drive the process. Two points are particularly noteworthy. First, the IAF is now equipped primarily with American weapons systems, including two of the best strike-fighters in the world, the McDonnell Douglas F-15 Eagle and the Lockheed Martin F-16 Fighting Falcon. Whether or not those American aircraft are superior to their Russian equivalents in the hands of competent operators is debatable, but they are unquestionably superior to the contemporary fighters of Israel's previous major supplier, France. Second, additions to the IAF's order of battle since 1967 include air-to-air refuelling and airborne early warning and control aircraft, perhaps the two most significant force multipliers to emerge in recent years. In other words, the IAF has continued to complement its highly successful threat-specific force structuring process with an unwavering commitment to quality.

As noted earlier, structuring to meet a specific threat and/or adversary should be a relatively straightforward task, at least compared to shaping a force in a threat-ambiguous environment. Nevertheless, many nations have failed abysmally to prepare their air forces logically for clear and present danger: for example, the United Kingdom, the United States and their allies prior to the Second World War; and indeed those Arab states which have sought Israel's demise for nearly 50 years. The point here is that, for the reasons outlined at the start of this chapter, force structuring is a difficult and complex business, almost invariably riven by political, economic and personal biases. It is never easy.

Before turning to the intellectually most challenging situation – that is, where there is no obvious threat – the experience of the Republic of Singapore Air Force provides a worthwhile case study as the RSAF's approach to force structuring falls half-way between the 'threat-specific' and 'threat-ambiguous' models. On the one hand, Singapore is not subject to the kind of overt hostility that exists between, say, Greece and Turkey, North and South Korea, and India and Pakistan. On the other hand, Singaporeans are highly sensitive to their position as an economically extraordinarily successful nation which, lacking both natural resources and a large domestic market, has built its wealth almost entirely on intellectual capital. They are also keenly aware that they are a small, predominantly Chinese society bordered by large, less-developed Islamic nations (Indonesia and Malaysia) with an historical distrust of expatriate Chinese communities. Finally, Singapore has almost no strategic depth – a jet fighter can cross the island from north to south in only three minutes and from east to west in a few seconds more.

Consequently, Singapore's leaders have worked assiduously to ameliorate their perceived vulnerability by developing an air force which sends a powerful message to any potential aggressor. Specifically, the RSAF is designed in the first instance for pre-emptive strikes, to be conducted as far away from the city-state as possible. If pre-emption is precluded, offensive (as opposed to defensive) operations, again at the maximum distance from Singapore, are clearly the RSAF's preferred option.

The RSAF was established as an independent Service in 1968. From almost the first day its commanders have concentrated above all else on building a formidable, high quality strike force, a process which is neither quick nor easy. After four years the RSAF comprised only 500 people with 48 combat aircraft, primarily obsolescent fighter/ground attack (FGA) aircraft and armed trainers. But the foundations for the future were being laid as the RSAF drew on some of the world's best air forces, including those of the United States, Australia and Israel, for training, equipment, advice and support.

By 1987 the RSAF had expanded to 6,000 people and 180 combat aircraft. Today the cutting edge of the RSAF is its four FGA squadrons armed with McDonnell Douglas A-4S/S-1 Skyhawks and F-16s. Air defence is provided by two squadrons of lightweight Northrop F-5 Tigers while strategic reach has been added with airborne early warning and air-to-air refuelling aircraft. The 'Super' Skyhawks represent a particularly interesting capability. Modified in-country by Singapore Technologies Aerospace (STA), the aircraft have been fitted with upgraded weapons and navigation systems and a newer General Electric F404 engine in place of the original J85. The end result is a formidable strike platform which belies the A-4's apparent age. It is also noteworthy that the RSAF's F-5s were the first in the world to return to squadron service after receiving an extensive cockpit upgrade, again completed in-country by STA. The ethos of quality has been extended to the indigenous infrastructure. It has also been extended to fast-jet pilots, who are paid far more than other RSAF aircrew in an attempt to keep them from joining a civil airline.[17]

There is no doubt that the general (as opposed to specific) threat posed by the RSAF is well-understood throughout the region, not least by the Malaysians, with whom Singapore has had an ambivalent relationship. Nor is there any doubt that the RSAF is capable of performing the task for which it has been structured.

It could be argued that the Singaporeans have eased their planning problems by, in effect, concocting a threat where none exists. Nevertheless, the threat they perceive is real enough to them, and in that context their response has been logical. And in purely military terms it is also credible.

Threat-Ambiguous Planning:

Force structure planning becomes most difficult when it is not possible even to concoct a threat. Britain's Royal Air Force illustrates the point. Unquestionably one of the world's premier air forces, for decades the RAF was structured primarily to fight as a member of NATO against the Eastern bloc. Because NATO's strategy rested on defeating the immensely powerful Soviet Army on the plains of Germany, the RAF gradually acquired the form – and perhaps the mentality – of a tactical rather than a strategic air force. The transfer of the United Kingdom's nuclear deterrent role from the RAF to the Royal Navy in 1969 perhaps added to the RAF's predisposition to limit its strategic outlook.

In the circumstances that may have been understandable. However, following the collapse of the Soviet Union and the Warsaw Pact, the RAF found itself doctrinally exposed and, therefore, vulnerable. After decades of preparing their Service materially and mentally to meet a specific threat essentially as a tactical player, the RAF's leaders suddenly found their certainty of outlook had evaporated. Subsequent operations in Bosnia in 1995–96 may have provided the RAF with temporary relief from its identity crisis, but sooner or later the Service will have to confront two fundamental questions: What is its purpose? And does it have a strategic future? The RAF's hierarchy doubtless draw cold comfort from the knowledge that they are in good company as a number of other European air forces also search for an identity in an environment which has suddenly become 'threat-free'.

The leaders of those air forces could do worse than examine the Australian experience of defence planning in threat-free, or at least threat-ambiguous, circumstances. That happy situation has been Australia's lot for more than two decades now, from the time it first became apparent that the numerous communist insurgencies which had shaped Asian security attitudes since the end of the Second World War did not represent a genuine threat either to the liberal democracies or to most of the emerging states of South-East Asia. Having spent 30 years structuring their Services to fight as an expeditionary force alongside Western allies in some distant land, in the mid-1970s Australian defence strategists had to confront the intellectually uncomfortable truth that there was no immediate physical threat to their country. [18]

After a good deal of uncertainty, two key planning judgements were eventually made. The most important was that the core business of the Australian Defence Force was (and remains) the direct defence of Australian territory. That judgement is not as self-evident as it may seem. In some parts of the world, notably the South Pacific, the idea of armed attacks by one state against another with the intention of subverting sovereignty is so remote as almost to seem incredible. (Nor indeed is it very credible in relation to many countries closer to the globe's strategic heartland.) Nevertheless, it is a fact that, at the end of the 20th Century, international relations and national security assessments are, like economics, a dismal science, characterised by uncertainty and rapid change. It may well be the case that in about 15 years nations will feel sufficiently confident not to worry about their territorial integrity, noting, however, that a very high level of confidence is likely to be demanded by voters before any kind of unilateral disarmament is endorsed. In the meantime, determining the core business of the defence forces is the essential first step in force structuring. Where that core business is defined as the defence of sovereignty, it must not be allowed to blind decision-makers to other national responsibilities such as regional co-operation and support for United Nations activities. It must however assume superseding importance.

Decision-makers who conclude that protecting national sovereignty is *not* the core business of their defence forces should, before proceeding any further, reconsider their need for an air force, and think instead about coast guards and the like, with which they can still conduct policing tasks but at a fraction of the cost of a military service.

Having defined the defence force's core business, the second key step is to test that business against the nation's enduring strategic characteristics of geography, economy, population and infrastructure. In Australia's case it seems almost blindingly obvious that the country is an island continent surrounded – and therefore protected by – an air/sea gap; and that it has a medium-sized economy, a small population and a limited infrastructure. The strategic implications of those characteristics were not, however, obvious to those Australian planners who for years believed their country could not be defended without British or American help. Japanese planners who examined the problem less emotionally reached a different conclusion. When staff officers at the Imperial General Headquarters in Tokyo did their sums in the Second World War, they found that they would need 12 divisions and 'more shipping than Japan could provide' to cross the air/sea gap and make a lodgement in Australia.[19] In other words, the effort was enormous, primarily because the air/ sea gap was a formidable barrier which would not be excessively difficult to defend independently. Yet it has only been in the past 20 years that the independent defence of the air/sea gap has become central to Australian defence strategy.

Two points should be made at this stage. First, cases of the seemingly blindingly obvious are not always so. Consequently, defence planning needs to proceed on a basis of rigour and process rather than intuition, bias, visceral fear and the like. Second, the methodology being outlined here is general, not specific. The idea is to structure the defence forces to maximise one's enduring comparative advantages. A comparison of Switzerland and Australia illustrates the point. The Swiss, who also define their core defence business as the protection of national territory, exploit their land-locked, mountainous terrain by maintaining a huge citizen-based army which would literally take to the hills to make any attempted invasion so difficult and potentially costly as to be irrational.[20] Australia, by contrast, has given priority to the surveillance, reconnaissance, air superiority and strike forces needed to mount operations in its air/sea gap, to the extent that it is now recognised as having the most potent maritime strike force in the Asia-Pacific region. Although using the same approach, Australia and Switzerland have arrived at two fundamentally different national defence strategies, the one naturally favouring defensive land forces and the other offensive air power. Each strategy is suitable for its particular circumstances.

It may of course be the case that for economic reasons a particular country's leaders will decide that their nation cannot be defended independently against a major external threat; or they may decide that internal pressures constitute the greatest danger to their regime. If they are rational they will shape their air force accordingly, in the first instance perhaps by trying to bolster their security through alliances; and in the second by giving priority to counter-insurgency capabilities such as fixed- and rotary-wing tactical transport and close air support aircraft. Regardless of individual circumstances, the defence strategy should be based on an assessment of core business and enduring strategic circumstances.

Once those judgements have been made the question becomes one of defining systems, numbers and preparedness of states.[21] To use the example of Australia again: What is the best way to defend a large air/sea gap? How many platforms/weapons systems/people will be needed to provide an acceptable level of confidence on the one hand and to deter potential aggressors on the other? How long will various rates of effort have to be sustained? How much money should be spent bringing and keeping those forces up to the appropriate level of preparedness? Those questions are germane to force structure planning in any country, with due alteration of detail.

Three key concepts have been developed by Australian defence analysts to help generate informed answers to those questions. Those concepts are: warning time and defence preparation time; the nature of credible military contingencies; and the role of the expansion base.[22]

Warning time is the most contentious of those concepts. A 'threat' is generally regarded as having three components: motive, intent and military capabilities. The first two are notoriously hard to measure. The motivation for one country to attack another may or may not be apparent; while the intention to attack is likely to be even more obscure, as events such as Pearl Harbor, the start of the Six-Day War and Iraq's invasion of Kuwait have demonstrated. Military capabilities, however, can be measured fairly accurately. The fact that the countries which possess those capabilities may have no hostile motives or intentions whatsoever is, under this methodology, effectively irrelevant. The only 'credible' defence contingencies are those based on *existing* military capabilities (rather than ethereal motives and intentions) within the relevant geographic area of strategic interest. By focusing on existing capabilities, so the argument goes, defence planners should be able to determine the force structure they themselves will need both to counter those generic capabilities and to prosecute their own defence strategy. The corollary of basing a force structure on existing regional capabilities is that a 'threat' which is not supported by the right capabilities is not credible.

Clearly, military capabilities can change through the acquisition of new weapons, or better training, and so on. It is a fundamental assumption of the threat-ambiguous methodology that any significant change in regional capabilities will be detected in sufficient time for the appropriate force structure adjustments to be made, an assumption which indicates the prime importance of comprehensive, high quality surveillance and intelligence services.[23] The reliance on warning time also assumes that substantial military capabilities cannot be acquired so quickly that an appropriate response is not possible.

Some analysts find the assumptions relating to warning time troubling. For example, there have been occasions when dramatic increases in capabilities have occurred undetected, as when Saudi Arabia obtained approximately 30 Chinese CSS-2 Intermediate Range Ballistic Missiles in 1988. By any standards ballistic missiles with a 3,000-kilometre range represent a major offensive capability, with the potential to disturb prevailing regional balances and stability. Because the acquisition of the CSS-2s did not require any of the in-country development and testing which reconnaissance systems look for and generally detect, the missiles were discovered by the United States only after they had arrived in Saudi Arabia; that is, too late for any preventive action to be taken.[24] Similarly, following the reunification of Germany, NATO security planners were startled to discover that some East German army units held stockpiles of supplies, including weapons, three times greater than those reported by Western intelligence.

However, there have not been any disturbing revelations of that kind in recent years in relation to major capabilities such as aircraft, ships, divisions and armour. On balance, given the open nature of the international arms market since the collapse of the Soviet Union and the increasing effectiveness of commercially available global surveillance systems, the use of warning time as a key concept for force structuring, as it applies to conventional weapons and conventional threats, is valid.

So much for warning time and 'credible' contingencies. The final variable planners must factor into their deliberations is the size and role of the expansion base. Here again the issue is one of quality, defined in terms of operational preparedness. In ideal circumstances a nation's standing air force will have been structured to meet credible contingencies, no more, no less. Should, however, threat assessments indicate a deteriorating security outlook, the standing force may have to be strengthened, which is where the size and shape of the expansion base comes in. Do we want to maintain a highly-trained reserve force, ready to supplement the regulars at a moment's notice, an approach which will be comparatively expensive; or do we, for the same money, want a larger but less-ready reserve? General threat assessments (including warning time) and finances will drive the answer.

A final caution, which derives from the same kinds of pressures applying to the size and role of the expansion base, must be sounded. In the Yom Kippur War of 1973 and the Falklands War of 1982, the IAF and the RAF – two of the best air forces in the world – were critically dependent on the United States, particularly for intelligence and resupplies of advanced weapons. It would seem that, given the furious pace of modern conventional war, no matter how good the force structure, any 'small' air force without a powerful mentor is likely to find itself in serious trouble.

CONCLUDING THOUGHTS

In broad terms, either of two diametrically opposed methodologies can be used to shape an air force. Those methodologies have general relevance, but the end result of applying one or the other will be determined by individual geostrategic circumstances. For example, in the case of the Israeli Air Force, which was used in this chapter to illustrate the threat-specific model, its commanders have built an air force which is especially proficient in air-to-air combat and offensive strike operations. Those are precisely the kinds of capabilities one would expect in an air force defending a country with little strategic depth and bordered by states overtly hostile to its existence. By contrast, charged with defending an island continent located in a threat-ambiguous environment, the Royal Australian Air Force has structured itself as the Asia-Pacific region's most potent maritime strike force. Again, that posture, which is based on existing, generic regional capabilities rather than any specific threat, is appropriate to the prevailing strategic circumstances.

Regardless of which approach is used, there must be an uncompromising emphasis on quality. Military strategy is an art. While its practitioners must be comprehensively informed by specific knowledge (orders of battle, platform capabilities, weapons effects and so on), in the final analysis a commander's decisions will rest on subjective judgements. The single best means of reducing the risks associated with such judgements is to provide commanders with high quality forces. Nowhere does that axiom have greater application than in the war in the air.

'Quality' by itself may represent a dubious investment if it is not related to a particular purpose. But when it is superimposed on the kinds of rational methodologies described in this chapter, it will provide air force leaders with the force structure best suited to meet their solemn national defence responsibilities.

NOTES

1   The effect of the combined bomber offensive against Germany has been a controversial subject, a situation largely attributable to selective reading of the United States Strategic Bombing Survey. That survey in fact concluded that the offensive made an important contribution to Germany's defeat, but many commentators, for presumably subjective reasons, have preferred to remember only John Kenneth Galbraith's extraordinary statement that the allied bombing somehow accelerated German war production. Recent, more intelligent assessments of what was by 1944 a devastating campaign include Richard Overy's *Why the Allies Won* (London: Jonathan Cape, 1995), pp.123–133.

2   See Paul Mann, 'Mass Weapons Threat Deepens Worldwide', in *Aviation Week & Space Technology*, 17 June 1996, pp.58–9.

3   'Instructions Issued by Headquarters Royal Flying Corps, 14th January 1916', in Alan Stephens and Brendan O'Loghlin (eds), *The Decisive Factor* (Canberra: Australian Government Publishing Service, 1990), p.167.

4   See Richard P Hallion, *Storm Over Iraq* (Washington: Smithsonian Institution Press, 1992), esp. pp.201–240.

5   It seems probable that Syrian losses amounted to at least 86 and possibly even 100 aircraft. See MJ Armitage and RA Mason, *Air Power in the Nuclear Age* (Urbana and Chicago: University of Illinois Press, 1985), p.139.

6   See Kenneth W Allen, Glenn Krumel and Jonathan D Pollack, *China's Air Force Enters the 21st Century*, (Santa Monica: RAND, 1995). The approximate number of 4,000 aircraft was in 1994. That total is expected to decrease over the next decade as modernisation is effected.

7   For an excellent analysis of the challenges associated with maintaining an indigenous aerospace industry in a small economy, see Air Commodore Neil Smith, 'An Industrial Strategy in Support of Fighter Aircraft for Industrially Developing Nations', *Air Power Studies Centre Paper No. 41*, February 1996.

8   Writing in 1919, Giulio Douhet claimed that it was time for 'the army and navy [to] recognize in the air force the birth of a third brother – younger

but nonetheless important in the great military family'.

9   Colonel Phillip S Meilinger, quoted in Group Captain John Harvey, 'Maritime Air Operations', Presentation to the Royal Australian Navy Sea Power Conference, Sydney, 1995. The figure of 60 per cent includes space systems.

10 Royal Australian Air Force, *The Air Power Manual* (2nd ed) (Canberra: APSC, 1994) p.44.

11 The Australian Army currently has 152 aircraft compared to the RAAF's 284, but while the RAAF's fleet is reducing the Army's helicopter numbers are growing. The US Army operates 7,761 aircraft (mostly helicopters) against the USAF's 7,126. All figures come from *Aviation Week & Space Technology*, 8 January 1996, pp.179 & 193. (Note that *AW&ST* double-counted the Australian Army's light observation helicopters, listing them once as Bell 206s and again as OH-58s.)

12 Sir Hugh Trenchard, quoted in Air Vice-Marshal R A Mason, 'Current Air Power Developments', in Desmond Ball (ed), *Air Power: Global Developments and Australian Perspectives* (Rushcutters Bay: Pergamon-Brassey's, 1988), p.62.

13 See RAF, AP1300, *Operations* (4th ed), Air Ministry, 1957. *Operations* was the successor to the RAF's 'War Manual', which was first published in July 1928 when Sir Hugh Trenchard was still chief of the air staff.

14 See pp. 206–7 above.

15 These figures come from Peter Young, *The Israeli Campaign 1967* (London: William Kimber, 1967), pp.42–57. They do not include the 20 combat aircraft and 30,000 troops from Saudi Arabia which in the event played almost no part in the war but had to be factored in to Israeli planning.

16 The IAF was equipped primarily with French Mirage, Mystère, Super-Mystère, Vautour and Ouragan strike/fighter aircraft.

17 Experienced RSAF strike/fighter pilots are paid at about the same rate as an international airline Boeing 747 captain.

18 Although as a member of the Western alliance Australia was theoretically still exposed to the threat of the Soviet Union's nuclear arsenal, that apocalyptic contingency was not a factor in force structure considerations. Like most members of the alliance, Australia rejected ownership of nuclear weapons by becoming a signatory to the Nuclear Non-Proliferation Treaty, relying instead on the shelter of the American nuclear umbrella.

19 John Robertson, *Australia at War 1939-1945* (Melbourne: William Heinemann, 1981), p.104.

20 Switzerland's army, which is based predominantly on a militia, comprises 363,800 personnel on mobilisation. Also indicative of the defence strategy is the fact that the Air Corps is an integral part of the army, ie, it is not independent. *The Military Balance 1995-1996*, (London: IISS, 1995), p.99.

21 Preparedness for military operations is the sum of 'readiness' (eg, quality of equipment, standard of training, etc.) and 'sustainability' (ie, how long the operations can be continued at various rates of effort).

22 For a detailed account of this process see Paul Dibb, *The Conceptual Basis of Australia's Defence Planning and Force Structure Development* (Canberra: Strategic and Defence Studies Centre, 1992). See also Thomas-Durrell Young, *Threat-ambiguous Defense Planning: The Australian Experience*, Strategic Studies Institute, US Army War College, 1993.

23 See Dibb, *op. cit.*, pp.1–8.

24 Jeffrey T Richelson, 'US Space Reconnaissance After the War', a paper presented at the conference *Australia and Space*, Strategic and Defence Studies Centre, Canberra, 1991, p.20.

8

THE NEW CALCULUS: THE FUTURE OF AIR POWER IN LIGHT OF ITS GROWING QUALITATIVE EDGE

by
Frederick L Frostic
FORMER DEPUTY ASSISTANT SECRETARY OF DEFENSE
(REQUIREMENTS AND PLANS), WASHINGTON, DC

T here is a new calculus in military affairs, in the roles that air power can – and will – play in the future security environment. This shift is the product of an evolutionary revolution brought about by the merging of new operational concepts, fielded capabilities and technological opportunities. The changes have amounted to a significant step forward which has taken place against the backdrop of the demise of the Soviet Union and the Warsaw Pact, and the regional instabilities that have followed this profound transformation of the international security environment. Because so many important changes have occurred simultaneously, it is difficult to fully recognise and appreciate both the magnitude of these changes and the impact that they can have in the future if planners and defence leaders are made aware and remain cognisant of them. Briefly stated, a unique combination of capabilities and opportunities have coincided to make it possible for air power to fulfil the role that many airman have dreamed about for years and perhaps, equally important, to open a path to new missions and expanding roles. Examining what might be possible in the future is best undertaken by looking at some of the capabilities of air power demonstrated since the end of the Cold War and the collapse of the Soviet system. More precisely, it is profitable to explore the new concepts and possibilities for the application of air power in the next century against the backdrop of both experience – the missions that have been accomplished and demonstrated since that 40-year stand-off – and the opportunities offered by rapidly advancing and available technologies.

The watershed in thinking about air power and its impact on military affairs was, undeniably, Operation DESERT STORM. It constituted a veritable showcase of air power in action; those who followed the war even casually are still mesmerised by the picture of laser-guided bombs going down the air shaft of the Iraqi air defence headquarters building, the burning hulks of vehicles along the road north of Kuwait City, and Iraqi soldiers surrendering at the first opportunity. The success of air power surprised even the true believers, somewhat like a football team who knew they were good, but not really sure how good. Sports metaphors are almost always misleading, but the DESERT STORM air campaign constitutes one of the rare exceptions to this general rule. Las Vegas oddsmakers probably would have made the Coalition air forces a 17 point favourite in a game that was, in American sports parlance, a 'blowout'. In retrospect, such an outcome should have been obvious: in fact, it was, but then again, it wasn't. Since the air power revolution is still a work in progress and the enabling factors of the Coalition's victory – factors still very much a part of the present and future air power scene – are wound together in a gigantic tangle, it is useful to review the significance of events over the past few years and their implications for future operations.

THE EVOLUTIONARY REVOLUTION
AS SEEN THROUGH THE LENS OF DESERT STORM

Air power in the present day has benefited from a steady and evolutionary progression of development that has occurred in a largely unspectacular fashion but which, nevertheless, constitutes a general revolution. If there is, as some allege, a 'revolution in military affairs', it is a revolution that is primarily one involving air power. This quiet internal revolution gained momentum in the late 1970s and throughout the decade of the 1980s, and affected virtually all aspects of military air power use.

A key aspect of the Gulf victory was the tremendous advantage accruing to the Coalition from robust airlift and air refuelling forces, particularly those of the United States. The short-notice intercontinental airlift of forces following the Iraqi invasion of Kuwait itself constituted significant proof that a revolution in air power's capabilities had occurred. Prior to DESERT STORM, such rapid-response airlift had existed as a plan but had never been demonstrated. Civil airlines cross the ocean all the time; however, these flights are on well-planned flight routes with bases organised and stocked to handle the flight operations. The plans for a 'come as you are' NATO-Warsaw Pact conflict in Europe or a war in the Middle East or Korea all called for a massive strategic mobility operation, but it hadn't been practised on any realistic scale. The existing plans for South-West Asia were in the process of being updated, but didn't match the situation. The American Civil Reserve Air Fleet (CRAF), consisting of airliners and aircrews mobilised to meet airlift requirements, had never been exercised since its creation almost 40 years before. In addition, though fighter squadrons had deployed overseas using aerial refuelling for years, a constant stream of fighter and attack aircraft squadrons from all the Services hadn't been organised and practised before. But despite many complexities and operations that had been planned, but not fully exercised, the concept of intercontinental strategic airlift was proven in DESERT SHIELD. Furthermore this capability has been refined in the numerous contingency operations that have occurred since that conflict.

Another of the indicators that the revolution had indeed occurred was manifested in the night skies over Iraq as the Coalition began its air campaign, slicing seemingly effortlessly through Iraq's formidable and daunting air defences to achieve air superiority. Before the Gulf War, theorists expounded about the need for air superiority in modern warfare, but like strategic airlift it, too, had not been demonstrated on a large scale. In an operation that matched the textbook recipe for attaining air superiority, local air superiority was quickly and decisively established in the areas where Coalition air forces were operating on the first night. This transitory condition was then extended throughout the region on a more enduring basis and, like a rampaging virus, rapidly expanded beyond superiority to become overwhelming air supremacy. Once air superiority had been established, all of the Coalition air forces operated from that point on with their bases a virtual sanctuary. Subsequently all Iraqi air and land movements were faced with the constant threat of attack – a condition that had a virtue all of its own for the Coalition.

Air superiority meant more than the classic image of fighter aircraft locked in a deadly 'furball'. Decades ago the concepts for employing an air superiority (ie air-to-air fighters) force paralleled the concept for the isolation of the Normandy beachhead: the principle of mass. Prior to the introduction of AWACS and effective pulse doppler radars with user-friendly displays, the general approach for employing an air superiority force was to distribute fighter combat air patrols (CAPs) across the span of the battlespace and hope that some of the CAPs would be in the right place to engage enemy aircraft, or employ fighter sweeps with the hope of encountering the enemy fighters. Knowledge of the likely routes the enemy would take made this concept better than a random draw, but it took a lot of assets to cover the battlespace. With the introduction of a wide-area sensor like AWACS, fighter radars which could be counted on to detect most aircraft at relatively long ranges and at low altitudes, and the electronic means to separate friend from foe, the counter-air mission became a planned event making far more efficient use of fighters, allowing greater areas to be covered with less aircraft while retaining the capacity to mass fighters when large threats occurred.

However, the air superiority revolution revealed in the Gulf War went further than this. Precision attacks against command and control facilities and Iraqi airfields played a key role in ensuring Coalition air supremacy. The Iraqi Air Force was attacked in the air and on the ground. Within a week their only option was to flee to Iran and the escape routes were along a perilous flight path. The theory that had been practised in Red Flags and training exercises for more than a decade proved to be sound in combat. The detailed air campaign planning permitted Coalition air-to-air forces to initially engage from beyond visual range by isolating the Iraqis in the airspace and identifying them through electronic means by airborne AWACS aircraft. Even if the Iraqis were competent in the air, they would have started the fights from a great disadvantage. The air-to-air missiles, older brothers of their predecessors which didn't meet the test over Vietnam, achieved a success rate that was about an order of magnitude higher than in Vietnam. Air base attacks were conducted at the outset and continued throughout the war. As predicted, air bases are hard, complex targets and consequently were never completely shut down. However, the air base attacks did slow the rate at which the Iraqis could even attempt to launch sorties to defend their airspace. The effectiveness of the Coalition in air combat offers new possibilities in the balance of offensive counter-air (OCA) mission planning. Indeed, against an inept opponent it is possible to be selective about air base attacks and let the air defenders take-off rather than trying to shut down the relatively hard air bases themselves via strikes against their runways and hangar or hardened aircraft shelter facilities..

Probably the most challenging task in the air superiority mission is suppressing, or negating, surface-to-air defences. Because the Iraqis realised beforehand that they couldn't compete in air combat, they had acquired and fielded a massive array of surface-to-air missiles (SAMs) and conventional anti-aircraft artillery (AAA). Surface-to-air defences are numerous, mobile, and can be hidden until they choose to engage and, if cleverly used, are capable (against even a sophisticated opponent) of establishing conditions of air denial. This occurred, for example, in the opening stages of the 1973 Arab-Israeli war, when the combination of the Soviet-built SA-6 and SA-7 SAMs and the low-level ZSU-23-4 radar-directed gun carriage briefly inflicted conditions of air denial for the Israeli Air Force as it attempted to attack Syrian forces on the Golan Heights. Several choices are available in establishing air superiority against a surface-to-air defence network: defences can be destroyed, negated through stand-off jamming and self-protection measures, or avoided by staying out of their effective range. In the stealth era, of course, there is the option of operating within threat range but outside the detection range of enemy radar systems. The roots of the Coalition's technical ability to confront and handily defeat the wide array of Iraqi surface-to-air defences (for example, the

Coalition's – and particularly the United States' – tremendous investment in electronic warfare, stealth, and anti-radiation missile technology) dated to the Vietnam war; the apparent ease of the Coalition's efforts against Iraq should not disguise what was both a difficult undertaking and the product of intensive investment, research, trials and training.

DESERT STORM demonstrated how creative use of new or refined capabilities can achieve an overwhelming advantage against an opponent who does not appreciate or possess the air power advantage. In one important aspect, the Iraqis departed from the doctrine of their former Soviet sponsors: they concentrated their SAM defences around Baghdad and critical research and manufacturing complexes rather than defending their deployed forces in the field. Not surprisingly, the approaches taken by Coalition airmen in DESERT STORM to establish air superiority against the surface-to-air threat differed depending upon the target being struck. Defences around Baghdad were sometimes jammed, but mostly avoided. Thus, throughout the war, the concentration of defences in Baghdad remained largely intact, for it would have been extremely difficult to destroy the defences in Baghdad without substantial collateral damage and risk of large numbers of civilian casualties. (One only has to recall the pictures of rapid-fire anti-aircraft guns firing from every rooftop to appreciate the magnitude of this problem). Further, anti-radiation missiles such as the American HARM and the British ALARM are not as precise as the laser-guided bombs used within the city. However, it wasn't necessary to destroy the SAMs in the city since the critical targets in Baghdad could be attacked with precision from sanctuary using the remarkable Lockheed F-117A stealth fighter, and Tomahawk cruise missiles.

But the situation was quite different in the Kuwait theatre of operations (KTO). Since the density of SAMs protecting the Iraqi forces in the KTO was lower, concentrated attacks were used to take out the radar-guided SAMs early. Throughout the campaign, continual patrols of aircraft were used to engage or (by their presence) intimidate any remaining radars in classic suppression of enemy air defence (SEAD) operations. Instead of using stealth and stand-off weapons to create a sanctuary (as in the Baghdad case), SEAD missions confronted and overcame medium- and high-altitude SAM threats, and Coalition strike aircraft operated at medium altitude to stay out of range of low level man-portable infra-red guided SAMs and light mobile AAA guns such as the ZSU-23-4. In sum, then, the Iraqi war demanded different approaches depending on what planners were targeting, but they both worked synergistically to achieve a spectacular result.

DESERT STORM did show that air power can play a significant role in the defeat of an army in the field. The persistent pounding from the air rendered the Iraqi army largely incapable of action. Interdiction slowly strangled any attempts at resupply. The Iraqis had two choices: remaining in fixed positions (the choice they generally adopted, relying on concealment, deception and digging in) and being slowly and methodically destroyed in those positions; or, secondly, venturing from cover and being destroyed on the move. It was, in short, a devilish proposition; during the two times they did move (at the Battle of Khafji and during the panicked retreat along the highway north out of Kuwait City), massed air power cued by airborne command and control aircraft inflicted massive destruction of their columns.

As with many other lessons of the Gulf War this, too, should not be considered surprising, for the relative speed and manoeuvre of air power compared to ground forces permits the combined effects of manoeuvre and firepower from the air to be brought to bear quickly and overwhelmingly: more so than other forms of military attack. The fact that the fourth largest army in the world was overwhelmed by a counter-offensive in four days with minimal Coalition casualties shows that the capabilities of air power to defeat ground forces have undergone a significant shift and constitutes itself proof that air power was, in fact, the decisive form of military power projection in the Gulf War.

That said, it is important to assess things that couldn't be done in 1991, beginning with strategic attacks. Strategic attacks are conducted to destroy the enemy's ability to fight. The massive attacks throughout the theatre in the first week of DESERT STORM certainly demonstrated that we could attack any set of targets with relative impunity, in parallel. Some of the specific objectives of the attack on strategic targets were achieved and it is intuitively clear that the scope and effectiveness of these attacks in conjunction with other air operations set the stage for the overall victory. However, there is little evidence that strategic attacks on their own exclusively abetted the end of the war. Virtually all knowledgeable air power authorities believe that these attacks played a significant role in the ultimate defeat of Iraq, but on their own they did not force an Iraqi surrender: even though the Iraqi leadership had ample opportunities to surrender prior to the ground offensive, it chose not to do so. It is also unclear what actions Iraqi forces were unable to take because of these attacks. In essence, the strategic centre of the Iraqi nation simply remained static and rode out the attacks much like the Iraqi leadership has ridden out another form of strategic attack – the embargo and UN sanctions – in the years since the end of the war. To a degree this unhappy result reflected the circumstances of the war and its aftermath, for if the Iraqis had been forced to take actions with their strategic infrastructure, their system may have imploded. As it was, they had the option to remain static and we can only speculate on the actual effectiveness of the strategic attack missions.

Likewise, the 'Scud' missile launcher hunt was also 'too hard to do' with the assets available in DESERT STORM. Fleeting targets that can move quickly in and out of cover present a difficult challenge. A systematic means to detect and destroy the missile launchers didn't exist at the start of the war and there wasn't enough time to formulate a successful combination of sensors and strike platforms in the short war. Coalition air campaign planners may have made the launch problem more complicated for Iraqi rocketeers through persistent combat air patrols in the known launch areas – launch rates dropped precipitously through the war once air patrols started – but the race wasn't won in DESERT STORM. Similarly, the Coalition air forces were not able to attack and destroy those targets and capabilities they didn't know about. The chemical and biological weapons, Iraq's nuclear weapons programme facilities and their leaders' locations were not known to Coalition intelligence and therefore couldn't be attacked. The operating principle for DESERT STORM was that the things that could be found could be successfully attacked; those that were unknown remained untouched. This lesson, of course, was not new to DESERT STORM – but it does highlight the increasing importance of linking intelligence with air campaign operations.

Summing up, the fruits of the evolutionary revolution of air power, particularly as it applied to the US military but evident also in the operations of Coalition forces, produced a rich harvest in DESERT STORM and, incidentally, raised the level of expectations for air power's contributions in future conflicts and military operations. Air power came of age in the Persian Gulf. Historians and advocates will argue for years to come over the relative contribution of air power and the land and sea forces to the Coalition's victory. The contribution of air power was undoubtedly far greater than in any previous encounter and far exceeded the contributions predicted by any prewar simulation. If, despite its very significant role, air power did not win the war alone, the war nevertheless was far from merely the 100-hour land campaign; the die was cast long before the ground offensive began. Rather, as with virtually all major conflicts in this century, it was the combination of air, land, and sea forces acting together that produced victory, with the air weapon being the linchpin of that victory.

If one would say with caution that air power was not the exclusive agent of the Coalition's victory over Iraq, nevertheless the overall contribution of air power in the defeat of the Iraqis was significantly greater than any analysis would have predicted and greater than in any previous conflict. Some capabilities were clearly demonstrated; some weren't; and some provided an interesting taste of things that may be, but remain to be fully proven. Beyond DESERT STORM, air power has been used in several new and potentially interesting ways which serve as indicators of its future employment. Strategic airlift, air superiority and the direct attack of land forces in the field, all shown to be important in previous wars, were reaffirmed in the crucible of the war with Iraq, and shown to be more significant than at any previous time. They will continue to mature as essential and core characteristics of air power in the future and, of course, have been validated since the Gulf War by the NATO experience in Bosnia.

AIR POWER'S CONTRIBUTIONS
TO SANCTIONS ENFORCEMENT

Since DESERT STORM, the world has experienced a period of instability and challenge and air power has shown that it can build upon its demonstrated capabilities to perform new functions in a changing world. The end of conflict usually brings with it a series of sanctions and constraints that are placed upon the loser. For example, a set of United Nations resolutions were enacted to limit Iraq's ability to act and its sovereignty. Normally, sanctions are enforced by ground forces acting in a police role or naval forces restricting commerce. But this is a new era and air power has new and growing capabilities. As the Iraqi forces moved to subdue the Shia rebellion in the south-eastern corner of Iraq and the Kurds in the north, no-fly zones were established in the northern and southern parts of Iraq to restrict their ability to carry out these operations. Because Coalition air forces possessed the capability to attain air superiority over Iraq, they have been able to enforce these sanctions on a continuing basis for over six years. The no-fly restrictions included restrictions on emitting for surface-to-air defence radars, a natural extension of the air superiority mission. The use of air power as a means of sanctions enforcement is a relatively efficient means of accomplishing the task in terms of manpower, risk and national expenditure. In effect it is the rediscovery of the 'air policing' experience of the British, French, and Spanish air arms during the 1920s and 1930s, but with a degree of leverage over an opponent that is far more profound than that achieved by those earlier efforts. Because using air power for sanctions enforcement has proven to be effective, it was also applied as a means to control the situation in the former Yugoslavia. As the level of NATO and the international communities' commitments increased, another no-fly zone was established under Operation Deny Flight. Considering the relative ease of implementation and the level of risk, the enforcement of no-fly zones will undoubtedly be an inherent role of air power in the future. However, as the shoot-down of Captain Scott O'Grady and his F-16 clearly indicate, 'low risk' does not equate to 'no risk'.

Enforcement also requires that action be taken when violations occur. An important precedent has been set in the period since the end of DESERT STORM with the use of unmanned stand-off weapons – air and sea-launched cruise missiles – to punish violations. These weapons provide a largely invulnerable means of striking an aggressor without exposing personnel to capture or loss of life. Conventional cruise missiles are costly (approximately $1.5 million per missile), limited in the number that can be used, are generally most effective against fixed and definable targets, and, despite rising expectations, are not 100 per cent effective: at present their accuracy is less than that of a laser-guided or electro-optical bomb dropped from a piloted strike aircraft. Tomahawk Land Attack Missiles (TLAMs) have been the principal cruise missile used to conduct these attacks so far, but the menu of available conventional cruise missiles with greater accuracy and less cost per missile will grow substantially in the near future. We can expect that the growing family of unmanned stand-off weapons will provide a new dimension for using air power in the future. Already it is hard to imagine a potential aggressor, or rogue nation, failing to anticipate or ignoring the possible use of cruise missiles against its territory before deciding to commit aggression.

In the case of Iraq, near-continuous and frustrating provocations resulted in extending the sanctions in the south to include a 'no-drive' zone where the introduction of new ground force military units and equipment was also prohibited. As might be expected, the air power capabilities needed to enforce a 'no-drive' zone are more complex than for a 'no-fly' zone. The effectiveness of air power to control activities on the ground depends on a near continuous system of sensors for detection of vehicle movements, and, because of the potential level of effort required to stop a large violation of the 'no-drive' zone, responsive airlift is critical to bring in additional forces to support the enforcement. The verdict is not complete on this role for air power, but already we have witnessed an emerging capability to prevent nations from massing land forces along their neighbour's borders using air power as the primary means of deterrence and border enforcement.

As the crisis and bloodshed increased in Bosnia, the spectre of the number of ground troops that would be needed to control the situation acted as a damper on the willingness of the US and Western Europe to act to resolve the situation. Most were convinced that, while interesting, the 'no-fly' zone activities would not really affect the outcome, since none of the warring factions relied on air power. There was a reluctance to use air power against either (on both) sides, due to the difficulty of finding targets and the danger of collateral damage and civilian casualities. While air power may not deserve full credit for solving the crisis, when the two-week bombing operation was conducted in September 1995 it did have the effect of balancing the level of military power in Bosnia-Herzegovina and it demonstrated Coalition resolve to end the conflict. In these types of situation, air power alone may not solve the root causes of the conflict, but in a stalemated situation it can dramatically tip the scales in one direction. Provided there is adequate preparation (including realistic planning, determination of desired outcomes, adequate forces, appropriate rules of engagement, clear lines of command, and so on), modern air power has clearly demonstrated that it can produce circumstances and results which justify expectations that air power will dramatically contribute to the security needs of the 21st Century and have even greater capacity to adapt as the challenges and conditions change in the years ahead.

That adequate preparation can benefit to a remarkable degree from using battlespace knowledge derived from a wide-area common picture produced from an intelligence, surveillance, and reconnaissance (ISR) network. Indeed, as the operations in the Gulf and elsewhere of the Boeing E-8 Joint STARS surveillance aircraft have shown, it may soon be possible to have a pretty comprehensive picture of ground movements, much as we have been able to monitor and control air traffic over the past decade. This offers opportunities to create new categories of sanctions against potential aggressors and air power can play a large part in enforcing these restrictions. Of course, there are limitations, particularly if the environment involves movements of people on foot and urban areas. However, to accomplish most activities on the ground, organised vehicle movements are needed for sustenance, if not the activity itself. An enforcement regime built around an airborne ISR system augmented with some ground presence to observe activity in the seams of the ISR network and sized to be able to protect itself with the assistance of air cover could be plausible in the not-too-distant future. Additional air power with precision weapons can be used to engage violators accurately from a virtual sanctuary. The use of an integrated ISR network with air power in an enforcement role can also bring new dimensions to the tasks of treaty monitoring and compliance, and to restricting commerce and trade within an aggressor nation.

Finally, the surveillance capability inherent in the sensor packages carried on various airborne platforms has provided a somewhat unexpected service in enforcing peace and international sanctions. In Bosnia, ground commanders have used attack helicopters to detect armour and artillery pieces which the warring parties thought they could hide. Video recordings taken from the sensor packages on US attack helicopters is shown directly to commanders of the national forces to give them an 'understanding' of our ability to find hidden military assets and, by implication, to destroy them from sanctuary if they are not moved into designated areas. The growing capability of sensor platforms on manned and unmanned aerial vehicles and on space platforms will enhance the ability of air power to contribute to the efficiency of stability operations in the future. The combinations of endurance, wide area coverage and the ability to shift the focus across the theatre of operations will clearly increase air power's capability in the future.

TECHNOLOGY AND THE EMERGENCE
OF AN AIR POWER QUALITATIVE EDGE

Not surprisingly, the key to the transformation of modern air power has been the integration of technology into the world's most advanced air forces. The rate at which new technologies and concepts are introduced and assimilated is increasingly rapid, particularly as information technology expands, and is characteristic of modern society at large, not merely the defence aerospace community. This should open new opportunities for the application of air power in the 21st Century, because the foundations for the integration of new capabilities are inherent in a professional, well-trained, technically-oriented force. But the challenge lies ahead, and though the accomplishments of the past are encouraging, they should not be considered an affirmation that the path ahead will be particularly easy or preordained for success.

The competition and subsequent demise of the Soviet Union also contributed its own dimension to setting the stage for the emerging age of air power. Until the walls came down, the United States and its allies were in a seemingly never-ending race to gain a qualitative edge, but the goal seemed always a bit too far ahead to reach. The competition with the Soviets provided a strong impetus for a qualitative technological advantage since individual Western nations didn't have the capacity to field numerically superior forces. It is clear, in retrospect, that the qualitative gap was increasing in the West's favour from the mid-1970s onwards. However, more than one would like, numbers *do* count in combat, and the Western bloc's qualitative advantages would probably not have been sufficient to overcome the Eastern bloc's quantitative advantage.

For example, large numbers of surface-to-air missiles employed in a co-ordinated manner can overcome even the most sophisticated electronic countermeasures and concentrated defences can make operations with stealth aircraft and cruise missiles difficult. With the demise of the Soviet Union, the number of systems likely adversaries might possess has been pared down to a size that technology can handle and it is much more difficult (though far from impossible) for rogue nations to replace the equipment that they currently have. In addition, as the Soviet Union reached the limits of its acquisition process, the quality of their equipment similarly levelled off except in a few areas. The consequence is that Western nations – particularly the United States – have a generational advantage in fielded equipment which should last against future adversaries for a decade or more. Indeed, the most dangerous technologies for the West will be those the Western nations have developed themselves: a powerful argument for prudent and cautious arms sales, particularly to countries that may have profound internal instabilities (Iran in the 1970s being a case in point). Having a decade or more of qualitative advantage permits a unique

213

opportunity to experiment with new concepts for air power.

So, the last two decades have created an environment in which air power has the capability to achieve the potential envisioned by the early pioneers. The combination of a highly-trained force which has demonstrated it possesses the knowledge to apply air power with devastating effectiveness, new technologies which have been applied under the stress of a wide range of operational conditions and a threat which for now is limited, have all come together to make this environment not merely a possibility, but a reality. Each of these is highly significant, but again, the most important element in promoting the new air power-conducive era has been the exploitation of high technology. For sowing two decades of technological effort and investment, the US and its most sophisticated allies have reaped a full decade of advantage.

A review of selected programme areas clearly shows that this technological development did not itself proceed with great smoothness and there were combat systems introduced along the way – for example the Rockwell B-1B Lancer, the LANTIRN night navigation and targeting system, the AIM-120 advanced medium-range air-to-air missile (AMRAAM) and the air defence variant of the Tornado fighter—that had more than their share of problems before evolving into supremely capable weapons. Some, such as the US Army's Aquila Unmanned Aerial Vehicle (UAV), the Israeli Lavi fighter programme and the USAF's Tacit Rainbow anti-SAM system, simply offered too many problems to warrant further development. (Nor were even relatively simple surface warfare systems immune, as the example of the US Army's abortive Sergeant York air defence system demonstrated.)

A good example of both the potentialities and problems of high technology is the quest for precision air weapons, particularly air-to-air missiles and air-to-surface guided bombs. In the missile case, the performance advocates anticipated from air-to-air missiles lagged behind the real-world experience. Perhaps not surprisingly, simpler heat-seeking missiles such as the Sidewinder performed better at an earlier date than more complex radar-guided missiles such as the Sparrow, but at this early stage in air-to-air missile development and use neither could be relied upon to turn the tide in air warfare except in the hands of a select few who could master the systems. In retrospect, these missiles *were* a revolutionary development (as evidenced by reactions to their first employment by Taiwanese F-86Fs against Chinese MiG-17s during fighting over Quemoy and Matsu in 1958), but the first generation didn't work very well in the dynamic environment of 1960s tactical air combat. (The probability of a successful kill with these missiles was less than one in ten in South-East Asia.) Similarly, the first generation of precision-guided air-to-surface weapons were used in South-East Asia and the 1973 Arab-Israeli war. Laser-guided bombs and Maverick missiles were employed in limited numbers in what were almost operational test and evaluation conditions. Essentially all of these air-to-air and air-to-surface weapons gave hints of their potential when employed by the technically and tactically proficient few. But if the promise was evident, much more work needed to be done to turn that promise into a combat reality. That work occupied much of the 1970s and 1980s, and the success of this effort was demonstrated in combat in the Falklands, the raid on Libya, the Gulf War and Bosnia.

This effort occurred in spite of a chorus of well-meaning if ill-informed 'defence reform' critics who argued that field performance showed that technically simpler systems were the answer. In reality, the right combinations of technology made 'complex' systems simpler to employ and much more reliable in demanding operational conditions and their overwhelming superiority clearly qualitatively outmatched less sophisticated opponents. Several factors facilitated the process. The electronics revolution generated advanced avionics in the 1970s and 1980s that greatly simplified the employment of air-to-air missiles and precision air-to-surface weapons. These avionics were incorporated as an integral part of the avionics suite carried by the new generation of fighter aircraft such as the F-15, F-16, Sea Harrier and Tornado, and were added to older generations through modifications and self-contained pods. They aided target acquisition and let aircrews know when they were 'in the envelope' to employ the weapons. Improvements to the munitions themselves (such as improved sensors, aerodynamics, fuses and guidance units) made their real-world combat performance match test-range and theoretical predictions. Finally, putting the weapons in the hands of operational forces to train with and use for a decade or more guaranteed that when they had to be used, they would be employed to good effect.

Thus the emerging technologies of the late 1950s and 1960s were honed and refined in the 1970s and 1980s to became the integrated force capabilities that made air power live up to its potential throughout the dynamic environment of the late 1980s and into DESERT STORM and Bosnia. Today, new technologies with their roots in the 1980s provide promise for the late 1990s and beyond. Some examples of these include:

- The common precision reference system from the array of Global Positioning System (GPS) satellites;

- Multi-spectral sensors operating from space, in high endurance unmanned aerial vehicles, and manned aircraft;

- Broad-band communications to distribute information throughout the battle space;

- Information acquisition, processing, and exploitation technologies that can contribute to what is loosely referred to as 'information warfare' and, by some, as 'cyberwar'.

- High-power laser technologies capable of being applied to new combat aircraft and suitable for a range of missions, most notably stand-off anti-ballistic missile defence during the boost-phase when such a missile is at its most vulnerable over an enemy's own territory.

These are just some of the new tools that are now coming out of the technological concept stage and rapidly spreading into the acquisition and, indeed, operational world.

TRAINING AND DOCTRINE

Technology and training go hand-in-hand and a force lacking either is in serious trouble. Accompanying the technology revolution that had transformed military power by the time of the Gulf War was a training revolution of almost equal profundity. The training revolution emerged from the notable 'lack of success' experienced in air combat over North Vietnam by the US Navy and the USAF. During the Korean War, F-86 victory-loss ratios over MiG-15 fighters exceeded 10:1, and occasionally topped 14:1; in Vietnam, the victory-loss ratio hovered for much of the war at just above 1:1, clearly unacceptable. Both the Navy and the Air Force had lost the edge in air combat training.

Out of the Vietnam experience came two notable programmes, the Navy's Top Gun and a strengthened air combat training programme at the Air Force's Fighter Weapons School. These initial efforts generated a small cadre of individual pilots who mastered the air combat business in time for the climatic air combats of late 1972, when Air Force and Navy F-4 crews shattered the North Vietnamese Air Force. The next step was the Air Force's development of Red Flag at Nellis Air Force Base in the mid-1970s, which served as both an inspiration and model for establishing the Navy's 'Strike University' programme of the mid-1980s, following a disastrous Navy air strike over Lebanon in 1983. The original purpose of Red Flag was to let individual pilots experience the stress and demands of combat in a structured training environment, so that they would have the equivalent of the statistically dangerous first ten combat missions (when, historically, most losses occur) under their belt before they went to war. It met this purpose well, as the nearly unanimous testimony of pilots in DESERT STORM observing that 'Nellis was a lot tougher' affirms. However, an even more important capability emerged from this experience. Units from throughout the air forces of the United States and other nations gained an instinctive proficiency in planning and conducting large-scale composite force operations. By the time squadrons completed local preparation

216

for Red Flags and went through the exercise, their ability to undertake co-ordinated composite force operations became more refined and effective. While Red Flag was created to improve individual skills, its contribution in developing composite force operations was an extra payoff.

The experience base widened throughout the 1980s. A family of 'Flag' training exercises grew from the original Red Flag to meet a wider variety of purposes: Green Flag for Electronic Warfare; Blue Flag for Command and Control; Chequered Flag for unit mission deployment; and Maple Flag in Canada. These exercises, combined with training emphasising 'surge' sorties (to get as many aircraft in the air as possible and then maintain a high sortie rate over mutiple training missions), live weapons firing, and a rigorous system of inspection and evaluation, produced a Coalition air force that was ready for DESERT STORM, not merely from an 'in the cockpit' standpoint but from an organisational and structural standpoint as well. The Air Tasking Order is a good example. Though the format is certainly not a 'user-friendly' one, the 200+ page daily Air Tasking Order (ATO) used in DESERT STORM was a document that all Coalition airmen could sift their way through to know their own specific missions and understand the battle plan for the coming day. A decade or more of demanding composite force operations in a widening variety of situations accelerated spreading the knowledge of how to do it throughout the force, from the very highest echelons of the senior leadership through to the crew chiefs sweating on the flight line. In the United States and in many NATO and Pacific forces, every squadron in both the active and reserve forces has a leadership cadre who have been through multiple Red Flag-like composite force exercises and who, in turn, are prepared to pass their first-hand experience along to the next generation of airmen under their command or tutelage.

Ironically, air power doctrine has not really advanced at the same pace as the technology and experience of the air forces. Unlike the land forces which first develop and test detailed doctrinal concepts and then practise and train according to the doctrine, air power doctrine traditionally has been the last thing that changes. The approach used by airmen has been more to try new equipment, and operational and tactical concepts and ideas, out first and then let the doctrine follow later. Indeed, a 1978 study conducted by the Air Force Systems Command (now Air Force Material Command) showed that over three-fourths of the systems under development had their origins in technological opportunity rather than a clearly defined requirements or doctrinal base. The doctrine is something that follows later for airmen rather than driving the development of new concepts and tactics. Perhaps that is appropriate in an age where technology and the dynamic defence environment move at a pace that makes it hard for the doctrine developers to keep up. However, it is necessary to step back and bring the doctrine forward both to codify the progress that has been made, and to clarify and focus thinking on future problems. Even without recourse to the reinvigorated doctrinal thinking that has so profoundly influenced the international air power community since the mid-1980s, the field and training experience of the 1970s and 1980s have produced a *de facto* doctrinal reference base for air power that is now validated, and which provides a solid foundation to expand the missions and capabilities of air power in the years ahead.

FOUR CASES: STRATEGIC MOBILITY, MANOEUVRE, AWARENESS, AND PRECISION ATTACK

Intercontinental deployability (which may be termed strategic mobility), the manoeuvre implications of air power, a common picture available to all (awareness), and near-universal, all-weather precision attack are changing the way in which air power is used. The relatively rapid intercontinental mobility of air power means that it will almost always be the first requirement for short-notice operations and will be the enabler for virtually all operations. Air power is now the dominant form of manoeuvre warfare, a development that itself has been evolving over the half-century since it first showed its ability to profoundly influence the manoeuvre of friendly and opposing forces. The distributed common picture of the battlefield derived from airborne sensors provides battlespace knowledge which permits integrated planning and battle management. Precision attack is redefining the meaning of strategic and tactical air war, and has already established itself as the new 'gold standard' of air power application. Each of these is worth a discussion in turn.

Strategic mobility

The capabilities of the modern high-capacity, air-refuelled, long-range jet transport has generated the potential for the envelopment of an opponent over global distances and the ability to respond rapidly within hours to a crisis virtually anywhere in the world. As a result, air power is now the decisive opener in almost any military or humanitarian operation; in today's world, virtually all military operations, those of an armoured cavalry regiment on the earth's surface or a carrier battle group far out to sea, are dependent to a greater or lesser degree upon continuous land-based air mobility operations.

Just as the parallel warfare strike concepts used in DESERT STORM confounded the enemy's means to resist, the use of air power for a parallel strategic, operational and tactical deployment of forces into a theatre can provide an overwhelming initial edge in a campaign by creating a near-simultaneous envelopment throughout the theatre of operations. For larger nations, air mobility can be critical to the execution of foreign policy objectives and regional presence. For the USA, for example, the refined capability to plan strategic airlift operations direct from the continental USA increasingly permits the rapid delivery (defined as delivery within hours) of the lead elements of a composite force package (for example, fighters, strike aircraft and airborne combat forces) and its associated initial logistics support anywhere in the world. In a joint and coalition warfare sense, the combination of forces brought in by an integrated airlift package together with those that are permanently stationed overseas, those which might be deployed in the region, and those that can meet up with pre-positioned equipment permit the bringing together of substantial forces almost anywhere in the world. (Indeed, advanced nations possessing the air power qualitative edge have a realistic hope of deploying locally dominant combat power across an ocean before most nations can generate it within their own borders.)

The result is dominant presence on short notice to overwhelm potential adversaries within their own territory before they can respond, or to meet the rapidly unfolding needs of an emergency humanitarian operation. For example, one could imagine the arrival of a dozen or more C-17A Globemaster IIIs at an austere location like Tuzla, Mogadishu or some locale in Central Asia with a dominant leading edge ground force. At the same time, C-5B Galaxies and civil reserve air fleet aircraft would arrive at a nearby forward staging base with initial logistic support, elements of the surveillance and reconnaissance network, and air support. Boeing tilt-rotor MV-22s and heavy lift helicopters arriving on the final leg of a staged deployment (flying into theatre with multiple stops and/or air refuellings *en route*) would establish a tactical lift operation providing direct delivery throughout the area. Within a few days an air-and-land operation could be in progress with assets fed either by direct delivery from the continental United States or moved through the forward staging base. Phased arrivals planned in advance would complete the intercontinental envelopment and establish a lodgement sufficient for sustained operations.

Thus, as can be seen, in any likely future scenario, direct delivery of combat and support assets into the theatre can become the norm. Further, on call and reliable airlift available within hours can significantly reduce the sustainment traditionally required to be pre-positioned in theatre to conduct both peacetime and combat operations. Increased confidence in conducting these rapid intercontinental operations should also permit units such as Marine Expeditionary Units to deploy regular peacetime operations with a much lighter logistics load and rely on dedicated strategic airlift to bring in sustaining logistics and other combat forces needed to conduct a specific mission, obviating the need for cumbersome pre-positioning and pre-stocking of supplies aboard ship. Similarly, forces that are permanently stationed overseas can rely on military and contract airlift to shift many traditional maintenance and depot activities back to the continental USA. This can then reduce the number of personnel stationed outside the USA and the 'footprint' of peacetime and contingency deployments. In short, the growing efficiency of air power makes it feasible to achieve global presence within hours largely from a continental-based force.

Air Power as Manoeuvre Warfare

Air power is inherently manoeuvre warfare. Integrated planning between the Joint Air Force Component Commander and the Joint Land Force Component Commander, which can link together air power's manoeuvre and precision attack with ground manoeuvre and artillery systems such as the ATACMS (the US Army Tactical Missile System), is possible with the advent of the common picture of the battlespace. With a common picture, the control and co-ordination lines which have historically been used to deconflict (i.e. prevent interference between) operations (but which have often complicated or confused them as well) can be eliminated. It also makes strategic and operational sense to establish a process to plan and execute the air and surface battles as one integrated plan. With a common picture shared by all, a common plan and process for battle management for air and surface forces is the natural byproduct.

Within this context, the use of air power as a manoeuvre force to bring a concentrated application of precision firepower rapidly anywhere in the battlespace from a distance that furnishes a virtual sanctuary from counter-attack should be a key factor in the development of the theatre commander's battle plans. With the emergence of comprehensive, or even only 'pretty good' situational awareness and battlefield knowledge available from a shared common picture, air power can rightfully be thought of as a critical operational and tactical manoeuvre force, a manoeuvre force with long, indeed global-range precision firepower. Traditionally, when manoeuvre forces are talked about, pictures of the 'Left Hook' of DESERT STORM, or the massing of the Republican Guards along the Kuwaiti border, or tanks rumbling through a burned-out city in Bosnia come to mind. With a common wide-area picture of the ground environment, air power should also be considered a manoeuvre force, for the essence of manoeuvre is to bring a critical mass to a position on the battlefield at the right time and the right place.

In the past, it was difficult to know where the right places were over the ranges that air power operated, so plans for the application of air power tended to distribute it across the battlefield. Having lots of aircraft that were almost everywhere when the weather was good helped to isolate the Normandy beachhead for the D-Day invasion. Being everywhere works if one has a big quantitative advantage, but it is not an efficient use of critical assets. But even with this qualification, and allowing that air power in earlier times – notably the Second World War – operated with only a fraction of the effectiveness it now possesses, no less an authority on manoeuvre than Field Marshal Erwin Rommel, the famed 'Desert Fox', grumbled in frustration to his naval aide

Admiral Friedrich Ruge, in 1944 that Allied air power was the new way of manoeuvre warfare, turning a flank from above. (At the same time, in Italy, Allied air power was dramatically hindering German mobility, so much so that one German general complained he was in the position of a chess player who could only make one move to his opponent's three.)

The extreme mobility of air power compared to the relative immobility of ground forces – as demonstrated at Khafji and the 'Highway of Death' in Kuwait – show that a critical mass of air power can already be brought to bear at the right time and place, if appropriate command and control systems (such as Joint STARS) are in place. It is a simple matter of the kinematics of the speed at which air and ground forces move; air forces move at over 500 miles per hour, approximately 20 times faster than the typical unobstructed mechanised surface warfare force and over 200 times faster than the unobstructed infantryman on the ground.

Awareness, the Common Picture, and the Integrated Battlespace

The intelligence, surveillance and reconnaissance (ISR) systems, which provide both a framework for building a 'system of systems', and generate the common picture of the battlespace, all operate in the aerospace environment: they are carried in flight by aircraft operating within the atmosphere or by spacecraft in orbit hundreds of miles, or more, above the earth. Most of these systems possess the rapidly deployable characteristics that are common to air power today with the exception of some of the ground support facilities. The ground support facilities that make the pieces of the 'system of systems' difficult to deploy efficiently today may be reduced in size and complexity through information technology or may be replaced by facilities far removed from the theatre of operations, linked by using satellite communications to pipe their products to the theatre commander and key staff. In DESERT STORM and Bosnia, the ISR network had to be built up slowly over time as needs were identified and the system was incomplete since critical elements which provide continuous multi-spectral coverage were in the design stages. Now the individual elements of the ISR system are becoming a reality and we have the experience of putting together the disparate elements which make the system function effectively across a wide span of operating environments. Joint STARS now gives wide area coverage of activity on the ground and focused coverage across the battlespace can be enhanced with the growing family of Unmanned Aerial Vehicles (UAVs) carrying sensors tailored to the specific operational environment. The atmospheric sensors are complemented by space sensors. The tools are also maturing which facilitate the planning and dynamic control for coverage which provides the 'common battlespace picture' that leads to battlefield knowledge.

One of the challenges for commanders in the integrated battlespace of the future will be the allocation and positioning of ISR assets. Fortunately, computer visualisations are now reaching the point where they can simulate the disposition and coverage of multiple sensors on a real time basis. These visualisations will furnish commanders at every level with a clear picture of the area of sensor coverage, as well as any gaps that may exist. It is not difficult to imagine future commanders fighting as hard over the availability and positioning of ISR assets in the future as they do today over combat force allocations. This is the new world of air power where knowledge is the critical part of the equation.

The common picture provides the capability to monitor activities on the ground and in the air over a wide area. For more than a decade, we have had a reasonable common picture of air activities. That is one reason for the relatively swift attainment of air supremacy in DESERT STORM, and the expansion of air power's role in peacetime through the creation and enforcement of 'No Fly' zones in Iraq and Bosnia. The use of air power to constrain the ability of aggressor nations to act with 'No Fly' zones is a harbinger of other new roles for air power. 'No Fly' zones are possible because we could attain air superiority and because sensors are available to monitor activities over wide areas at times and places of our choosing from relatively safe bases. In Bosnia, ground commanders are using sensors on helicopters and sometimes from UAVs to place movement restrictions on the forces of the warring parties and civilians (one would guess that the ground commanders prefer using helicopters for control of ground movements since the helicopters are directly controlled by them whereas UAVs must be requested from the theatre commander). The restrictions are locally imposed since the sensor coverage available from helicopter, and UAVs can only cover a small area – larger than a ground commander can see himself, but still relatively small.

Soon, it will be possible to link and correlate the products of the ISR network in an integrated manner to produce a common picture. The fielding of the Global Positioning System (GPS) allows multiple sensors to be fused together into a common picture in space and time. This is essential when building a picture which necessarily contains many moving parts. Even allowing for existing and anticipated capabilities, advances in computers and information technology will be necessary to correlate the inputs from multiple sensors ranging from satellites in orbit to antennae at fixed points spread over a wide area on the ground, and reporting at different times and on different frequencies as part of a global network. Additionally, automatic recognition and assessment tools will be needed to filter, store and display the vast array of sensor inputs that the ISR network provides. Finally, a direct, global broadcast system is necessary to spread the common picture not only throughout the theatre, but worldwide.

There are profound command implications from the common picture capabilities that future ISR network technology is likely to produce. The global broadcast communications attribute will certainly offer challenges and complications to the authority of the theatre commander, for there will be a strong temptation for someone at a distance to participate or intervene in theatre decision-making. Thus, at a minimum, new roles and responsibilities will have to be worked out to accommodate the capabilities of new technologies. In fact, the geographical requirement to have the theatre commander in-theatre may completely change. As a result of these new capabilities the assessment, planning, and battle management functions no longer need necessarily to be conducted in the theatre of operations. It is not hard to imagine a future crisis where the Joint Task Force Headquarters and the Joint Force Air Component Commander are busily conducting the initial phase of contingency operations from a location in the continental United States or from a CINC's permanent peacetime facilities overseas. This can permit integrated operations, while the buildup is occurring, with a battle staff that is in place, has worked as an established team and has had the opportunity to rehearse the operation. This can enhance the capacity for intercontinental envelopment made possible by the growing effectiveness of airlift. Additionally, this capability will reduce mobility requirements in the critical initial phases of the operation. Limited airlift assets can be used to bring combat and essential logistics elements in first rather than dedicating part of the lift to command elements. Then, as the operation matures, the assessment, planning and battle management functions can be electronically transferred to the theatre for sustained operations.

Some of the ISR developments that have appeared in rudimentary form will assist the accomplishment of traditional missions and enable new ones in the near future. The universal dissemination of a common picture of the battlespace displayed on a common reference system and providing wide area and focused coverage almost *demands* integrated planning at the Joint Task Force level. Information technology will facilitate multi-dimensional planning and battle management for air and surface forces. Finally, precision weapons permit precise objectives. These capabilities can largely eliminate the lines and sectors which have characteristically segmented the battlespace to provide co-ordination, deconfliction, and interoperability. The integrated battlespace can provide more flexibility for all of the forces in the theatre of operations and will enhance the contribution of air power. However, the independent status airmen have historically accorded air power should disappear as integrated operations are made possible. The tighter knitting of the operational environment will demand a revisiting of air power doctrine to accommodate the possibilities available in the integrated battlespace. Air power will continue to grow as an instrument of national power, but at the same time the independence which characterised air power and airmen will fade in the common vision of integrated battlespace management. Integrated battlespace management makes air power become a strategic, operational and tactical manoeuvre force that can bring massed precision firepower throughout the battlespace, and will also open a wide range of new opportunities in enforcing sanctions and peacetime controls on warring parties.

Precision Attack

Much has been made over the profound demonstrations of precision attack in the Gulf and Bosnia, and its ability to shatter deployed forces and force an opponent virtually immediately into a defence posture. Despite some critics, the strong evidence that precision weapons do significantly add to the credibility and effectiveness of an attacker indicates that strategic attack is an air power concept that needs to be reconsidered, particularly in light of the new synergy of rapid airlift, refined targeting and precision weapon development. Against Germany and Japan, the concept of massive urban strategic attacks against the enemy homeland and their industrial war-sustaining capacity was a sensible approach when bombing accuracy was not good, precision weapons did not exist and the war would, in any case, last for a long time. The pressure of continual bombing raids in the enemy's heartland may have worn the enemy down over time and reduced his war-making potential through attrition of his wartime industrial base. While postwar bombing studies can quantify the productive capacity of industrial bases, it is not clear that populations can be successfully worn down, except by the most strenuous (i.e., a Hamburg-, Dresden-, or Hiroshima-level) attack. As shown by the studies of Group Captain Andrew Lambert of the Royal Air Force Staff College, the probable effect of the far less intensive German bombing in the Battle of Britain was to make the British more determined to win the war at any cost.

Strategic attack has traditionally carried with it the implication that long-term effects are desired. The combat phases of modern war seem to be getting shorter and the time and political will may not often be in place to conduct a successful strategic air campaign against an enemy's heartland. Finally, the 'CNN factor', whereby every bomb is a 'political' bomb, may limit the capability of any nation to undertake a strategic air campaign as traditionally assumed. However, the combination of precise targeting with precision weapons is transforming the nature of strategic attack, reinvigorating the concept even if not in the same sense – massive urban-oriented attacks – that it has usually been viewed.

With the improving capability to find and categorise targets and then to attack them with precision weapons, similarly precise objectives can be set for the types of target sets included in this category. If the goal is to destroy the enemy's industrial capacity to manufacture chemical agents, and known stocks of chemical weapons and their means of delivery then, through a systematic analysis of likely targets, planners can identify a finite number of aim points to meet this specific objective. Similarly, an objective might be to shut down electrical power to a definable area for a specific time period. Instead of relying on traditional general categories of strategic targets, it is now possible to choose precise objectives and, in the process, develop quantifiable, focused measures of success. With precision objectives for precision missions that are related to larger campaign objectives, it is also possible to produce a systematic battle damage assessment (BDA) process to determine when the objective is met. This should focus BDA much as the objectives are focused and bring precision to all parts of the general mission area that used to be called strategic attack. In short, guided weapons, integrated planning, and a good common picture will allow more narrowly focused and defined precision objectives to be reached which satisfy the aims of a strategic attack campaign.

CLOSING THOUGHTS:
LOOKING AHEAD TO THE 21ST CENTURY

Air power has come of age, but there is a lot of room to grow. The combat capabilities of air power that have been practised and refined intensely in the 1970s and 1980s are now mature and have been proven in the test of combat. The process and systems that make intercontinental strategic airlift, air superiority and the defeat of ground forces possible have enabled the accomplishment of new missions in the types of stability operations which have occupied US and allied military forces since DESERT STORM. Space is a natural extension of air power and as hypersonic trans-atmospheric space-lift vehicles are developed and fielded in the early years of the next century, the boundaries between these media will blur into a single operational continuum.

The challenge is to absorb and extend existing capabilities along with new ones enabled by technologies that are ready for use now, or which will be ready in the foreseeable future. The affirmation of the traditional missions for air power in contingency operations; the demonstration of new mission capabilities; and new possibilities offered by technology that will soon be an integral part of the force, will open the door for the application of air power in even wider missions and roles after the turn of the century. As the common picture permits worldwide integrated battle management, air power will play an ever-increasing role, but while the role increases for air power even beyond its remarkable contributions in the present-day, the independence that has characterised air power, air operations, and airmen since the aircraft was invented will be blurred in the new and more pivotal joint and combined roles that 21st Century air power will assume.

AFTERWORD:
CHALLENGES AND
OPPORTUNITIES

Colonel John A Warden III, USAF (ret.)

PRESIDENT, VENTURIST, INC., MONTGOMERY, ALABAMA

A s the 20th Century draws to a close, air power dominates warfare. Those who have air power overwhelm those who don't; those who don't have it spend their energies trying to get it, thwart it or escape it. It is control of the high ground writ large – but unlike the old days when high ground was largely an accident of the situation, in the new world, air power allows the user to move the high ground to wherever it is needed. Air power, when measured in terms of output per dollar or life invested, is the cheapest, most effective method of fighting in human history – and the advent of precision makes it even cheaper.

Air power and the precision technologies adopted by it have given birth to the first new type of war in human experience, 'parallel warfare'. In the past, military operations had to be serial with concomitant action, reaction, and uncertainty. Today, precision weapons coupled with high bandwidth communications and individual aircraft make it possible to attack multiple key enemy strategic and operational centres of gravity almost simultaneously. This simultaneity dramatically changes the nature of war and reduces significantly the uncertainties that were inherent in serial operations. Even before the advent of precision weapons delivery which made parallel war possible, air power had upset the delicate balance of the offence and defence. Now, with the advent of parallel war, offence has become so powerful that the outcome of a war between two adversaries capable of waging it will depend almost entirely on who attacks first.

With all this said, air power ought to be at the dawn of a long, golden age. Despite all the indications, however, precisely the opposite may be the case. Its success has reduced the probability of major war. This in turn leads electorates around the world to call for reductions in defence spending, and air power, because of its apparent high cost, is likely to feel the brunt. As air forces become smaller, the analysts who are still committed to old ideas of sequential combat and who still see air power as a supporting arm will argue that even less air power is needed because the air power threat has diminished. These two events alone can easily lead to a hiatus in new weapons development and even to renewed challenges to the whole concept of independent air forces.

On a geopolitical scale, the very success of air power may have created an environment which will also contribute to its demise as a dominant concept and to its independence around the world. For example, independent air forces are not the only owners and users of air power. In the United States, the Navy and Army spend more money for air power vehicles or their support than any other category of weapons; and the Navy has most of its combat power in manned or unmanned air vehicles. Despite their dependence on air power, navy and army cultures make air power a support tool for traditional sea or land operations. Independent air forces, however, need not be burdened by a cultural requirement to perpetuate old ways of fighting and are free to pursue new concepts.

With the collapse of the Soviet Union – an event certainly hastened by air power's rapid defeat of Iraq – the United States became the undisputed single superpower of the world by all measures. Although it is hard to measure degrees of superiority, the United States today appears relatively stronger compared to potential adversaries than has any state at least since the height of Rome. This in turn suggests that the world – on a global scale – could be more stable than at any time since the fall of Rome. For the first time in almost two millennia, the probability of two major powers going to war with each other is almost zero. This does not suggest that war and conflict are banished; what it does suggest is that the conflicts which do take place will be different and at a lower level which will not seem to threaten the vital interests of any major power and will certainly not threaten the vital interests of the United States.

Some readers will take exception to the premise of existing and projected stability by citing the Bosnias, Sudans, and Liberias of the world as evidence that instability is building, not declining. These readers, however, should consider that the same degree of instability in these areas would have ignited – and normally did ignite – a much wider war in every period of history up to the present. Even those who question the stability hypothesis, however, know that public opinion in the wealthier countries around the world generally reflects a view that major war is unlikely in the foreseeable future. Regardless of where the truth lies, the effect on the development of new air power systems is obvious: almost all countries will reduce their defence spending to include reductions of their existing air forces, and all will slow down their development of new systems. In the United States, we have seen both.

A reduction in size by itself means nothing if we measure effectiveness by what we can accomplish. If the trend of slowing or stopping new system development continues, however, air power will gradually lose its offensive dominance simply because defensive technologies and concepts can catch up if offensive technologies and concepts stagnate. Thus, in another two decades, the United States, for example, could easily find itself unable to defeat an Iraq-like enemy at an acceptably low cost in blood, treasure and time. Such an event would have grave consequences for world peace and stability. This entirely feasible future need not be; indeed, airmen around the world can avoid it – but only if they reassess and redefine themselves, their purposes, and their tools.

A century ago, some of the great American railroads issued bonds which had no maturity. The implication was obvious; the railroads were so vital, so powerful, so right and so profitable that they would exist forever. A half-century later, the majority of those great companies were gone, the industry was in shambles and many fortunes big and small were no more. As with the collapse of empires, the railroad industry fell apart for many reasons; the primary one, however, was a failure to realise that railroads were in the transportation business, not in the steel and locomotive business. So it is with air power: our first order of business is to define our business.

Air power developed from nothing at the beginning of this century because of the allure and excitement of flight. The Wright brothers certainly didn't invent the aircraft to compete with railroads and ships. It was only after those first successful flights that people began to see the real commercial and military potential associated with flying. Over the course of the years, the excitement and attraction of flying has not diminished. Most air forces are run by pilots and most pilots have an emotional attachment to the machines they have mastered. They tend, then, to see themselves as being in the aircraft business, although some are willing to tolerate minor deviations into unmanned vehicles. But are we really in the aircraft business, or is there a higher potential for us just as transportation was for the railroads?

To understand our potential, we must ask ourselves what we do which is different enough to justify a separate, independent organisation. To answer this question, we must think about war, evaluate the environment in which we find ourselves and see what our air power ideas and concepts can achieve. In other words, we look for new business opportunities which stem from our core competencies.

Our very reason for being is to wage and win the wars our countries assign to us. But what is war? Is it shooting down other aircraft? Is it destruction of enemy equipment? Is it killing enemy troops? War may include all these things, but they no more define war than sawing boards define house construction. A good, broad, working definition which includes all the range of operations currently undertaken by military forces is this: war is the use of physical force, or the threat of its use, to change an environment, in the face of opposition, to something in consonance with our desires. This definition encompasses traditional wars, peacekeeping and peacemaking, and disaster relief. In each case we alter with physical means a system, or environment, that does not want to be altered or would not alter in the absence of outside intervention.

In the simplest of terms, we affect an environment by changing its energy states. Traditionally, we have changed an enemy's energy state by killing his soldiers or laying waste his land and we did it with swords, bullets and bombs, which we can label as negative energy devices. That is, their purpose was to take energy out of the enemy system. In the case of a natural disaster, our goal is to put energy back into the system by giving it food, communications and structure. When we do this, we are inserting energy and we can think of the devices we use to accomplish these ends as positive energy devices. With this broad definition, we can see that the basic tools and concepts of air power have very wide applicability across a range of circumstances. Furthermore, moving from peacekeeping to disaster relief to large-scale war does not require superhuman mental agility for all these are the same – we use more or less, negative or positive, energy as the situation requires.

Our next problem is to define the environment in which we will be operating. First, it will be quite peaceful at the global level, so the chances of our using our equipment or skills on a large-scale, life or death struggle are relatively small. We can expect our country, though, to ask us to solve less dramatic, less traditional problems. We can further expect that we will be asked to solve them quickly, at minimum cost and with little loss of life. If we can bring our air power ideas and tools to bear on these problems, we will be offering a great service; if we cannot, if we can only fight the great air battles of the past, we will have little to offer.

War defined and the new environment outlined, we must next ask what it is that we as airmen do that soldiers and sailors (classically defined) don't do. The answer is simple: we take with us our high ground from which we inject energy in relative safety into the heart of the contesting system or environment. In other words, we put energy either negative or positive directly where it does the most good, where it changes the target system as quickly and accurately as possible. Classic ground and sea power, on the other hand, are constrained by the necessity to move serially on a two dimensional plane from the outside to the inside of the target system. The cost of the classic approach is quite high in terms of time, people at risk, logistic support and extrication.

As airmen, if we think of our contribution in these more encompassing terms, we have something very valuable to offer, something which potentially justifies our independence and continuing investment in technology. To this point, we have identified two challenges. The first challenge is to ensure that stagnation of technology and thinking do not allow the defence to catch up with the extraordinary offensive advantage now enjoyed by air power. The second challenge is to show that air forces are relevant to today's problems. In reality, we are blessed with having both challenges; without the first, it would be difficult to convince taxpaying publics to finance continued technology development and without the second, we would have nothing contemporaneous to offer an electorate unaccustomed to spending money for illusory benefits a half lifetime into the future.

In the big sweep of future history, nothing could be more important than for the United States to maintain its global stability-inducing dominance. No precise measure of necessary dominance exists, but some subjective criteria stand out. First, for dominance to induce and maintain stability, the dominator ought to be superior to every individual contender and superior to any conceivable coalition. Absent this degree of domination, potential enemies may decide that a little luck will swing a contest in their favour. Second, the dominance must be dynamic. That is, given enough time, any number of contending states can equal a power that is fixed. On the other hand, if the dominant state becomes effectively more powerful every day, then catching it is nearly impossible. Third, the dominating power must use its strength with great caution. If it indulges in imperialism or in willy-nilly interventions, it will create enemies at an impressive pace. At some point, enough Lilliputians can subdue a Gulliver of any size. Likewise, it must ensure that its interventions are seen by all to be just, proportionate, humane and always successful. Fourth, the amount of wealth in the world must be growing fast enough to give everyone a visible chance for a better standard of living. Absent a growth in wealth, ambitious men and nations will take great risks to seize what they see as their part of a fixed amount of wealth. The problem for the dominant power is to make all these things happen at the same time; Rome failed to do so.

The preceding paragraph should make it clear that if the United States is to lead the world into a long period of peace and prosperity, she must have an integrated grand strategy. Neither political, military, nor economic success is uniquely sufficient.

Just as the United States must have an integrated grand strategy, so must American air power, and the air power forces of states which want to contribute to the golden age which beckons. The American air power strategy must derive directly from American grand strategy.

At first glance, making American air power superior to any potential contender or coalition may seem prohibitively expensive. Indeed, it would be if our measure of security were numbers of aircraft or missiles. Numbers, however, are no longer the right measure for the strength of an air force; instead, the right measure is output, or effect on the enemy. A thousand aircraft with inaccurate bombs are unlikely to achieve what a single stealth aircraft with an accurate bomb can do. The real measure of power is how quickly an air force can impose strategic or operational paralysis on opponents of varying sizes. Unfortunately, we are still at the stage where many military and civilian leaders are still stuck in an old world mentality where numbers of aircraft, numbers of sorties per day or tons of bombs per week are the real measure. This old world mentality creates two problems: first, political leaders need to be educated so they understand that high technology systems are extraordinarily inexpensive when measured against output; and second, potential enemies need to understand what air power will do to them if provoked. For both groups stuck in this old world, convincing demonstrations are a necessity.

Our air force does not need to be numerically superior to be dominant, but it must be technologically above every other. This means technologically superior across the board, from delivering weapons to exploiting space. It must be superior today and all must believe that it will be at least as superior five, ten, twenty, and fifty years into the future, in other words, dynamic technological superiority. To put the concept in still another way, our air force must be a technological revolution ahead of everyone else in virtually every area. Thus, by the time someone has begun to figure out a way to counter the first generation of stealth aircraft, our air force should be fielding the second and third generations which are sufficiently different that the defences developed against the first generation are irrelevant against the second and third generation.

Many will argue that across-the-board technological superiority is too expensive; they will cite the B-2 and F-22 programmes as examples. It might actually be too expensive if we tried to follow the old world model for systems development where we assumed that we needed many aircraft of any given type and that buying many would reduce the unit cost. Buying lots of something will frequently reduce the unit cost as ever larger numbers share research and development and tooling costs. Unless we define success and our measure of merit as merely producing a lot of something, however, what really matters is the programme cost – and the programme cost should be evaluated against what effect the entire programme can produce on an opponent. Consider the F-117: for a programme cost of $4–5bn, the USAF received 60 aircraft which changed the face of warfare. These 60 aircraft, of which about 40 were used in the Gulf War, imposed far more deleterious effects on Iraq and achieved more with fewer aircraft and pilots exposed to hostile fire than did aircraft with somewhat lower unit costs but with hugely higher programme costs.

Our model for the future should be rapid acquisition of small numbers of revolutionary technology systems as rapidly as possible. With small numbers (a squadron or two of aircraft), we avoid the extraordinary costs of decades-long programmes engendered by huge production facilities and bureaucracies.

By building small numbers of new platforms or major weapons every three years or so, we can give the taxpaying public proof that it is receiving something of value. Again, it is tough to convince taxpayers to spend lots of money now on a design which may be superfluous or inappropriate 20 years later when it finally becomes operational. Conversely, a process which sees a new programme become operational three years or so from inception (like the F-117 and the Boeing 777) satisfies the public that its money is being well spent. Likewise, with a little thought, every one of our new systems can play a role in daily operations which fit under the war definition used at the beginning of this chapter. In this way the public receives constant demonstrations that its money is being well spent – as opposed to 20 years of 'trust me'. Note that this approach also creates a terrible problem for would-be challengers: how can they conceivably develop defences against radical new systems which pop up frequently? In technology as in modern war, the offence has the overwhelming advantage.

Our new air force must support the American grand strategic imperative to intervene rarely, but always successfully, proportionately and humanely. The principle which accompanies all of our rapid system and weapon development is one which demands improvements in accuracy and lethality control similar to the improvements in computer power guided by Moore's Law. It should be as easy to deliver positive energy as negative energy, as easy to disable as to destroy and as easy to control destruction radii as to leave it uncontrolled.

The last grand strategic imperative for the United States is to adopt and follow policies which generate worldwide wealth. Revolutionary air force development can make a contribution to the extent that a new system may have significant commercial value. With a little thought, most new systems will have commercial utility, but a few have clear and immediate payoff. For example, in the world of tomorrow, the need for speed will increase dramatically. Since speed is always of inestimable value for military – and commercial – purposes (the faster you go, the sooner you get there, and the faster you go the harder you are to hit), development of very fast vehicles will certainly have a dual payoff. In addition to their value in moving people, goods and services faster and thus more profitably, significantly higher vehicle speeds will probably require non-carbon fuels; discovering a way to develop and field new fuels will also add wealth to the world economy.

Preceding paragraphs have alluded to the potential for immediate application of new technologies to 'small war' problems (recalling our definition that war is the use of physical force, or the threat of its use, to change an environment in the face of opposition to something in consonance with our desires). The 'small war' problem facing the United States and its friends includes such actions as: emergency food and medical relief following a natural or man-made disaster; separating warring parties when choosing one side or another might be counterproductive; neutralising or destroying criminal or terrorist organisations; protecting citizens abroad; stopping offensive behaviour by states; restoring order in a city or state; imposing strategic or operational paralysis on a state attempting to conduct or threaten significant cross-border operations; or 'occupying' a state in order to enforce a prescribed form of behaviour. In every one of these instances, speed, precision, low cost, low risk and low or zero collateral effects will be of the utmost importance.

Air forces around the world which share the American view of the future know with utter certainty that they will be asked to participate in one or all these contingencies. Knowing the requirement, they can and must develop the specific tools needed to succeed with all. Unfortunately, as we approach the end of the century, air forces are relying on relics of attrition war to deal with problems unrelated to attrition. A quick look at each of the scenarios will illustrate the point and suggest solutions.

Our ability to deliver food and medicine from the air is not much improved over what it was in the Second World War. We rely primarily on parachuting crates of material into an objective area even when we know that the most serious requirements for emergency food and medicine occur when local distribution mechanisms cannot or do not work either because of physical damage to the distribution mechanism or because some other party is deliberately restricting distribution. If air power is to be useful in these very common situations, it simply must develop the wherewithal to take care of distribution directly from the air – home delivery, in other words. If we can drop a 2,000-pound bomb down a smoke stack and if we can put a small packet of lethal explosives on every square yard of a football field, we can surely figure out a way to deliver a two pound loaf of bread (or more likely its calorific equivalent) to someone's doorstep.

Separation of warring parties who don't want to be separated is almost impossible with today's equipment unless we are prepared to take sides or to attack both parties for infringements. Defeating one side is not normally a good idea and tends to create long-lasting enmities; likewise, we rarely have the will to attack both sides equally. The solution to the problem, however, is conceptually simple: you can 'attack' both sides equally if the consequences are reversible or if no one suffers unacceptably as a result of the attack. Reversible and bloodless consequences are attainable with non-lethal weapons – and non lethal-weapons are best delivered by air (faster delivery and far higher probability of producing a strategic- or operational level-effect). For air power to be able to make this contribution, it must begin now to think in terms of non-lethal weapons and to develop them specifically for air application. Unfortunately, most air forces have failed to grasp that non-lethal weapons would make them the tool of choice for what are often called peacemaking or peace enforcement operations.

In preceding centuries, navies and armies played a key role in destroying pirates and brigands. It is only in very recent times that that mission has fallen from the military repertoire in the United States. And yet, we can predict with certainty that nations will become increasingly frustrated with criminal organisations and will turn to the military for resolution. Can air power play a key role?

Air power can not only play a role but can easily play the major role, especially when the target organisation is some distance removed from the offended state. Air power can reach any point on earth quickly with little or no need for a potentially objectionable presence on the ground. With current weapon ideas, it can render unusable the criminal organisation's facilities and it can make the movement of criminal goods and services difficult. It can also interfere effectively with the flow of information which is critical to any criminal group with more than local operations. It can, of course, attack criminal personnel directly; with non-lethal weapons it could immobilise them for pickup by ground personnel. Its ability to arrest criminals without ground help is currently non-existent – but that doesn't mean that it must remain so. Very-long-range stealthy helicopters would be useful, as would small helicopters able to leave and rejoin a long-range mother ship. Almost certainly there is a solution; of equal certainty is the fact that it won't be found unless someone looks for it.

Protection of citizens abroad is a difficult air power task especially if the threatened individuals are dispersed. As they become less dispersed and are brought together in a single place, air power solutions become clearer. There are even excellent models such as the Israeli rescue of hijacked passengers at Entebbe, an operation based on technology now 30 years old.

Stopping the offensive behaviour of states is an area where air power has a proven record of success dating back to the British air control operations in Mesopotamia and extending through the very short American war against Libya in 1986. In the 1986 operation, the United States wanted something specific and relatively limited from Libya – to reduce its support of international terrorism – and achieved its objectives by making it very clear to Quadaffi that he was in mortal danger unless he acceded to American demands. The EL DORADO CANYON mission was quite successful but it depended for its success on a single capability – the high explosive bomb. There were no gradations of bombs, no capability to impose reversible effects and no ability to seize and control the Libyan datasphere. Although the absence of these capabilities in the Libyan situation was acceptable, it is hard to imagine a scenario some months or years in the future where their absence would not be acutely felt. Here is another area where air forces must begin to think seriously about future requirements instead of merely improving existing capabilities.

Unacceptable disorder in a city occurs when groups bent on disruption can move freely. If groups cannot move freely, then disorder becomes localised and is no longer operationally (or even strategically) significant. Restricting mobility with surface forces is feasible if large numbers of troops are present. Large numbers are required because the topography of a city requires serial operations which means establishing multiple road blocks and strike forces. Conversely, a handful of drone-, helicopter- or gunship-type vehicles can cover a large city effectively, so long as we keep in mind our objectives.

The objective in restoring urban order is not to protect every facility or arrest individuals; rather, it is to establish and maintain a required degree of order. If we severely restrict the mobility of those wishing to cause disorder, we accomplish our ends – and we can certainly use air power effectively. Our willingness to use it, however, will be affected by the severity of the situation and the tools at our disposal. If the problem is a riot where the authorities are not willing to use lethal force, our options today are limited. At the other end of the spectrum, the use of lethal force may be entirely acceptable; in this case, we have many options.

To provide more options when lethal force is not appropriate, air forces must think again about non-lethal weapons and their delivery and concepts of operation. It doesn't take a lot of imagination to think of a dozen different kinds of non-lethal weapons which would force the majority of mobs or groups to disperse or to take shelter. A few tens of air vehicles and 100 or so crew members should be able to take care of most urban situations – *at operational levels*. Contrast this to the thousands of surface troops needed to do the same job and consider the high probability of casualties when thousands are operating in small units spread through the city.

The Gulf War of 1991 was the first true demonstration of how air power alone can impose operational and strategic paralysis on a large, well-equipped offensive power. Although the circumstances were less than ideal – for example, Iraqi facilities and forces were dispersed over broad geographic areas, Coalition planners had to contend with frequently unfavourable weather, and the majority of aircraft participating in the Coalition air war were neither stealthy nor capable of using precision weapons – parallel war made possible by precision weapons, stealth aircraft, and very high bandwidth communications presented Iraq with an impossible problem: within six weeks, they put her into a state of paralysis. The losses, though tragic and regrettable, were astoundingly low – about 30 airmen of whom over a third were lost when an AC-130 gunship went down while pursuing the remnants of the Iraqi 3rd Corps on the second morning of the Battle of Khafji.

In particular, the ratios between attackers and defenders was without precedent. Iraq had a population of about 15 million and had about 10 per cent under arms in one form or another; in Kuwait alone, she had fielded an army of 300,000-500,000 men. On the attacking air side, combat crew members numbered about 3,000 of which rarely more than 500-600 were in hostile air-space at any given time. It is more difficult to factor in the Navy cruise missile contribution; the Navy fired missiles from about ten different ships which had crews ranging from 100 to almost 1,000. Everyone aboard ship was at risk not only from hostile fire but also from the normal perils of the sea. Compounding the problem is the need to take into account all the support ships and their crews which constituted the groups of which the cruise missile launchers were a part. The degree of risk for personnel aboard ship is far higher than for support personnel at an air base. It is difficult to conceive of a circumstance where a single non-nuclear weapon is likely to kill hundreds of air base personnel; on the other hand, in the Gulf War, two single mines not only put major combatants out of action but came close to sinking two ships with many hundreds aboard.

Discounting the support personnel at risk on naval vessels, the ratio of attackers to defenders was in the vicinity of 1:200 if we count only the defenders in Kuwait. If we expand to count all of Iraq's armed forces (which could easily have taken part in the conflict if we had permitted it), the ratio becomes 1:500 or so. With these ratios, the Coalition air forces paralysed Iraq. To have accomplished the same end with surface forces would have required ratios ranging from an optimistic 1:3 to a pessimistic 3:1. Technology and the concept of parallel war have raised the productivity of the airman substantially; because ground forces are still constrained to serial, two-dimensional, force-on-force operations, technology has done little to change the relative productivity of the individual soldier.

Some will object by pointing out that today's M-1 tank can fire effectively at ranges three and four times those of its Second World War ancestors. Although true, it misses the point. The real point is this: modern armies use at least as many tanks and troops to accomplish a given job as they would have used decades ago. If the enemy is defending a sector with one division, an army planner will propose three divisions as an appropriate attacking force. If an army planner is asked to defend a sector, he will propose troop densities about the same as his Second World War counterpart in 1939–45 would have proposed. Contrast this with air operations: in the Gulf War, planners confidently dispatched one aircraft manned by one person to accomplish a job that either couldn't have been done at all in the Second World War or which would have required hundreds of aircraft with thousands of men aboard and at high risk.

The Gulf War saw handfuls of airmen impose operational and strategic paralysis on a well-equipped opponent; it also saw the most significant example to date of air power defeating a very large fielded army. It may have also been the last example of air power defeating a large fielded army for surely one of the key lessons of the Gulf is the terrifying vulnerability of large surface forces. One cannot imagine Iraq again trying to take over Kuwait by large-scale land invasion. Instead, the next time, Iraq will attempt to find a way to attack its opponent's strategic centres of gravity – or more likely, threaten to do so – such that she presents her potential opponents, and especially the United States, with a *fait accompli* sufficiently ambiguous as to reduce significantly the chances of a political decision leading to hostilities. For the United States, this new situation, where she can no longer depend on an opponent going through the cumbersome, slow, and highly visible assembly and dispatch of an invading army, dictates development of significantly faster attack and defence capabilities and the development of weapons which can be used in ambiguous situations.

In thinking about the force structure needed to attack and defend rapidly in order to prevent another state from imposing its will on a neighbour, we can approach the problem from a numbers or from an outcome methodology. In the first, we merely extend institutional desires and say we 'need' some number of wings (unlikely to be much less than those currently in existence). Whether that number is right or wrong is difficult to say. On the other hand, we can define the outcome we want and work backward to deriving the requisite force structure. A good starting point might be to say that the United States needs the ability to impose strategic paralysis on any opponent within 24 hours of the decision to do so. Likewise, the United States ought to have the standing capability to prevent or interdict aircraft or missile attacks on any state around the world. The time constraints suggest the need for very fast systems with global range. In addition, the political imperatives discussed earlier of proportionate reaction, minimum risk and no unintended casualties dictate a class of weapons with precision of impact and effect orders of magnitude beyond those currently available.

If we accept the need for a force structure capable of imposing strategic paralysis on an opponent within 24 hours and if we deploy it, the chances of using it are small. If we do use it, however, we may well be faced with the need to maintain pressure on the defeated state in order to force its conformity to war termination agreements. In other words, we may need to occupy it. When we speak of occupation, we need to understand that we are talking about an output measurement (the 'occupied' state follows imposed terms) not an input measurement.

The concept of occupation normally brings to mind large numbers of troops in the midst of a hostile, or at least sullen, population. By definition, the troops are imposing a regimen on the occupied state which is something different from what the state's inhabitants would do left to their own devices. Why does a postwar occupation take place? A brief historical review suggests four basic reasons: a conquering power may want the vanquished foe's land for its own long-term use; the winner may want to force transformation of the defeated state's government or even culture; the conqueror may want to put reins on the defeated state's ability to rearm and resume combat; or the winner may want the loser to adhere to restrictions on certain economic, political, or military activity. Air power has a role in each of these instances which varies from supporting to dominant.

If the victor wishes to take over the land of the defeated, it would appear that colonisers defended by troops on the ground would be necessary, although the mobility provided by air power in this case would still be most useful. At the other end of the spectrum, if the desire is to impose restriction on the loser, air power should be sufficient. The recent case of Iraq is instructive: a state which accepted no bounds to its behaviour before the Gulf War, has behaved acceptably and has done most of what was asked of it. Although there are still those adherents of the old order who insist that Iraq only suffered real defeat when ground troops took back Kuwait, nobody can argue that Iraq has been docile for the last five years because it feared that the Coalition would assemble a huge (half million, minimum) army to invade Iraq in the event the Iraqis refused access to UN inspectors. But they have granted access and the only threat has been the presence of 100 or so aircraft – backed by the demonstrated ability of the United States to dispatch hundreds more in a few days.

Between the two poles of occupation reasons, debate over the role of air power is proper. Can it force a defeated state to change its form of government and culture? Our answer is that it probably can't, but can contribute significantly. Can air power prevent rearmament and resumption of hostilities? Here, the answer is clearly affirmative.

The record of control from the air is a good one – probably at least as good as control from the ground. Air occupation becomes a significant role of air power, although it is not one in which any modern air forces have invested a lot of thinking or weapons system development efforts. In concluding discussion of this area, it is important to note that even if air occupation is not perfect—as it will not be in some circumstances – it will in many cases be the only occupation option available. At the end of the Gulf War, for example, the occupation of Iraq with ground forces would have meant overcoming enormous political, military and monetary obstacles. On the other hand, air occupation was easy on all three counts.

Earlier in this chapter, we discussed reaction to natural disasters by air operations. Left unaddressed, however, was the possibility of using air power to prevent them. We normally think of natural disasters as being terrestrial in origin and including earthquakes, volcanoes and wind storms. Our current knowledge of the earthquake suggests we are powerless to prevent them. The same may be true of volcanoes although it may be worth a little thought as to whether it might be possible to relieve volcanic pressures pre-emptively with some kind of high energy penetrating weapon. Likewise, there may be something which can be done about tornadoes and hurricanes. Without question, however, air forces have the potential ability, and arguably the responsibility, to prevent extra-terrestrial disasters.

The probability that the Earth will be hit by an errant asteroid or comet is close to one; indeed, we recently saw several such bodies hit Jupiter and impose on the Jovian planet damage which on Earth might have destroyed most life. Air forces unequivocally accept responsibility for intercepting airborne attackers; why should they not also be charged with protecting us from extra-terrestrial projectiles? The cost, if spread among the world's air forces, would be relatively low and would take advantage of multiple talents and observation positions.

Although the world in front of us looks quite peaceful in comparison to the millennia of strife we have suffered, the opportunities for air power are boundless. From ensuring a long period of stability to dealing with the inevitable localised disturbances, air power has the potential to be the most important, and importantly the least expensive, tool available. For it to be, however, airmen must become imaginative and innovative. They must rethink their business and realise that it is not flying aircraft but rather injecting energy into the heart of target systems from a conceptual high ground. Airmen must realise that their only purpose is not to fly and fight – for that is nothing more than a poor excuse for an industrial age input measure – but rather is to affect major change rapidly in a target system. They must realise that the manned aircraft is only a tool that must be discarded when it is no longer the best tool available. And airmen must be willing to engage in open, honest, brutal debate with the advocates of still older military tools who are fighting desperate battles to keep institutions alive.

The opportunities for air power are immense – as are the challenges. If we accept the challenges and overcome them, we will make a major contribution to world peace and stability. If we refuse to accept the challenges and continue to live in a long-gone world of flying scarves, our relevance will fade rapidly, and with it our best hope for the future.

INDEX